Touching the Wall –
Entering the Stream

By Karen J. Kobrin Cohen

Touching the Wall - Entering the Stream

Published by: Caprice Publishing/KKCohen
47593 Comer Square
Potomac Falls, VA 20165-7460

Cover Photography & Design by K.J. Kobrin Cohen

ISBN: 0-9717237-0-2
Library of Congress Control Number: 2002090141

Printed in the United States by:
Morris Publishing
3212 East Highway 30
Kearney, NE 68847
1-800-650-7888

Dedication

I dedicate this book to all those who have helped me along the path of my life's journey. Initially it was my mother, Audrey Weiss Kobrin, who instilled in me a love of learning. Then, to my children, Teleia and Arik, who are both wise beyond their years and hold the secret to a better future (as all children do). And finally, I dedicate this book to all the inspiring teachers I've met along the way. For every Being I have encountered has influenced me in some way and taught me more about living.

Table of Contents

List of Illustrations

Frontispiece

PREFACE

The scope of this book is actually quite narrow. In no way is the material to be taken as being all encompassing and definitive. The basic tenets of Buddhism and Jewish Mysticism (Kabbalah) presented here are just that, basic. Hopefully, the information given will intrigue the reader enough to go out and do more in order to learn and practice on his/her own. I have included a modest book list and some web sites that can be used to initiate this quest "to know."

As for my qualifications and background, it is openly presented within the covers of this book.

My reason for writing this book is quite simple. I had read numerous books about other people's spiritual journeys, especially those of Jewish men and women who wanted a more spiritual connection with Judaism and who ended up pursuing Eastern Philosophical systems to meet this need. I avidly read these biographically based stories searching for my self. However, I always ended up feeling dissatisfied with how they integrated their belief in Judaism and their Buddhist practice.

My frustration was due to the feeling I had that some how the core reason for their having delved into eastern meditation techniques, in the first place, had been glossed over. Consequently, I felt it was time to state it the way it is so that Jewish congregations, especially rabbis' and education directors, would bring the subject of Jewish mysticism and Jewish meditation techniques to the forefront of Jewish awareness and education.

Countless Jewish young people stray from their Jewish-ness in search of a deeper connection to life and G-d. It's time that they were told that Judaism also has a system for drawing closer to G-d, and becoming one with all creation. Why must our young people search elsewhere for some thing they can have within the context of Judaism, itself? Hopefully, my story will help educate the Jewish community as to how the neglect of introducing the subject of Kabbalah/Jewish Mysticism hinders the growth of Judaism and causes an exodus of our young people away from their religion.

For Buddhists, I hope I have shown what Buddhism does right. Buddha discovered the merit of meditation and taught all who desired to learn how to realize enlightenment for themselves. However, many Buddhists born into this tradition don't sit in meditation any more than the average Westerner. It is my hope that this book will encourage them to actively practice meditation, not just attend various temple functions and paying their respects to the monks. Buddhism is open about teaching meditation and you should take advantage of this.

And to the lay people of all the worlds various religious systems, those who question their beliefs and want a more direct experience, I encourage you to search within your own tradition first. You may be pleasantly surprised at what you find there.

Potomac Falls, Virginia
August 2000

K.K.C.

ACKNOWLEDGMENTS

I am truly grateful for the generous assistance, feedback, and support the following friends, family members, and teachers have given me in the course of my writing this book: Margeuritte McGee, Rabbi Daniel Ornstein, Bhante Yogavacara Rahula, Rabbi David A. Cooper, my daughter, Teleia Su-Fen Cohen Farrell, my husband, Matthew T. Cohen, the meditation group at Wat Yarnna Rangsee Si located in Sterling, Virginia, and the Buddhist monks and nuns residing at The Bhavana Society located in West Virginia. To those I haven't had an opportunity to thank; I take this opportunity to thank you now.

July 2001   Karen J. Kobrin Cohen
Virginia

Chapter 1
In the Meditation Hall

A distractingly noisy insect moves around my head several times and then lands on my left, upper arm. I can't see it as my eyes are closed, but I can feel it moving about exploring the territory. It tickles. I try to stay focused in the here and now with my attention fixated on the roaming explorer. What is it? A fly? A bee? Maybe it's not a flying insect at all. Maybe it's a spider. Anxiety sets in. Now I'm afraid I might be stung by a bee or bitten by a spider.

Should I open my eyes, look around, and check it out? One thought rushes by and then another and then another. Now I'm having an emotional debate with myself. Meanwhile, the fly or bee or whatever insect it is is busily exploring the contours of my inner elbow. Be in the moment, I say to myself. Stay calm. But my mind is racing ahead of me and I can't seem to put on the brakes.

So much for meditation. I open my eyes, glance to my left, lift my upturned right hand and wave the fly away. Yes, it was a fly. It was a very harmless fly. Now my mind is busy admonishing myself for letting my thoughts get away from me; for building one thought onto the next instead of just letting the thoughts pass by and staying in the moment.

Now my hearing is tuned in to detect any insect that may come within range. I try to pull my mind back to center, to dwell within the calm of my meditation again. I hear someone cough. Silence. Then I hear someone slowly switch positions. Is the fly exploring the domain of another person's leg or arm? Or is that person just switching position to avoid stiffness or cramps? Should I peek?

The gong is sounded and everyone, including myself, slowly sways back and forth. We uncross our legs, crawl off our black meditation cushions called *zafu's*, plump them back up, and then stiffly stand up and move into a line for walking meditation. My right leg is fine, but my left leg feels like it's filled with cement. I'm afraid I will lose my balance. I can't feel anything. I'm sure I will step down in the wrong place and fall. Slowly I make my way down the three steps to the floor below. As I reach the end of the line I feel that strange tingling sensation as feeling starts to return to my leg.

How do people do this? The last 45 minutes was an agony. I thought doing meditation was a simple thing and that it was supposed to be extremely enjoyable and pleasant. Was I the only person here to feel so wretched? Was I the only beginner? I was certainly the only Caucasian in the group. When I had first inquired where I could go to do meditation practice I was directed to the Zen Buddhist Soto Mission on Nuuanu Street in Honolulu, Hawaii. I rarely drove to that area of the island so decided to make my visit in the early afternoon to avoid rush hour traffic in both directions and so I would be driving in daylight.

I finally discovered the entrance into the parking lot after driving around the block several times. I parked my ever-so-humble, pale blue Datsun and slowly made my way down the pathway toward what I presumed was the entrance to the Mission's office. Part of me hoped someone, anyone, would come by whom I could inquire where the office was or who I should speak to. Another part of me hoped no one would see me doing this. I slowly climbed up the outside stairway to the door and hesitated a moment. Should I knock first or just walk in? I quietly knocked. No answer. I listened intently for any noise from inside. Nothing.

I turned around and started back down the stairs. How foolish of me to even think of doing this. Who in the world did I think I was? Sure, I studied Buddhist philosophy while attending the University studying for my Business degree, but reading about Buddhism is a lot different than showing up at a Buddhist Temple. Who was I kidding! Whoever was inside would probably laugh non-stop when I presented myself and asked to be taught how to meditate. What audacity!

Half way down the steps I stopped. I remained motionless while my thoughts debated within my head. I desperately wanted to learn, but I didn't want to be embarrassed or ridiculed. You have to take chances or you'll get no-where, I thought to myself. But this isn't taking a chance. It's being foolish. It's not foolish to ask for help when

Picture 1.1: Zen Buddhist Soto Mission on Nuuanu Street, Honolulu, Hawaii

you're trying to study and learn something new. That's what you think.

Suddenly, as if on their own, my feet turned me around, and I started up the stairs again. My hand grabbed the handle of the wood paneled door, opened it, and I propelled myself to the counter on the far side of the wall. It was a dreary room. The pale green from the walls blended with the pale green floor. There was a dining room size wood table set in the middle of the room with straight-backed matching chairs arranged neatly around it. On the wall next to the door I had just come in was a smaller table with booklets and other information sheets piled in even rows. Each pile had a rock set on top of it. A wise precaution against the wind blowing the papers off the table every time someone opened the door.

I waited, but no one came in. I knocked on the counter. The vibrations stayed in my ears for several minutes but I heard no other sounds. Finally, after what seemed like an eternity, but was probably only a few seconds, I called out, "Is anybody here?" The sound of my voice startled me as it broke the tomblike silence. I continued to wait wondering what to do. If I left now I didn't know when or if I'd return. I lived far from the Mission and it was difficult for me to get to. As I turned to leave a short, thin, Japanese man came up to the other side of the counter and said something to me in Japanese.

Feeling a sense of both relief and anxiety I turned about face and stepped back up to the counter. I asked him if he spoke English. After looking into my face for a few seconds, obviously trying to make out what I was saying, he shook his head no. He signaled for me to wait and then disappeared into a back room. I was committed now. There was no turning back. I had just plunged into the water. Would I drown?

A few moments later I was face to face with a very tiny Japanese woman with extremely short cropped, black hair, wearing the black robes of a priest. She stepped closer to me and looked up into my eyes with a look of wonder and friendliness. She gave me a small smile as she bowed and asked if she could help me. It was obvious that she was not totally fluent in English, but since I knew no Japanese I was more than relieved that we could communicate at all.

"I don't know how to put this, but I want to learn how to meditate." My words stumbled out quickly before I could change my mind about asking.

"Have you done any type of meditation before?" she asked in a soft voice.

"No, I haven't." I replied.

"This is a Buddhist place," she explained, "perhaps you have come to the wrong place."

Ah, I thought. Since I'm a Caucasian she thinks I must have made a mistake. Perhaps I was really looking for one of the many churches in the area. I was probably lost.

"Yes, I know this is a Buddhist mission." I answered. "That's why I'm here. I have studied a little about Buddhism but it always talks about meditating and I don't know how. So I thought I should find someplace to go in order to learn. Books can only go so far."

"That is true." she thoughtfully replied. "What do you know about Buddhism?"

I fell silent. Did she want me to tell her everything I knew about it from my college courses and my book reading? How could I tell her all of that now, standing here? Is she testing me? Does she think I'm making this up? Does she think I'm not sincere? I have to answer. I have to say something. I can hear the office clock ticking.

4

She stands there quietly, not moving, not hurrying me, just standing there.

"Well, I know about Siddharta, the Gautama Buddha. I'm familiar with the Four Noble Truths; the Truth of suffering, the Truth of the origin of suffering, the Truth of the cessation of suffering, and the Truth concerning the path leading to the cessation of suffering which is the Noble Eightfold Path. It makes sense to me. I have read many books on the subject such as <u>Buddhism in Translations</u>, by Henry Clarke Warren, <u>The History of Buddhist Thought</u>, by Edward Thomas, and <u>What the Buddha Taught</u>, by Walpola Rahula. Plus, I've read many books by D. T. Suzuki and Alan Watts."

"Books are good," she nods in approval, "but sometimes too much books is not so good. I think, maybe, you read too much. It is time to do practice. Don't read any more books. Come and meditate. A small group comes every Wednesday night at 8pm. Come and you can learn. I am Reverend Ichinose and your name?"

"I'm Karen, Karen Lee. Yes, I would like to come. Thank you." I replied excitedly. I was going to have a chance at this.

"Good. Now I must return to my work. You come. You don't read so much." Reverend Ichinose smiled, bowed, and disappeared behind the office.

On the way out the door I glanced down at the neat piles of booklets on the table. Quickly, I grabbed a couple of them and walked confidently back to my car. I'd done it. I had actually done it. My heart pounded hard in my chest as I pulled out of the parking lot and headed for home.

Chapter 2
Entering the Path

N
ow that the tingling sensation had subsided and I could walk with some feeling in my legs, I slowly followed the rest of the line. Slowly I placed one foot in front of the other, carefully placed the heel down and then slowly moved the foot down from heel to toe. Slowly I inhale, slowly exhale. Moved the other foot forward in the same way. Inhale, exhale, step, inhale, exhale, and step. Eyes focused on the person's back in front of me. Hands held against my stomach, my left hand folded into a fist with my thumb enclosed, my right hand cupping the left with the thumb resting on top of the left fist. Breathe, step, breathe, step.

It was a warm evening the Wednesday I returned to the Soto Mission to begin my meditation practice. The drive was much less stressful then the first time. I knew how to get there now, and I had been invited to attend. I listened to the soft music drift around me as the warm air wafted into the car. Luckily, it was late in the day, otherwise it would have been a very uncomfortable drive in this heat. My car didn't have air-conditioning. We depended on the trade winds on the island. Unfortunately, trade winds didn't necessarily blow into car windows the way one would like.

Evening was settling in by the time I turned into the Mission's parking lot. A few cars were already parked indicating that other meditators had arrived before me. Up until now I wasn't a bit nervous. Seeing those solitary cars sent waves of anxiety through me again. I felt exposed. Would everyone be staring at me? Would I make a fool of myself in front of all these strangers? I hoped Reverend Ichinose would be there so I would see at least one familiar, friendly face.

I walked into the office but no one was there. I heard some sounds coming from the left. Walking slowly out of the office door, I turned toward the noise. Double wooden doors were open into what appeared to be the main sanctuary. As I peered in I saw to my right a stunning display of gold and lacquer Buddha's, *Bodisattva's*, fresh cut flowers, incense, offering bowls and other Buddhist relics and devices of which I had read about. To my left were rows of wooden benches. In some way it did resemble a church or synagogue until you turned your eyes to the altar. I knew, then, that this was an unknown realm I was walking into, a realm with unknown rituals and rules of conduct. I was an alien here.

Picture 2.1: Meditation Hall at Soto Mission

As I stepped inside toward the four individuals seated in the front row, I felt even more alien. There was an elderly Japanese man and woman sitting together talking quietly to each other. A young man, probably in his early twenties, sat across the aisle from them and continued to look up at the golden Buddha statue on the altar. He looked like a local boy to me, a mix of different ethnic backgrounds. He was probably part Japanese, part Hawaiian, part something else. Next to him sat a young Japanese man who sat comfortably and was obviously relaxed. One could tell by just looking at him that he was

7

no stranger to this place or to the art of meditation.

As I made my way towards them they slowly looked up at me. I smiled wanly. Oh, boy, I was the only white person here. I sat down at the far end of the front bench. The elderly couple returned to their intimate conversation. The young Japanese man slowly turned his gaze to the altar. As I turned to do the same, the local boy said,

"New, huh?"

"Yes. And you?" I asked.

"My second time," he responded, "You from around here or tourist?"

"I live Ewa." I replied quickly. I certainly didn't want to be taken for a tourist. How absurd when I continued to think about it. What tourist from the mainland would come to this place outside of downtown Honolulu? How would they even know about it?

As I sat there feeling slightly indignant at the fact that I was thought of as a tourist *haole* (white person or foreigner), the elderly couple suddenly stopped talking. I looked up to see a bald headed Japanese man walking toward us. He, too, wore the same black robes of the Japanese Buddhist monk. His face was brilliant with a broad smile across his face. You couldn't help but smile back at a face that looked like that. I felt a little better being here until he started to speak. It was solely in Japanese. He walked over to me and spoke to me. I didn't understand a word he said and it was quite obvious that he knew no English. I assumed he was welcoming me and so I smiled up at him.

"Fujii," he said pointing to himself.

"I'm Karen." I responded in kind.

"Just . . . follow . . . others." he said haltingly.

Reverend Fujii then spoke to our small group and then mounted the steps up to the altar. The others silently stood up, walked up the few steps to the altar level, picked up a small, black, round looking pillow and a larger square black pillow from the closet behind the altar. I followed the others. They carried their pillows to the front of the altar and busily set themselves around the walls. Carefully, they placed the larger pillow on the floor. Then they set the smaller, round pillow on top of the square pillow. I found a spot to the left of the Buddha statue and did the same. They sat down on the small round pillow, facing the wall, and crossed their legs. I watched in amazement as the old man to my right quickly placed his left foot on top of his right thigh and then his right foot on top of his left thigh.

8

Later I was to find out this was called the full lotus position.

I sat down on my pillow and tried to do the same. Being a Westerner made a big difference. I was able to get my left foot on top of my right thigh, but I struggled quite a bit to get my right foot on top of my left thigh. I almost fell over and once I had gotten my legs in place I felt as if I was in a very unnatural, contorted position. My knees kept rising up in spite of my efforts to keep them steady and resting on the large cushion as I saw the others doing. They began to sway back and forth. I did the same trying not to fall off the small, round pillow. They stopped swaying and placed their left hand in their lap, palm facing up. Then they placed their right hand, also palm up, in their left hand. Their thumbs pressed gently together. I did the same.

A gong was struck several times. Then what sounded like a wooden mallet was hit over and over in a uniquely settling rhythm. As it faded, I heard the slow, melodious voice of Reverend Fujii, chanting in a language unfamiliar to me. Then it was silent. No one moved. No one spoke. I looked out of the corner of my eye to my left. The younger Japanese man was sitting erect, eyes half closed, staring down in front of him. His eyes didn't look as if they were focused on anything at all. His face was expressionless. What was he doing? What was he thinking?

I settled myself in the best I could mimicking the others. What I was supposed to do I still didn't know. I would just follow the form. I looked at the wall in front of me. I looked down until my eyes felt more comfortable and half closed my eyelids as I noticed the other man doing. Now what? I didn't know what to do. I was sitting like the others, but obviously they were doing something and I was unable to copy them, as I couldn't read minds. Think of nothing. That's what the books I had read said. But how do you think of nothing at all?

Chapter 3
My Search Begins

I t was 1967. I was attending my first year of college at the University of Miami in Coral Gables, Florida. At that time there was very little surrounding the campus. A major highway, a few buildings, but that was pretty much it. This was my first time away from home. I had grown up in Massachusetts and I had come to live in a warm climate and to study Marine Biology Oceanography.

The first year at college and away from family and familiar friends catapults the unsuspecting teenager into a maelstrom of conflict. Up until now I pretty much lived the way my parents expected me to, embodying their ethic, religion, thoughts, and basic view of the world. Suddenly, I was surrounded by people from all over the country and various parts of the world. People who had different belief systems, different ways of seeing the world around them then I did. Finding one's balance in this alien world was to be very challenging and, sometimes, frightening.

I was a nice Jewish girl who was, naturally, brought up Jewish. The only anomaly was that my mother was a Reform Jew and my father remained Conservative. It was difficult as my father preferred to go to a Conservative Synagogue for services and my mother refused to go anywhere but to a Reform Temple. According to her those in the Conservative movement were hypocrites. They were neither observant nor modern.

My brother and I went to Sunday school in an old church that the newly founded Temple my mother affiliated with rented to hold services and classes. Naturally, the young congregation hoped to build their own Temple, one day, but for now this arrangement worked. They called their newly established congregation Temple Beth Am and their church location was in Framingham, Massachusetts.

Framingham was only one town over from where we lived, but the drive there always seemed to take forever to me.

I must admit I hated going to Sunday school. I would have much rather been outside playing with my friends. At that time they didn't have professional teachers, but parent volunteers who would teach the children what they knew of Judaism. So, depending on the luck of the draw you either spent the school year with someone who knew something and was able to teach it to you in a fun and interesting way. Or, you ended up with someone who knew practically nothing (or seemed to know practically nothing) as they couldn't communicate or relate to young children. I always seemed to hit the later type.

Every Sunday morning was a struggle. I just didn't want to go. Every year was the same to me. Holidays were studied as they came up on the calendar and we tasted, once again, the traditional foods for that particular holiday. One day, however, I must have been misbehaving and was sent to the Rabbi's office. This wasn't good. I dreaded having to face him. Who knew what was behind his office door? The only people I ever saw go in there were adults who didn't look so happy going in and sometimes looked worse when they came out.

Slowly I made my way down the dark stairway to the even darker lower landing. A quick turn to the right and I was facing the Rabbi's office door. I timidly knocked. A moment later the door opened and the Rabbi smiled down at me. He invited me to enter. I walked in.

Immediately, I was in awe. Directly in front of me was a huge dark wood desk covered in books, magazines, papers and writing implements. There was a large window directly behind the Rabbi's desk where rays of morning light slipped in and fell across the top of the desk and into my eyes. Surrounding the walls were books. There were hundreds and thousands of books on ceiling to floor bookshelves. I looked down to see my feet covering a flower sort of design in deep reds. Later I was told it was an Oriental rug. I liked it.

The Rabbi asked me to sit down in an oversized brown leather chair facing his desk. As I pulled myself up into the chair as directed, the Rabbi walked around his desk and sat down in a similar chair across from me.

"So," he asked, "what happened?"

I didn't know what to say. I certainly didn't want the Rabbi to be angry with me but I didn't really remember what had happened.

11

Whatever it was happened so fast.

"I don't know." I answered slowly.

"Come, come," the Rabbi exclaimed kindly, "you must have some idea. No one is sent to me unless they acted in some inappropriate way. Don't worry. I will not hurt you. I just want to understand, to help."

This was a new twist. He looked sincere. He had a kind and gentle smile on his smooth shaven face. He certainly didn't look mean.

"Well," I volunteered, "I guess I was talking when I shouldn't have been talking and I wasn't paying attention to the teacher."

"Ah," he exclaimed softly as he moved his head up and down in apparent understanding, "and why did you behave in this manner?"

My brain was speeding in all directions and my heart was pounding. Should I tell this man the truth or make something up that might not get me into as much trouble? I opted for the truth, as I saw it.

"It's boring." I told him. "I'm tired of hearing about all the holidays over and over again. I want to learn about real Judaism. I want to learn about the Torah (Five Books of Moses). I want to know, to understand things."

"I see." The Rabbi rubbed his chin thoughtfully.

I decided not to say anymore. I waited for his reprimand, a suitable punishment. It never came. Instead, he pointed around the room at all his books and told me that he, too, wanted to learn about real Judaism. That he wanted to understand the Torah and to understand things. He told me that was why he had so many books. He read all the time trying to learn, to understand, to know. He told me that I should be patient. That it takes a lifetime of learning to understand even a little. He then pulled out a couple of books from a shelf, leafed through them a bit, and then handed them to me.

"Why don't you read what you can from these two books?" he kindly said as he handed the books to me. "I realize the words may not be easy to understand for you, but I think you would enjoy learning these things. Don't lose those books. All books are precious and have to be given the greatest respect. Knowledge is contained in books. I rarely loan out my books but I think you are trustworthy." He smiled down at me again. "If you don't understand something, please come and visit me. I will try to explain what I can. Later, we can talk about what you have read. Would this be okay with you, Chidle Rochel?"

Chidle Rochel was the name they called me in Sunday school.

Sometimes I didn't recognize it as being a reference to me. I was Karen. Anyway, I nodded my head in acceptance.

"Good." the Rabbi said in obvious pleasure, "you sit here for now and look through the books I have given you. You have my permission to stay in my office today until school is over. If you want to look at any other books in here please do so, but don't take any without my permission first. Okay?"

"Okay." I replied.

The Rabbi excused himself and left me alone in his office. It was so peaceful in this place. It had the feeling of the sanctuary during prayer. It was a safe place, a place of learning. I loved it in the Rabbi's office and didn't want to ever return to Sunday school class. I wanted to stay, surrounded by all this wisdom. I wanted to read every book on the Rabbi's bookshelves so that I could learn all there was to learn and so I could, finally, understand things. I wanted to stay and talk with this Rabbi who was so kind, who treated me like a real person, and who was willing to talk to me about important things

To me, Judaism was that Rabbi in that special room called the Rabbi's office. The smells in that room were the smells of Judaism, of learning and wisdom. All those books were as a universe to be explored. This was what I had been longing for. This was what I wanted to be doing. Not wasting my time in a class with other kids who didn't want to be there either, being taught by someone who didn't know much more than we did. I wanted to stay with this Rabbi.

Chapter 4
To Know G-d

Unfortunately, it didn't work out that way. Rabbi Rosen was a very busy man, and he didn't have much free time to spend with a little girl. He was kind and understanding. He did allow me access to many of his books and, from time to time, would discuss some of them with me. But, usually I spent my Sunday mornings with the other children and studied, once again, the holidays as they came up on the calendar. I would see him during the abbreviated services held for the benefit of the Sunday school students. His tall, heavy-set frame swaying as his dark haired head moved in prayer. What did he feel as he prayed, I wondered?

By the time I was in high school and college bound, I had long since stopped going to Sunday school. I picked up the Torah on my own and started to read. The Torah is what the Christians call the "Old Testament" although the Torah only includes the first five books referred to as Genesis, Exodus, Leviticus, Numbers, and Deuteronomy (or what we call *Bereshith, Shemoth, Vayyikra, Bemidbar, and Devarim*). I read and reread the Torah and then picked up a Bible so that I could read the other stories such as those contained in the Prophets that included the Judges, the Kings, as well as the twelve prophets, and the Writings that included Psalms, Proverbs, the Book of Job and the Song of Songs.

At some point during all this reading an extreme restlessness over-took me. I became impatient with my reading, yet I kept going back. I would reread sections, especially those verses where G-d was in direct relationship with various personages such as Moses, King David, the various Prophets, etc. I found myself feeling jealousy. What was this? I was frustrated but I didn't know why. I stubbornly kept going back and rereading even though it heightened my frustration.

14

Whenever I would attend Friday night or Saturday morning services, which wasn't all that frequent, I must admit I would go in feeling calmly expectant and would leave in an agitated and frustrated state. I went back to the Torah. I reread it, this time trying to figure out what had me so upset. Was it finding out that my ancestors, the Israelites, weren't all pacifists and certainly not perfect? Was it the discovery that they were all too human? No. What was it then?

Suddenly it came to me. My frustration came because I felt somehow excluded. I didn't have a personal relationship with G-d. I would pray to Him, but never did I ever recall hearing an answer. I was told to live a certain way, to uphold certain values, laws and rituals, to be moral. I behaved myself. I tried to be a good daughter. After all, G-d was always watching, always aware of what was going on in His world. He wouldn't like it if we didn't do as we were expected to do.

This is where all the ritual came from. We made sure we fulfilled G-d's will in this way. The Israelites ended up with 613 *mitzvot* or actions they were required to uphold and perform. Many of the *mitzvot* involved the Temple in Jerusalem and so we were currently exempted from those, but it still left plenty of *mitzvot* to perform. But G-d never said thank you or acknowledged being pleased in any way.

Then the next thought popped into my mind. Obviously G-d was either not listening or didn't care. After all, in biblical times he certainly made His opinions and directives known. His silence might mean that he was no longer interested. Or, maybe, people today just weren't listening properly. Maybe G-d was trying to speak, but no one was listening.

The reason for my frustration became apparent at last. I, too, wanted a personal relationship with G-d. Moses, Noah, King David, the Prophets all appeared to have had an informed and intimate relationship with G-d. Why couldn't I have this experience, too? What good were all these rituals and laws, what relevancy to ones prayers if you never received a reply, some approval, some response?

Obviously, these rituals and laws came about after certain individuals became conversant with G-d. These particular people had a relationship with G-d and through this relationship they were not only enriched, but they enriched others. How did they come to have this personal relationship with G-d? What had they done? What had they experienced? I went back to my reading. Now I was searching to find out what these people had done to become intimates of G-d.

Chapter 5
The Quest Continues

I decided to take a religion course during my freshman year at the University of Miami. I enrolled in "An Introduction to Religion" course aptly referred to as Religion 101. It was a general overview of the world's main religions. We studied Christianity, Judaism, Taoism, Confucianism, Buddhism, Hinduism, Islam, Shinto, Jainism, Sikhism, and others I can't recall. It was a whirlwind course. Through it all I continued to search for the answer to the question I had asked when I was in high school. How was someone to become connected to, intimate with, G-d?

What did Abraham, Moses, and the Prophets do? How did they experience G-d? I would pick up my worn Bible, again and again, to read more. Late one evening, while pondering over what the possible common factors could be between all these well-known people of the Bible, it hit me. Each and every one of these famous Biblical personalities had either gone up a mountain or into the desert for an extended amount of time. In the majority of cases they went alone into the wilderness. After a period of time, usually not so brief a time period either, they returned to civilization. But when they returned they were no longer the same as when they had left. What happened to them up on that mountaintop or out in the harsh desert? That must hold the answer. I figured something must have happened. If I could find that out the mystery would be solved and I, too, could learn how to commune with G-d in a two-way dialog rather then in one- way prayer.

Our religion Professor had just completed the overview of our next area of study, Buddhism. It sounded interesting, but so did all the others so far. In fact, I had concluded long ago that depending on how you looked at something, anything could be true. This was terribly unsettling at times when friends would get together to debate over some issue and I would see the truth in all of their viewpoints. When I was once challenged as to what I believed to be true, I really couldn't say. Depending on the argument, anything could be thought of as true. Be your self, they would plead. You must have an opinion of your own. But I really couldn't be myself. I honestly didn't know who I was.

Sitting in class, the Professor started to discuss in detail the Four Noble Truths of the Buddha. He started with a little background history as to the man Siddhartha, who would eventually become the "Enlightened One," or the one who saw reality as it really was/is. He also delved into the Noble Eightfold Path leading to a manifestation of the Middle Way as practiced by and taught by the Buddha, as well as, the nuances of all the philosophical twists and turns.

Siddhattha (Siddhartha in Sanskrit) was born of royal blood into the Sakya clan having the family name Gotama (Gautama in Sanskrit). This clan lived in an area of Northern India, which is now part of Nepal. His father, Suddhodana, was the ruler of this kingdom and his mother, Maya, was the queen. According to the custom of the time, Siddhattha was married at an early age, probably at 16 years, to the young princess Yasodhara.

During his boyhood and young adult life Siddhattha lived in luxury, sheltered from the heartbreak and deprivation of everyday existence. He was unaware of the hardship, pain, and suffering that befell the people who lived outside his palace walls. He was raised a prince who would eventually be king and so wanted for nothing

As the story goes, one day Siddhattha requested to take a journey outside the palace. His father, fearful that Siddhattha would be exposed to the realities of life, ordered all the sick and aged to be removed from the path Siddhattha was to take on his excursion. All matter of filth and pestilence were ordered cleaned up and all roads made ready for the young prince's retinue.

Unfortunately for Suddhodana, his plan didn't quite work out as expected. Along the way Siddhattha was to come upon a sick man, a man dying, and to see other forms of suffering and pain. This was a shock to Siddhattha as he had never known of or seen such things before. When he returned home, he was haunted by the images he had seen outside his father's palace gates.

Being confronted by the existence and reality of sickness, old age, pain, suffering, and death, Siddhattha questioned the purpose of it all.   He wanted to find a solution to this torment of mankind, a way out of this universal suffering he had seen.   Siddhattha was pained to realize that all things would eventually fall ill, become old and eventually die. What was the point of life if all one could look forward to were old age, sickness and death? And this didn't include other forms of suffering that people appeared to be prone to.   Even Siddhattha, himself, was subject to these same phenomena and conditions.

His mind in turmoil, he recalled a yellow robed ascetic he had seen during one of his brief excursions. This mendicant had walked slowly, his facial expression peaceful and serene. When Siddhattha had asked about them he had been told that they were men who had gone from the home to homeless state in order to find the path to liberation in order to overcome suffering.

At 29 years of age and shortly after Yasodhara had given birth to their only child, Rahula, Siddharttha left his home and his kingdom to enter into the homeless state. He became an ascetic and wandered for six years along the Ganges River searching for a solution. He studied under various religious teachers and followed their methods. He practiced rigorous ascetic practices. He was so good a student that several of his teachers even offered him a standing and leadership role equal to their own.   Siddharttha always refused these honors, and remained dissatisfied that he felt no closer to a solution then when he had first entered the homeless state.

At this stage Siddharttha abandoned his teachers, all the current traditional religious practices of that time and their methods, and decided to continue his search alone. It was during this period of his life that he was to sit under a tree on the bank of the river Neranjara at Buddha-Gaya and attain enlightenment. He was 35 years old, and the tree under which he had sat in meditation was henceforth known as the Bodhi or Bo Tree (Tree of Wisdom). From that moment on, he became known as the Buddha, or "The Enlightened One."

Two months later Siddharttha, now the Buddha, left his place under the Bodhi Tree and traveled to the Deer Park at Isipatana (now Sarnath) near Benares. It was here that he found the five ascetics who used to practice with him. He delivered his first discourse, to them, which came to be known as the "First Turning of the Wheel of Dhamma" (*Dhammacakka Pavatthana Sutta*).   In this discourse he explained his solution to the problem of suffering by teaching the Four Noble Truths, and the Noble Eightfold Path.

He spoke to them about avoiding the two extremes of indulgence, on the one hand, and self-mortification on the other. By avoiding either extreme he came to realize the Middle Way, or Middle Path. What was this Middle Path? It was simply living according to the Noble Eightfold Path. Through living and practicing in this way, the reality and truth of the Four Noble Truths would be realized first hand, intuitively from within, and so would lead to higher knowledge and enlightenment.

One could start by learning the Four Noble Truths. But until one experienced the reality of them for oneself, it would only be more bits of information collected in the mind. In order to experience it for oneself, one must follow the practice of the Middle Path as described by the Noble Eightfold Path.

The Four Noble Truths

1. *Dukkha-* The Noble Truth of Suffering: That birth, aging, sickness, and death are suffering. That sorrow, lamentation, pain, grief, despair, and depression are suffering. Not getting what one wants and getting what one does not want is suffering. *Dukkha* or Suffering also involves the deeper concepts and awareness of emptiness, imperfection, impermanence, and insubstantiality.

2. *Samudaya-* The Noble Truth of the Origin or Arising of Suffering: It is the craving and/or clinging that creates rebirth. It is tied up with pleasure, greed, and even avoidance. It is the activity of grasping for that which one desires and avoiding that which one does not want. And yet, this origin of suffering isn't the first cause as there really isn't a first cause. The origin of *dukkha* is ignorance which gives rise to mental activity (*samudaya*), consciousness (*vedana*), contact with the world (*phassa*), craving, karmic actions and further suffering. This on-going circle is called Conditioned Genesis (*Paticca-samuppada*).

3. *Nirodha-*The Noble Truth of the Cessation of Suffering: That it is possible to completely eliminate suffering by letting go, developing wisdom, renouncing, and overcoming craving. There is a way to realize this freedom from suffering. However, in order to eliminate suffering completely one has to eliminate the root cause, ignorance, which has initiated the craving or "thirst," in the first place. This involves the complete halting of the on-going circle called Conditioned

19

Genesis stated above. When a being has completely cut off the root of suffering there is *Nibbana* (*Nirvana*), known as Enlightenment. It is also known as *Tanhakkhaya* or "Extinction of Thirst."

4. *Magga*-The Noble Truth of the Way Leading to the Cessation of Suffering (*Dukkha*): It is the path one follows. It is the way to live, think and meditate in this very life. It is the Middle Path also known as the Noble Eightfold Path.

And what is this Middle or <u>Noble Eightfold Path</u>? It is:

1. Right Understanding (*Samma ditthi*): the realization of the Four Noble Truths; that there is suffering, the origin of suffering, that suffering can be eliminated, and that it is eliminated by following the Noble Eightfold Path.

2. Right Thought (*Samma sankappa*): thoughts free from ill will, sensuous desires, and cruelty. Promoting thoughts of goodwill, compassion, non-violence, and being considerate.

3. Right Speech (*Samma vaca*): the avoidance of telling lies, slandering others, using abusive or hateful words, gossip and useless/frivolous talk.

4. Right Action (*Samma kammanta*): abstaining from stealing from others, killing, sexual misconduct and basically any misuse of the senses.

5. Right Livelihood (*Samma ajiva*): engaging in work that does not cause you to commit wrong speech or wrong action.

6. Right Effort (*Samma vayama*): actively exerting oneself and striving to prevent any evil or unwholesome thoughts to arise, to dispel any evil or unwholesome thoughts that has already arisen, to bring about pure and wholesome thoughts which haven't all ready occurred, and to maintain the good, pure, and wholesome things that have already arisen.

7. Right Mindfulness (*Samma sati*): being mindful and aware of the body, feelings, states of mind, and the objects of the mind.

8. Right Concentration (*Samma samadhi*): mental calmness and the ability to remain concentrated on a

particular topic or single object without letting the attention wander or to be distracted.

The Noble Eightfold Path can be viewed as a means of purification. Moral conduct or self-discipline (*sila*) involves right speech, right action, and right livelihood. Concentration or mental discipline (*samadhi*) involves right effort, right mindfulness, and right concentration. These factors are developed through the practice of meditation. Wisdom (*panna*) involves right understanding and right thought. These factors lead to insight (*vipassana*) and transcendental knowledge (*maggaphalanana*).

In its essence this is what Buddhism is all about. For 45 years Gautama Buddha taught the Way to anyone who desired to learn. He made no distinction between men and women, rich and poor, law-abiding and criminal. The Middle Path was open to everyone. After a long career devoted to showing others how to transcend the rounds of birth and death and how to find inner peace by following The Noble Eight-Fold Path, Siddhartha attained final nibbana (upon his death) at the age of 80 in an area of Uttar Pradesh, India, an area known at that time as Kusinara.

Enlightenment, meditation, enlightenment, meditation. Could this be the key I was looking so hard to find? Could the activity these Biblical personages had in common, the activity that appeared to be the catalyst for a two-way communication with G-d, be meditation? The prospect excited me but I still wasn't sure if it was just wishful thinking on my part. Besides, what exactly was meditation? How did one "do" meditation? Back to my Bible, but I couldn't find the answer I was looking for.

Chapter 6
Rediscovering Buddhism

Years went by and large segments of time passed without my being haunted by my quest to find out how the patriarchs had come to know G-d. I was involved with other aspects of life. I had transferred to the University of Hawaii and was now majoring in Business Administration. I was experiencing a new culture although I was still living in the United States. The majority of people living in Hawaii, at that time, were Japanese, Chinese, Portuguese, Hawaiian and a mix of all of the above. However, there was a definite oriental influence.

I rediscovered Buddhism there. The University had an outstanding Eastern Philosophy department. I decided to take select courses in Buddhism as possible electives. However, as I began to study Buddhism more, its importance to me became more apparent. By my junior year I was taking many more courses in Eastern Philosophy then was warranted by the required business major electives.

Meanwhile, I decided to look up the Jewish temple in the area. I discovered it was located on the Pali Highway on the way to Kailua from Honolulu. The drive was beautiful. The foliage was green and lush. Going up the Pali the air became dense and moist and you could some times see the mist of moving clouds being combed through the mountains tops. It had a spiritual feeling to me. I thought it was a very appropriate place for a House of G-d. I was pursuing my quest, again, and so had decided to try to speak with the Rabbi there. Perhaps he could suggest some reading material from the Temple's library or even answer some of my questions him self.

The parking lot was empty on that sultry early afternoon. It was mid-week and nothing much happens at Synagogues during that time. It was a deliberate choice. I walked up the flower-bordered walkway toward the back of the building on the left side of the sanctuary where I had noticed the sign pointing to the "Office." A middle-aged woman was sitting at a small desk. She looked up at me as I entered.

Her hair was cut short and she wore a brightly colored muumuu (the local Hawaiian style of dress originally introduced to the islanders by the missionaries from New England). The orange and yellow flowers drew my attention away from her eyes. I asked if it were possible to see the Rabbi. She asked me if I had an appointment. I told her that I didn't, but that I was a student at UH and had specifically gotten a lift over here to see the Rabbi. She told me to wait and she would see what she could do.

As I waited I browsed through the booklets and the temple's newsletter. It appeared that they did pretty much what most Jewish places of worship do. I also found out it was a Reform Temple. My mother, at least, would approve. I smiled to myself.

As the Rabbi entered I walked toward him, thanked him for taking time to meet with me, and introduced myself. He, too, was middle aged. He appeared to be about 50 years old. His dark brown hair displayed gray, and the wrinkles around his equally brown eyes gave him the look of a Bedouin who had spent too many years roaming in the sun. He extended his hand and asked how he could help me.

I asked him the question that had been burning in my heart for so long.

"Rabbi, I would like to know what Abraham, Moses, David, the Prophets, experienced so that they were able to communicate directly with G-d. I've read the Torah and it seems they either went up in the mountains or out into the desert and when they returned from there they were changed in some way."

The Rabbi was silent. Then he replied, "One can't know these mysteries. We do, however, have a code of law and ritual which can help you to be a good Jew." He then went on to advise me to come to services as often as I could, to join the Youth Group and meet other nice Jewish students and, perhaps, to avail myself of their Temple library.

That was not why I had come. I was feeling frustrated. I knew the answer was out there but no one seemed to be willing or able to supply it. I had already attended Jewish Sunday school (I knew all the holidays and their significance, the traditions, the special foods). I had attended services (they rarely strayed from the usual form). I had listened to the Rabbis discourses (usually relevant to some political issue of the time and/or to clarify some learning from the Torah portion just read).

"What about meditation?" I ventured.

"What about it?" the Rabbi asked in return.

"Do you think the patriarchs went to meditate and it was meditation that stimulated their relationship with G-d?" I wouldn't give up so easily.

The Rabbi appeared to be a little uncomfortable. I'll never know if it was because he couldn't or wouldn't answer me, or if it was because I had taken up so much of his time without an appointment. In either case my question went unanswered.

Chapter 7
Study versus Experience

ntuitively, if one could call it that, I truly felt that somehow meditation was the key I was searching for. As I continued taking undergraduate courses in Eastern Philosophy and especially in anything to do with Buddhism and Taoism I became convinced that meditation was what I had to pursue. What I was learning from my Professors was profound, but I also read anything and everything I could lay my hands on regarding Buddhism and meditation. I was no stranger to the university library and bookstore or the local bookshop at Ala Moana Shopping Center.

One day while doing my usual browsing I came across James Michener's latest book at that time, The Source. I wasn't reading any books for pleasure of late so I decided this might be a good thing to do over my Spring break. A little switch in mental focus can be a very therapeutic process. I was still interested in my Jewish roots and Jewish history so I figured this book would also be informative as well as entertaining. It certainly sounded interesting. It involved an archeological dig located in the Holy Land. What intrigued me was Michener's style of using the excavation as a stepping off point for going back into history and describing the daily lives of people from those Biblical times. Little did I know at that time what an enormous effect that book would have on me.

At the same time I continued searching out and reading books concerning Buddhism and especially Buddhist meditation practices. I initially focused on any works by Daisetz Teitaro Suzuki, also known as D. T. Suzuki. I read What is Zen?, The Field of Zen, An Introduction to Zen Buddhism, Studies in Zen, and Essays in Zen Buddhism (first edition). Every book I could find by Alan Watts, including Meditation, was also purchased and poured over.

I then discovered other authors and other books. I read

<u>Concentration and Meditation: A Manual of Mind Development</u> by Christmas Humphreys, <u>Meditation Gut Enlightenment: the Way of Hara</u>, by Haruo Yamaoka, <u>Buddhist Meditation</u> by Edward Conze, <u>Meditation: The Art of Ecstasy</u> by Bhagwan Shree Rajneesh, <u>Meditation in Action</u> by Chogyam Trungpa, and <u>Zen Training: Methods and Philosophy</u> by Katsuki Sekida.

I was now taking college courses during summer breaks, as well, trying to cram in as many eastern philosophy classes as I could. I even thought I would go for a second degree in Eastern Philosophy if I could take the course work required along with my Business Degree requirements without my father finding out about it. Even though I worked part time as a waitress, it certainly wouldn't pay for college. My parents would gladly pay for my education, yet my father was the pragmatic type. Although more than willing to pay for a Business degree that I could use, I couldn't see him approving of and paying for further semesters to earn a Philosophy degree that, according to his way of thinking, would be useless and a total waste of money.

So, I continued to take Philosophy courses as I pursued my B.B.A. hoping my father would be none the wiser even though I was taking courses year round. It worked until my senior year when the college must have sent home my grade report. My father isn't a fool and when he saw all the philosophy course grades I immediately received a long distance phone call from him.

Nervous would have been an understatement. My father wasn't upset about my grades (although he was a little concerned that my philosophy grades were all "A's" whereas my business grades weren't so good). He wanted to know why I was taking so many philosophy courses, as it was apparent that I had fulfilled all my elective requirements. He also wanted to know if I planned to graduate on time (that coming May). I took the plunge and asked him if I could continue so as to earn two degrees: the business degree as originally planned, and a degree in Eastern Philosophy, too. My father must have been shaking his head on the other side of the continent, but I couldn't see it over the phone. Then he emphatically replied, "Karen, I expect you to graduate on time." Case closed.

I graduated that following spring in 1971. My father was pleased as I graduated on time. I started training for work with a major airline in Honolulu and I married right after the two week training session held in Los Angeles. A weekend honeymoon and I trotted off to work early Monday morning.

26

I had met my husband, Evan, during my second year at the University of Hawaii. We were both juniors and we were both majoring in business administration although his emphasis was on Hotel and Restaurant management and mine was in travel agency management. He was a nice Chinese guy from South America. One of my first big challenges was to explain to my parents who this man was when I wrote about him in a letter. Evan was Chinese, but a Dutch citizen, but was born and raised in a country called Surinam located on the north coast of South America. His parents were from Mainland China and he, himself, spoke several languages included two dialects of Chinese, German, Dutch, a little French, *Taki Taki* (a local Surinam dialect), and English.

Since he was Chinese it was assumed by many that I became a Buddhist because of him. This was totally untrue. As a matter of fact, he had been raised Catholic and if pressed, considered himself Catholic. Now how do you explain all of this to your parents?

A year later we had a beautiful little girl who we named Teleia. In Hawaii a person who is of mixed blood is called "*hapa*." Since Teleia was half-Chinese and half-Jewish she definitely fit into that category. And like the majority of *hapa*'s, she was absolutely beautiful. But, of coarse, I'm her mother and so must be accused of being biased.

Neither of us had changed our religious beliefs nor did we expect it of each other. We did, however, have the dilemma of how to raise Teleia. We compromised and decided to raise her Buddhist with the understanding that we would both follow our own beliefs and that we would answer any questions Teleia may have when watching us in our own practice. However, we promised we would not try to unduly influence her in either religion. I kept that promise until after our subsequent divorce and Teleia's request for a Jewish education.

My University days were currently over, but not my reading of books. I was still searching. I was a familiar face in all the bookstores on the island. I even frequented the University bookstore, roaming up and down the aisles to see what new books the Professors were using. Sometimes I would purchase a text, feeling guilty while doing so. I couldn't help but think that I might have been preventing one of the enrolled students from purchasing his/her text in time, for the start of his class.

It was two years after this period in my life that I decided that reading about Buddhism, reading about meditation, just wasn't going to get me where I wanted to go. Of coarse, I still wasn't clear as to where I was heading, but I figured I was walking in the right direction at least. I wrote to the Honolulu Star Bulletin, the major newspaper on the island, and asked if they knew of any place where I could learn to do Buddhist meditation practice. There was a question and answer column and I hoped they could help me, as I didn't really know whom to ask. I waited several weeks and then found an envelope from the newspaper in my mailbox.

I rushed upstairs to my apartment and carefully opened the envelope. Inside was a very short note, typewritten, telling me I should try the Soto Zen Mission on Nuuanu Street. That was it. I reread this small bit of information several times. That was it? There was no more information then that? I knew what "Zen" was, but what was "Soto?"

I pulled down the telephone directory from the top of my closet. Flipping through the "S" section I finally found it. I copied down the full address and phone number. At first I was going to call, but hesitated and changed my mind. No, I would just go down there, introduce myself, and ask for some lessons in meditation.

Chapter 8
Dogen Zenji and Soto Zen Practice

The transmission of the "Right Law" as rediscovered by Sakyamuni Buddha in India, was passed on to Venerable Mahakasyapa, who in turn transmitted it to Ananda. It was then passed down to Sanawasa and continued being transmitted from teacher to disciple all the way to Bodhidharma who was the 28th Patriarch. Bodhidharma was attributed as being the monk who brought the teaching of the Dharma to China in 520A.D., and so became known as the First Patriarch in China.

It was in China that the Zen Sects of Buddhism first developed. The term "Zen" is Japanese and means, as closely as possible, meditation. The Chinese term is *Ch'an*. *Dhyana* is the Sanskrit and actually has a meaning closer to "to think," from the Brahman tradition, or "thought and practice" in the Chinese tradition. It also comes close to the meaning "quiet reflection." Because *Dhyana* is not easily translated, the term "meditation" is used to describe it although it isn't totally accurate. The term *Samadhi* is the Pali, which came close to "no thought" or what we would say was just experience.

The three sects that developed, at that time, were Soto, Rinzai, and Obaku. In 1191 C.E, the Japanese, Buddhist, monk Eisai, introduced Rinzai in Japan. It is best known by its "sudden enlightenment" methodology, of using the system of problem solving called *koan*. A *koan* is a problem given to an individual to meditate on the solution. A *koan* can't be solved using our logical mind. D. T. Suzuki, the well-known writer, is attributed with introducing Rinzai Buddhism to the West.

Soto Zen was founded by Dogen Zenji who studied for many years in China under the Soto Zen Master, Ju-Ching (Nyojo). In 1223

CE, Dogen (also known as Joyo Daishi) was disappointed and concerned about the highly scholastic form Buddhism had taken in Japan. He felt that Enlightenment or Awakening was to be attained from within oneself, not some thing that can be obtained from an outside source. Consequently, learning alone would not take you there. It wasn't a case of coming to "know about Buddhism", but to "become Buddhism."

Because of Soto's emphasis on meditation practice and de-emphasis on book learning and scholarship, it became quite popular with the masses and is currently the second largest Buddhist sect in Japan. The Soto Zen Buddhist Mission of Honolulu was established in 1913, by the Missions first Bishop, Venerable Hosen Isobe It was here that I was to have my first contact with Buddhist meditation practice after immersing myself in reading books about Buddhism for so many years.

It was this method of deep meditation, called *Za-zen*, which I was to practice for the next 25 years. *Za-zen* or "sitting in meditation" involved sitting in concentration with mind control, beyond thought. It was a method often referred to as "right thinking" although thinking in the usual sense was not to be implied. While attending *Za-zen* at the Soto Mission I was to learn of the various requisites required for productive sitting. The meditator should be physically fit. What this meant was that one was to be well nourished, but not over indulged. One was to be mentally fit. This meant that you came to meditation with deep conviction and a quiet-ness of mind. And, you must be morally fit which entailed observing the precepts. The five most common precepts were, put simply: not to kill, not to steal, to be chaste, not to lie, and not to indulge in intoxicating liquors or drugs.

Next, an environment conducive to meditation was to be sought. This involved finding a place where one wasn't likely to be disturbed. It could be a location were one would be alone, in solitude, or with a group of like-minded individuals who would also be sitting quietly. One should be in a well-ventilated room or in the open air. The temperature should not be too cold or too hot, and one should sit in an upright, comfortable position.

The method I was taught involved sitting on a small, black, round cushion called a *zafu*. You placed the *zafu* under your buttocks, slightly in back, and you crossed your legs in a full or half lotus position. The full lotus involved placing your right foot on your left thigh, and then placing your left foot on your right thigh. In the half

30

lotus position you would place only your right foot on your left thigh.

As for your hands, they were placed palms up with the right hand placed on the left foot while resting the left hand on the palm of the right hand. Next, an oval was formed with your hands as you brought the tips of your thumbs together until they touched lightly. In this way it was felt that your hands would act as an indicator. If you became too relaxed your thumbs with fall forward, if too tense your thumbs would press themselves firmly together. In this way you could monitor the intensity of your meditation and make the necessary mental adjustments.

Once in position you were to sit upright with your spine erect, your ears parallel with your shoulders, and your nose in line with the navel. Your mouth was to be closed with the tongue gently held against the roof of the mouth or palate. The positioning of the tongue in this way made it possible to sit for quite a long time without feeling the need to constantly swallow which could be distracting.

Finally, your eyes were to be kept slightly opened and focused about three feet ahead of you. This was to keep you grounded in the here and now and to help prevent one from falling asleep. In the Soto tradition meditation was done while facing a wall in order to cut down on distraction, especially since one meditated with one's eyes opened slightly. To begin you would inhale deeply, than exhale all the breath just inhaled. This would be repeated several times and then you would settle into a quiet breathing pattern.

In the Soto tradition you were to sit in silent meditation while maintaining a mental attitude of "no thought." No *koans* or riddles were given as it was felt that life, itself, was the *koan* or problem to be solved. Therefore, all activity was to be done in the spirit of meditation. Meditation was not considered a means to an end, but as an end in itself.

Once *Satori* or "Awakening" occurred, the Zen practitioner not only continued his/her meditation practice, but also returned to the world of multiplicity in order to fulfill his/her vow to help liberate all beings. This was the *Boddhisattva* ideal. One dedicated one's life toward helping all other beings to realize Nirvana. You practiced in order to be able to help others. This is the cornerstone of Mahayana Buddhist practice.

To stop thinking was impossible. So, we were told to practice singleness of thought. To quietly sit without clinging to thoughts, allowing thoughts to come and go of their own accord without attaching anything to them.   In this way, eventually, the thoughts would cease to appear and in its place, from within the framework of the mental equilibrium so established, the *Samadhi* of No Thought or Emptiness would spontaneously reveal itself from within. This form of meditation was referred to as Tranquillity, Concentration, or Mindfulness meditation.

Let me mention here that Buddha was not a God or an incarnation of God. He was and is revered solely because of his great accomplishment in becoming "the Awakened One," and because he was compassionate enough to spend his life teaching this *Dharma* to others. He is revered as Buddha, "The Fully Awakened One," not as Siddharttha Gotama, the prince. The religion of Buddhism is based on the principle of Nirvana or *Nibbana* ("inner illumination" or "realization"), not on a particular person.

Chapter 9
Entering the Stream

I had been going to the Soto Mission on Nuuanu Street for over two years now. I would enter the *zendo*, take my *zabuton* and *zafu*, find a place to sit facing the wall, and I would meditate. Some times it would be a good session. I would remain still. My mind would be still. I would follow my thoughts without attaching anything to them, without getting attached. I would follow noises, movements, and bodily or mental sensations without actively thinking about them or analyzing them. Time would enter time-less-ness. I would just sit. The feeling in my legs would sometimes disappear. Sometimes it would tingle, become numb. It didn't matter. Only sitting mattered.

Some times it would be a difficult session. My body would feel restless and want to move around even though I forced it to stay still. My mind would be restless as well and would rush to catch any thought, any distraction. I would keep my eyes lowered, but my vision would see a bump or mark on the wall and my mind would start thinking about and embellishing whatever I saw on that wall. I would be aware of every uncomfortable sensation. My mind would continue a two-way dialog in my head. One side of my mind would tell me to forget meditation. That it was getting me nowhere and that, besides, my legs hurt. The other side of my mind would tell me to be still, to refocus and to just sit, to just watch as my thoughts went by and not to attach anything to anything.

In either case the gong would sound, we would do walking meditation called *kinhin* and then we would be invited to join the Priest at the table in the office to have some tea and to discuss whatever we liked. I would always stay for tea. To me, it was another highlight to the meditation session. I had an opportunity to meet and talk with the others who were meditating along side me. It allowed me to ask questions about my meditation and to see that my mind wasn't the only one that resisted being trained in this way.

No other Caucasian ever found their way to this Mission, but often someone would attend that knew English as well as Japanese. This would be exciting for me. For at those times I could actually ask the Priest questions and be given answers I could comprehend. I enjoyed sipping Japanese tea in little cups, sitting around the heavy wood table I had seen the first time I had come to the Soto Mission, and having something in common with those other men and women who sat around the table with me. We had nothing in common racially, but we all felt somehow connected through our meditation practice and in our belief in Buddhism.

Yes, I had come to the point where I was feeling more Buddhist than Jewish. At least in terms of practice. I would always feel and be a Jew. I believed in the one G-d. I believed in the long and rich history of the Jewish people and so was connected by roots that grew in many directions. But, I also felt I was part of a Buddhist lineage. It was a feeling. Nothing I could put into words. I just felt strongly that I belonged there, in that Buddhist Temple, with the other practicing Buddhists, with that Buddhist priest.

Shortly after, I decided it was time to become a Lay Buddhist. How does one go about it? I hadn't a clue. After *zazen* one evening I left the office where we were having our tea and searched out Reverend Ichinose. I would have liked an opportunity to talk with the priest who had officiated at the meditation sessions. But, he knew very little English, and besides, I didn't want to ask this question in front of the others.

I found her in the back of the meditation hall. I went quietly up to her and asked if it would be okay to ask her something. She smiled, nodded in the affirmative and waited for me to go on.

"Reverend Ichinose, I would like to become a lay Buddhist. Could you please advise me as to what I would have to do?" I waited for her answer.

"All you need to do, " she replied, "is to take the Precepts. Then, you will be a Buddhist."

"Can I do that here?" I asked.

"We can do that here," she paused, than went on, "but it would be done all in Japanese. You wouldn't understand what was really going on. I would suggest you go some place else."

"Where should I go?" I asked, not a little disappointed. I felt at home here. I knew people here. It didn't matter to me that I couldn't understand Japanese. That I couldn't communicate easily with the others. There were other ways to communicate.

"There is a Soto Monastery in Northern California, I think. It is fairly new, but the Abbess trained and was given the transmission from the Very Reverend Keido Chisan Koho Zenji, Chief Abbot of Dai Hon Zan Soji-ji, one of the two chief training monasteries of Soto Zen in Japan. This Abbess was originally from England and so has adapted ritual to English so Westerners can more easily understand. I will find out how to contact her if you would like."

"If you wouldn't mind I would appreciate that information very much." I responded enthusiastically.

"See me next week after your meditation," said Rev. Ichinose, " and I will give you what information I can."

I couldn't wait for the week to go by so I could return to the Mission and find Rev. Ichinose. I hoped she would be able to find the name and address of this monastery. How and when I would get there would be another question, but for now I only wanted to get the process initiated.

I decided to find Rev. Ichinose before the *zazen* period began. I knew if I waited until after meditation, my mind would never be still. I found her in the office, bowed to her, and politely asked if she were able to find the information we had talked about last week.

"Ah, yes," she smiled warmly and reached into her black robe. She took out a small piece of lined paper and handed it to me.

I thanked her and looked at the paper. Written on it in very small, neat letters was: Reverend Jiyu Kennett Roshi, Zen Mission Society, Shasta Abbey, P.O. Box D, Mt. Shasta, California 96067 and the phone number was written below it. I bowed back to her, thanked her again, placed the piece of paper in my pants pocket and went into the *zendo* for meditation.

The next morning I composed a letter to Shasta Abbey. It was June of 1975, and I knew nothing about Shasta Abbey. I wrote my letter while struggling to formulate the words to use so that they would know that I was serious about becoming a lay Buddhist. After introducing myself, I advised them that I had been given my information about the Abbey by Reverend Ichinose. I explained how I had come to study Buddhism and how I had come to the Soto Mission in Honolulu to learn how to do *zazen*. I told them about my experience doing *zazen*. I asked if it would be possible for me to come to the

Abbey in order to take lay ordination and formally become a Buddhist. I made sure to tell them why I was asking to go to them rather then doing it locally at the mission. Placing a stamp on the envelope, I mailed my letter to California. Now I would have to patiently wait for their reply.

Chapter 10
Jukai

Within a week I received the letter from Shasta Abbey that I had been looking for daily in my mailbox. Taking it into the house I sat down immediately to read it. It was from Rev. Jitsudo Baran, the guest master. I was told that I was being sent a copy of the Abbey's monthly journal, some information about the Abbey and it's programs, and advised that I should read Kennett Roshi's book, <u>Selling Water by the River</u>.

A few days later a small packet arrived from California. It was the information Rev. Baran had sent to me. I greedily read through the journal and program information. The ordination ceremony was to be held during a *Jukai Sesshin*. A *Sesshin* is a 7-day period with a more intensified meditation schedule. *Sesshin* actually means, "to search the heart." *Jukai* refers to that ceremony which involves the taking or renewing of one's commitment to the Ten Precepts. *Jukai* means, "Ten Precepts Meeting" and is held for someone who wishes to formally become a Buddhist.

The dates for this *sesshin* were not as yet set, but according to them it would probably be in the fall. Reading the rest of the program information booklet I saw that the Abbey required that anyone wanting to attend a weeklong retreat, must attend a weekend retreat first. My heart sank.

Once again I wrote to Rev. Baran. As much as I would have liked to attend a weekend retreat at the Abbey, it would be impossible. Flying to California would be an expense I just couldn't afford to do twice in such a short period of time. I asked if there was any way I could attend the *Jukai Sesshin* without doing the weekend retreat. I tried to assure Rev. Baran that I wasn't new to *zazen* and even suggested that they contact Rev. Ichinose at the Zen Buddhist Soto Mission if they required any further information concerning my ability and sincerity.

Less then a week later I received another letter that advised me that they were unsure that a *Jukai Sesshin* would even be scheduled. I read the disappointing lines," . . .there is a possibility that instead of doing a full *Jukai*, we will only be doing the *Jukai* ordination ceremony on one day during a week *sesshin*. This ceremony essentially includes *Sange*, the Refuges and Precepts and becoming a lay Buddhist and is the ceremony that is done when it is not possible to do the whole of *Jukai*."

No mention was made as to whether or not I would even be allowed to attend without first attending a weekend retreat. I was advised to call them in mid-August concerning the program schedule for the fall, as it hadn't been formalized as yet. I quickly wrote back asking them to send me the information, by mail, as a telephone call would be expensive for me. I enclosed a self-addressed, stamped envelope for that purpose.

In a letter dated July 31, 1975, Rev. Baran advised me that the *Jukai sesshin* was definitely scheduled for September 6th through 13th. A tentative reservation had been made for me. I read the next line in a state of excitement. "It would be impractical for you to attend a retreat but that should not prevent your full participation in the *sesshin*." I was overjoyed.

A copy of <u>Becoming a Buddhist</u> had been enclosed and I was instructed to read it before the *sesshin*. I was also directed to read the sections on the *Shushogi* and the *Kyojukaimon* in <u>Selling Water by The River</u>. I posted a letter back that same day including my payment to confirm my reservation. I also enclosed an order to purchase the book I was directed to read sections of. Now it was a reality. Now I had to make all the necessary arrangements.

Shasta Abbey was not to be an easy place to get to. It was located in Siskiyou County, in a mountainous area of northern California along the Oregon border. First I would have to fly into San Francisco airport. From there I would connect to a commuter plane to take me up to Redding. Once in Redding, I would have to stay over night, as the last bus going north to Mt. Shasta would have already left before I landed. Once I arrived at Mt. Shasta bus terminal I would, hopefully, be picked up by someone from the Abbey.

On September 5th, and I boarded the DC-10 aircraft that was to take me on the first leg of my journey from Honolulu to San Francisco. I had been given a list of items I was instructed to bring with me; a sleeping bag, a foam pad or air mattress, clothing for sitting and outdoor work, toilet articles, my own eating utensils (dinner plate, soup bowl, tea cup, knife, fork and spoon), as well as a copy of Selling Water By The River: A Manual of Zen Training, written by Jiyu Kennett. I was told not to bring any other reading material and that musical instruments and radios should be left at home, as they weren't allowed at the Abbey. Yes, it was going to be quite an experience.

As the plane rose to its cruising altitude of some 34,000 feet, I realized that I was now involved in a most solemn event. This was the beginning of my journey to the temple. This journey was considered the first real ceremony performed by the Buddhist-to-be. There were five ceremonies or events involved in order to experience lay ordination and so become, formally, a Buddhist.

The second ceremony was that of *Sange* or a process of looking within. It was the activity of facing yourself and accepting the way you really are. Next would follow the Ceremony of the *Kyojukaimon* or the taking of the Precepts. Following next would be the fourth, the Ceremony of the *Ketchimyaku*. At this point one must make the solemn decision to actually live by the Precepts. It's one thing to accept the Precepts. It's another to live them. Finally there would be the Ceremony of Recognition. It is here that one comes to understand that . . . "the fifth great act of training is the decision that there is no final act of training." (Quote taken from Becoming a Buddhist, Vol. VI, No.3, March 1975 issue).

As I stepped off the Greyhound bus in Mt. Shasta, I saw a bald headed, black robed monk standing calmly next to a rather beat up car. In fact, it was so beat up that I couldn't even tell what color it was. Much relieved to see that I had a ride after all, I waved to the monk and hurriedly gathered my belongings. Once inside the car we drove to the Abbey in relative silence.

Entering the gate the monk advised me that I would be given a brief tour of the grounds and then given an overview of the mealtime ceremonies and protocols. After this I would be free to rest until the retreat formally began later that evening. I followed the monk into the *zendo* or meditation hall. Being informed that meals would be taken here, as well, I was introduced to another monk who went on to explain the mealtime ritual.

"Did you bring all your eating utensils as instructed?" she asked me.

"Yes, I did." I replied. "Should I take them out now?"

"Please do." she responded. "They will be left here during your stay with us."

I had placed my bag on the floor next to me. I quickly unzipped the side pocket and removed the plastic bag that contained my eating implements. Carefully I unzipped the bag and took out the plate, bowl, and coffee mug. Then I took out the knife, fork, and spoon and placed them on the bowl that I had placed on top of the plate.

"Very good." the monk responded. She then took out an off white cloth approximately two feet square and covered my eating utensils with it. "This will be your cloth to use while you are here. It will be used to cover your eating implements when not in use. It will be used as your napkin during meals, and as a drying cloth after meals when you wash your utensils."

I was then asked to move them to a shelf against the far wall where I would collect and return them at each meal. She then advised me that meals were taken in silence, that one was expected to eat all that was placed on one's plate or in one's bowl. That eating was also considered a form of meditation and so must be done in a state of awareness. I was instructed to place my hands together in *gassho* (bowing in gratitude) after each bite of food taken. That would mean placing my spoon or fork down after every mouthful.

"You will not begin to eat until all monks are seated and Kennett Roshi has arrived as well," she continued. "Once you have set up your plate on the table in front of you, you will bow to your seat as well as to the other trainees. This is to show gratitude for being here, having a place to sit and meditate, and as a sign of respect toward the others. Once everyone is ready, the chanting of the scriptures will begin. During this time the food will be served to everyone individually. One is to make *gassho* each time you are being served. Do you understand this so far or am I going too fast for you?"

"No, I understand."

"Once everyone has been served," she continued, "we will raise our bowls. We will offer the merit of our food, then recite the verse called *Five Thoughts*."

She then went on to recite them for me. "We must think deeply of the ways and means by which this food has come. We must consider our merit when accepting it. We must protect ourselves from error by excluding greed from our minds. We will eat lest we become lean and die. We accept this food so that we may become enlightened."

At this point she looked thoughtfully at me and then continued with her instruction. "You will then commence eating silently, keeping a meditational state of mind. You are permitted a second helping but should only eat what you need, no more, no less. After the meal a damp cloth will be passed along the surface of the table. You will need to lift your plates quickly." She pointed to my stack of eating implements. "Then another monk will pass by. You will present your bowl by holding it in front of you and making *gassho*. The monk will ladle some hot water into your bowl. You will swish the water around to clean your bowl and then drink the water. Using your cloth to wipe your utensils dry, you will then place the cloth over everything as it is now so that it may dry. Then it may be returned to the shelf until the next meal. Shall I go over anything again?"

I went over the steps in my head. After asking her to go over a couple of points, again, I thanked her and bowed. She gave me a small smile and bowed back to me. I was then meet by another female monk. She would give me a brief tour of the buildings and grounds.

Shasta Abbey was still in its construction phase. Because of this, a double- wide trailer had been set up and was being used as the meditation hall and where meals would be taken. Later, a more permanent structure would be built. Meanwhile, not all the covered pathways were covered, the Temple Bell was situated in the middle of a mostly empty space, and only a few small buildings were completed. One of these buildings was the library where we would sometimes meet for lectures or talks.

Several other buildings were located off to the side. I was to learn that they housed the monks in residence as well as accommodating guests such as myself. After my tour the monk escorted me to the small, wooden structure that I would call home while staying here. There were four beds with basic linens, a blanket, and a pillow resting on top. A door to a shared bathroom was to the left.

"This is where you will be staying." the monk advised me. "It would appear that you are the first to arrive. Please select a bed and set yourself up. Once the *sesshin* has begun you won't have much free time. We conduct services and do *zazen* up to 9:45 in the evening. Then it's time for lights out. The wake up gong is at 5:30 in the morning. At 5:45 a.m. we begin *zazen* in the meditation hall. You are expected to be dressed and in the *zendo* on time. The rest of the schedule you will learn by just following the others. Do you need anything else or do you have any questions before I leave you?"

"No, thank you." I replied. "I think you've covered most of it."

"Very well then." she smiled. "If you should need anything please ask one of the monks."

She quietly bowed, turned, and left the room. I stood in the doorway in silence. I was alone. I looked outside at the tall pine trees and listened as the wind blew threw the branches. I heard birds singing to each other and watched some squirrels run up and down a tree trunk nearby. Turning around, I dropped my bag next to the first bed I came to and made it mine.

As the day passed, others arrived for the weeklong *sesshin*. I had been instructed that this was a silent retreat. Consequently, we were asked to remain silent and to only speak when it was absolutely necessary. No idle chatter was to be tolerated. When the three women who were to be sharing my humble room arrived, I realized how difficult it was to "not talk." How much we rely on verbal communication. When this isn't available to you, you quickly learn the value of a smile, a nod of the head, a movement of a hand, and body language in general.

The gong was sounded. The *sesshin* had officially begun. We quietly left our dwelling and made our way to the *zendo*. There would be a lot to learn, a lot to experience, and a lot to discover about our selves during this week of intensive meditation. I hoped to complete everything successfully so as to become an "official lay Buddhist." I was to learn that to be a Buddhist, simply meant to live by the precepts and to follow what the Buddha taught.

Reverend Master Jiyu-Kennett, Roshi, was born in England in 1924. She originally became a Buddhist in the Theravada tradition. Kennett Roshi was later introduced to the Rinzai sect of Zen Buddhism by D.T. Suzuki. They had meet while he was visiting London. Jiyu Kennett began formal priesthood training in 1962, after having been ordained by the Very Reverend Seck Kim Seng, the Archbishop of Malacca. She was then considered a part of the Chinese Buddhist *Sanga* (community of Buddhist monks and nuns*)*.

The Very Reverend Keido Chisan Koho Zenji, the Chief Abbot of Soji-ji in Japan, invited her to come to train in the Soto tradition. In 1963, Juyi-Kennett received the *Dharma* Transmission from Koho Zenji and was then certified by him as a Zen Master or

Roshi. Koho Zenji encouraged her to bring Soto Zen to America. In 1969, Kennett Roshi came to the United States (along with two Western disciples) with the intention of doing just that.

The Zen Mission Society was founded in 1970, and in November of that year Shasta Abbey was started. The Abbey was to be set up as a Buddhist seminary and training monastery. In 1978 the "Zen Mission Society" was changed to "The Order of Buddhist Contemplatives." Emphasis at the Abbey was on the Serene Reflection Meditation Tradition (called Ts'ao-Tung Ch'an in China or Soto Zen in Japan), developing mindfulness in daily living, and adherence to the Buddhist Precepts.

Shasta Abbey sits on 16 acres of untouched forest between Mt. Shasta and Mt. Eddy in northern California. Centrally located on the property is the cloistered, oval compound complex which includes some twelve primary buildings such as the *Zendo* (Meditation Hall) and *Hondo* (Ceremony Hall) as well as some smaller buildings including the senior priests' residences. The primary function of the Abbey is to train priests and teachers of Buddhism. The California Superintendent of Public Instruction approved both of these programs. Shasta Abbey is, therefor, a state-recognized seminary.

Not only is Shasta Abbey a year round residence monastery for some 40 to 60 male and female monks training to become Zen Buddhist Priests, but it also has extensive programs for lay people. The weekend and weeklong retreats are part of that program. They also offer three-month training terms for those interested in pursuing it further. Kennett Roshi was the founder, Abbess, and Spiritual Director of the Abbey until her death in November 1996.

I will not bore you here with the minute-by-minute details of my *sesshin* experience. Rather I will present the daily schedule as we usually followed it and then get on with the spiritual or inner experiences each step of the *Jukai* process evoked in me.

The *Sesshin* Schedule

5:30 a.m.	Rising
5:45 a.m.	*Za-zen*
6:15 a.m.	Morning Service
7:30 a.m.	Temple Clean Up
8:20 a.m.	Breakfast
9:00 a.m.	Reading
9:30 a.m.	*Za-Zen, Kinhin*

	(walking meditation), *Za-Zen*
11:00 a.m.	Work
1:00 p.m.	Lunch
1:40 p.m.	Rest Period
2:30 p.m.	Work
3:30 p.m.	Evening Service/*Za-Zen*
4:15 p.m.	Work
5:30 p.m.	Reading
6:00 p.m.	Dinner
6:40 p.m.	Rest Period and Recollection
7:25 p.m.	*Za-Zen, Kinhin, Za-Zen*
8:40 p.m.	Vespers
8:50 p.m.	Tea for Monks/return to our quarters
9:15 p.m.	Lights Out
9:45 p.m.	Lights Out for the Monastery

The shower schedule for women was as follows:

| Monday, Tuesday, & Wednesday: | After Lunch |
| Thursday, Friday, Saturday & Sunday: | After Dinner |

During my second day of meditation, I found myself extremely restless. My mind just wouldn't be still. I tried as hard as I could to at least keep my body still. Perhaps if I were able to stay completely still physically, my mind would eventually follow. Unfortunately, this was not to happen so easily. My *Za-Zen* and *Kinhin* sessions became a battleground for me. I struggled to bring my mind into submission by making sure I didn't move a muscle and by constantly trying to stop my thoughts from hijacking me.

Unsettling thoughts and feelings swept through me each time I sat or walked in meditation. With nothing to distract me, everything seemed to come forward from the depth of my mind to torment me. I knew I wasn't perfect, who is? But I was still upset to see a long list of my faults and weakness' bubbling up into my consciousness. At this time I would attach to these thoughts instead of just watching them move across the screen of my awareness. I would try to rationalize and, sometimes, try to blame other people or various situations for my shortcomings.

It was the same the following day. Several times I felt the hot tears of sadness and frustration falling from my half-closed eyes. It was during this particular day that I noticed that I was not alone in my emotional state of mind. I would hear the muffled sobs of other people who were sitting in meditation. I didn't know if they were fellow lay-persons attending this retreat or if they were monks, but it hardly mattered. It was obvious that I was certainly not alone. Was this what was meant by being a part of a *Sanga*?

Za-zen became even more difficult. I started to feel a dull pain between my navel and chest. I continued to cry from within and to feel tears making trails across my cheeks. The next day I had cramping in my left shoulder and neck. I checked my sitting position, took an internal inventory, but found nothing incorrect in my posture. Now my mind hurried back and forth between seeing my shortcomings, and dwelling on the pain I was feeling. Would this never end? Maybe I should just call it a day, leave here, and go home.

That afternoon I decided to try to talk to a priest about all of this. I signed the San-Zen, or private interview request list, posted just outside the *Zendo*. Later that evening just before *Za-Zen* was to begin again, a priest came up to me and invited me to have a San-Zen session with him. He was one of the more senior priests. After following him into a sitting room obviously intended for the purpose, we sat down across from one another.

I told him what I had been experiencing during the last few days of meditation. I briefly told him about the unsettling thoughts that were constantly coming up and about the pain I was now feeling when I sat to meditate. I even told him about my thoughts concerning leaving the retreat and going home.

He listened to me thoughtfully. When I had finished he continued to sit in silence. I remained silent as well. Then he asked me to sit the way I did in the Zendo to do meditation. I did so. He examined my posture. He gently pushed the small of my back slightly forward. Then he asked if I always sat this way with my left foot on my right thigh. When I told him I did, he suggested that I place my right foot on my left thigh for a while and then to switch off so as not to cause damage to my spine. When sitting in the full lotus position this was rarely a problem, but it could present a problem when using the half-lotus position.

He went on to tell me that the cramping could be a result of either a poor sitting position or could be a result of karma, or a little of both. At this point he suggested that I change my sitting position and to continue to work on what was coming up within my mind, not to give up. He assured me that this was really a good sign as it meant I was starting to look within and that with perseverance great progress could be made. It was apparent from his body language (as subtle as it was) that the interview was over. I rose from the floor, bowed to him in gratitude, and left to return to the *Zendo*.

To look deep within and to find yourself-wanting is the first step in the next stage of *Jukai* that is called *Sange*. It is at this point that you realize what, and who, you really are, that you aren't perfect, that you have often caused pain and suffering not only to yourself, but to others as well. It is not a very pleasant realization to come to. While pressing on with *Za-zen* I came to see many things I hadn't wanted to see in myself. I also saw things in others that I didn't like. I felt hatred toward people who I had perceived as having slighted or hurt me either in the past or in the present. I was getting more frustrated. Wasn't meditation supposed to make you calm and at peace within yourself? It obviously wasn't working. Yet, I eventually found my mind slowing down and becoming still. Suddenly, a strong thought entered my mind, "Sometimes good intentions come out badly. We must have compassion."

Yes, we all have the potential for evil. All we can do is try our best at being good. We all have our karma to work on. It's not always easy either. I really shouldn't judge another. I'm in no position to judge another or their intentions. After all, I'm also not blameless. All I can do is take responsibility for my own actions and just accept those of other people with a compassionate heart. All beings suffer.

I came to realize from deep within my being how heavy a load hate is, and how very tiring. Instead of hatred, I should feel compassion and loving-kindness. It would make more sense to cultivate loving-kindness and compassion rather than hatred. My mind stilled even further and I felt an inner calm I had never known before. I became aware that the pain I had felt, both physically and emotionally, had disappeared. And I just sat.

The ceremony of *Sange* is symbolic of the event one experiences from within oneself. It is one of the most important and solemn ceremonies since it marks the moment when you recognize that you are not really satisfied with yourself, that you're not perfect, and that you must do something about it in order to improve. You take responsibility for yourself with no excuses.

The *Sange* verse is recited:

*All wrong actions, behavior and karma perpetrated by
me from time immemorial have been, and are, caused by
greed, anger and delusion which have no beginning, born
of my body, mouth and will; I now make full and open
confession thereof.*

Silently we all lined up for this most solemn procession. We walked quietly until we came to the first priest who represented *Kanzeon*, the Compassionate Buddha. In front of him, he held a bowl filled with folded pieces of paper which had written on them, "All the bad karma I have accrued, all my bad attitudes of mind, I wish to get rid of; I recognize that they are there." As each one of us stepped forward, we could choose to either take a piece of paper or not. The choice was ours and ours alone to make. When my turn arrived, I carefully took a small piece of paper from inside the bowl that was being offered to me. Placing it in the palm of my left hand, I resumed my place and continued to move with the silent procession.

The third ceremony, called *Kyojukaimon*, involves taking the Precepts. At the point of *Sange* when one decides one must do something about oneself, you realize that you must find a way to do so. This ceremony involves accepting the Precepts as a guide to assist you in your training. The Precepts are the foundation of Buddhism. It is the path the Buddha's and Patriarchs have shown us in order that we, too, may follow them and experience being "fully awake."

I was ready to hear and accept the Precepts. The ceremony was held just prior to the ceremony of *Sange* in order to allow the individual to keep them clearly in his/her mind and so instill a determination to live by them as a means of working on oneself. The Precepts of the Buddha's were then given and received.

The Three Treasures Precepts or Three Refuges
I take refuge in the Buddha.
I take refuge in the *Dharma*.
I take refuge in the *Sangha*.

The Three Pure Precepts
Cease from evil.
Do only good.
Do good for others.

The Ten Great Precepts
Do not kill.

Do not steal.

Do not covet.

Do not say that which is not true.

Do not sell the wine of delusion.

Do not speak against others.

Do not be proud of yourself and devalue others.

Do not be mean in giving either *Dharma* or wealth.

Do not be angry.

Do not defame the Three Treasures.

Once the act of *Sange* had been experienced and I had taken refuge in the Precepts, I was now considered to be Buddhist. At this point, I would be allowed to participate in the formal lay ordination and receive confirmation of that fact. I decided to do so.

I knelt in front of Jiyu Kennett, Roshi, and bowed. I remained in that position with my hands pressed together in *gassho*. She spoke as she placed a razor blade against the crown of my head. Symbolically shaving my head. She then asked me if I accepted the Three Refuges, the Three Pure Precepts, and the Ten Great Precepts of the Buddha's. I answered in the affirmative. She then placed a *wagesa*, a black mantle considered the simplest form of the monk's robe, over my head and around my neck. The following verse was then recited, and was to be recited whenever the *wagesa* was worn during *Za-zen*:

> *How great and wondrous are the cloths of enlightenment,*
> *Formless, yet embracing every treasure;*
> *I wish to unfold the Buddha's teaching*
> *That I may help all living things*

Now that the Precepts have been accepted, will you decide to actually live by them? Will you actually do something? The Ceremony of *Ketchimayaku* symbolizes the act of accepting training for the sake of training. It's making the Precepts a part of your self and putting them into continual practice day by day. It is in this way that the lay Buddhist joins the bloodline of the Buddha's and Patriarchs.

Now that the Precepts had been taken, there is another day of meditation. Then everyone reassembles in the ceremony hall for the

Ketchimayaku. It is evening and only candles illuminate the hall. Kennett Roshi enters, ascends the high altar, and sits in meditation. She is acting as Shakyamuni's representative. A torch is lit and held at her side as the *Ketchimayaku,* a silk manuscript listing her lineage from Shakyamuni Buddha to the present, is unrolled so that it falls across the full length of her left arm. The manuscript is read in its entirety and then she expresses to us her own understanding of the Truth of the Buddha's.

The manuscript is then rolled back up. A large tray is brought in which holds smaller versions of the manuscript just read. As each new lay Buddhist comes forward, Roshi hands him, or her, a copy of the manuscript, which has their name imprinted on it. They are now part of the bloodline of the Buddha's and Patriarchs. At the end of the ceremony, Roshi leaves the room. The rest of us resume *Za-zen.*

The following evening we return to the ceremony hall. It is time for the Ceremony of Recognition. This is when the trainee comes to realize that training is forever ongoing, forever practicing the Way, living by the Precepts. It's a time when the new lay Buddhist is shown that the Buddha's and Patriarchs respect you for having committed to this ongoing training and practice. It's when Buddha recognizes Buddha. The priests proceed to walk around us, ringing bells and chanting, "Buddha recognizes Buddha and Buddha bows to Buddha" After circling the hall three times the priests leave in procession. The trainees return to their meditation.

Jukai having ended, it was time to leave the Abbey. We were allowed to sleep in a little longer that morning. As we prepared to leave we exchanged addresses and phone numbers. Although we never had a chance to speak with one another, we felt connected within a special bond. Perhaps we would keep in touch. After breakfast we would each go our separate way. Each returning to the home we had left behind in order to come to this monastery, to experience *Jukai.*

Chapter 11
Eureka!

And so I returned home. The two-day trip was actually a good buffer for me as I reentered the mundane world of worry and work. I was still in a state of "spiritual high." Everyone seemed to be moving so very quickly, and appeared to be so intensely involved and restless. The talking never stopped and I found it difficult to keep up. It was obvious that my weeklong meditation retreat had slowed me down and made me much more introspective, thoughtful, and still.

The hustle and bustle around me tired me out. It was as if I were experiencing sensory overload. For the first time I realized how everyday life can become such a distraction that it is very difficult to stay focused and to keep the mind of *Za-zen/* the meditative mind. Once on the plane that was to take me back home to Honolulu, I slept.

Now home and back to my daily routine, I resumed going to the Soto Mission for weekly meditation as I had done before. Nothing had changed and yet I felt differently. I still sat in silence. I still joined the others for tea after *Za-zen*. But an inner stillness and calm was now a part of me that I hadn't noticed before. I was more apt to listen then to talk. Little things didn't seem to bother me as much although I would still find myself getting caught up in other things.

My parents called to see how I was doing. They knew I had taken a week to spend some time alone somewhere in California, but for what purpose they hadn't known. Not knowing exactly what I was going to experience, or even whether or not I would actually go through the entire process in order to formally become a lay Buddhist, I had decided not to tell my parents very much. But now that I had completed lay ordination, it was time to let my parents know about it.

How does one explain to one's parents that you have a belief that now differs from their own, the one they raised you within? It was easier to speak with my mother about it. She already knew that I had been studying about eastern religions and that I had enough of an interest in Buddhism that I was practicing a Buddhist form of meditation. We had even had discussions about Buddhism and my restlessness with Jewish traditional and ritual practices. She had even purchased and read various books that I had suggested to her. Consequently, she knew more about Buddhism then one would have expected. My father, however, had no interest in such things.

My mother was primarily concerned about my still being a Jew. Had I renounced Judaism for this? Did I choose to ignore over 4,000 years of Jewish history? No, I assured her. That wasn't the case. I was still a Jew. I felt connected to my ancestors all the way back to Abraham. I felt a special connection to the land of Israel as the land of my people. I had come to Buddhism by way of my meditation practice. I saw *Za-zen* as a means of finding G-d. It was a bridge, a way that could possibly lead me to a direct experience of the G-d of Israel, my G-d. My mother appeared to understand. Okay, I was a Buddhist-Jew. That may be okay and acceptable. She would keep an open mind.

My father kept silent. One didn't have deep philosophical or religious discussions with him. I really didn't know what he thought. His only concern at the time: was I getting involved in idol worship? Was I praying to the image of Buddha as a god? I assured him that I wasn't. I told him that Buddha was not a god, but a man who had discovered the Truth and had shown others the way to discover this Truth for them selves. He appeared satisfied but I knew he really didn't understand it. What was this *Za-zen*, this meditation I was so involved with? One just followed Jewish law, attended synagogue, and performed the rituals and traditions. You celebrated the holidays as they occurred throughout the yearly cycle, and did what was expected of you. He couldn't understand what more I could be looking for and I would never be able to explain it to him in a satisfactory way.

I still strove to hear the voice of G-d. To experience what I intuitively felt the Patriarchs, the Prophets, my ancient ancestors in Biblical times had experienced. If the method they used was not being taught in Judaism, I would practice the method of Buddha. I would do *Za-zen*, sit, listen, and wait. One realization I had come away with. You can't hear another voice if you are too busy talking. You must learn to be silent and to listen. This was what I was trying to do by practicing meditation. I would continue to practice listening until I was able, hopefully, to hear the small, still voice of G-d.

It was during that time in my life that I picked up the book by James A. Michener titled, <u>The Source,</u> which I had started to read some time ago, but had never finished. I found it on my bookshelf and took it down. Although I had read a couple of chapters a year of so ago, I didn't remember them, so I decided to start from the beginning. This time I became highly engrossed in the story. I was to read it straight through, all 1,188 pages.

It was when I was approximately 2/3 through the book that I was to discover something that would change the direction of my spiritual life. This was a story about the archeological excavation of a fictitious Tel in Makor, located in Israel that was supposedly located in Western Galilee. As the dig continues you were taken back in time as each layer of history was exposed. Although I found it very interesting, since it involved the daily life of the ancient and not so ancient Israelites, it wasn't until I entered the last 3rd of this phenomenal book that I was to be, literally, stopped in my tracks.

If someone had told me that a historically based novel would change my vision of Judaism, I would have laughed heartily at the very idea. Yet that was just what happened. As I read I became more and more entranced by the magnitude of what James A. Michener was writing about. But when I came to page 793 in the thick paperback copy I was reading I felt as if someone had come up from behind and hit me across the back of the head. The last paragraph on that page began as follows:

"Dr. Abulafia had met Ximeno twenty years ago, in the winter of 1522. It was an accident, an accident of words: at a formal dinner celebrating the patron saint of Avaro he had asked innocently, 'What is this Kabbala the Jewish people speak of?' And after a series of cautious probings the counselor had revealed himself as a master of the Kabbala, that esoteric body of mysticism that had grown up in Germany and Spain as a pathway to the understanding of the Hebrew God."

My reading slowed down almost to a halt. Intuitively, I sensed that something very important was about to manifest itself to me yet I didn't know what.

"Ximeno had given Dr. Abulafia a manuscript of the Zohar,

the arcane book of Kabbalism, believed to have been composed centuries before by a mystical Jew in Granada, and had initiated him into its mysteries."

What mysteries? Understanding G-d? What was this Zohar manuscript?

"There was in life, and his Spanish nature sensed it, an additional spirit of flight, the wild movement of the human soul seeking some kind of further identification with God; and only in the Zohar did Abulafia find a solution that satisfied him."

So, I wasn't alone in this search for a closer connection to God. I couldn't believe I was actually reading this in a novel written by James A. Michener. I reread what I had just finished reading and then continued on.

"Between the immensity of God and the insignificance of man the Zohar postulated ten spheres of divine manifestation, each of which man can approach or even encompass: the supreme crown of God, the wisdom of God, the intelligence, the love, the power, the compassion, the everlastingness, the majesty, the root foundation and the kingdom of God. These ten spheres, through which God emerges from his unknowable state, can be represented in the form of a tree, but it is known that the sap of this tree, the vitalizing power, is and must be the ultimate spirit of God. It was through the exploration and contemplation of these spheres that . . .the mystical point at which . . . they would come close to the ultimate secret of God Himself. Then . . . they would become aware of the actual presence of God Himself."

EUREKA! This was the missing component I had been searching for most of my life. This was the means by which a Jew could enter the spiritual realm of Judaism. This was the mystical side of Judaism that I sensed must exist but could never find. If this were true, and I determined I would immediately start researching it, then my path was clear. I must find out how the Jewish mystics practiced, and I must find the English translation of the Zohar to read for myself.

Chapter 12
Kabbalah

I decided to make another visit to the Reform Temple on Pali Hwy. This time to another Rabbi, much younger than the first one I had spoken to years before. We stood outside his office door within the courtyard that extended between his office and the main sanctuary. I introduced myself, thanked him for taking time away from his busy schedule to speak with me and then jumped in.

"Rabbi, I have been practicing meditation according to the Buddhist methodology as a way of being able to know G-d. For years now I thought that was my only way to go beyond one-sided prayer. Recently I've been reading The Source, by James Michener. Imagine my surprise when I came across something in Judaism that I never even knew existed. Kabbalah, Jewish Mysticism. Rabbi, I've been looking all my life for the answer of how I could experience first hand what Abraham, Moses, David, the Prophet's, etc., had experienced in order to know G-d intimately. I could never find it in Judaism so I ended up pursuing a path via Buddhism. Now I find there is a Jewish tradition similar to the Buddhist way of meditation, but I can find no one to help me. Do you know anything about Kabbalah?" I asked.

The Rabbi looked at me in disbelief verging on horror. After a moment taken to frame his response he replied, "Yes, I know of Kabbalah but that isn't anything you want to get into. Don't delve into such things. It is very dangerous. If you wish to know G-d then read the Torah, attend services, and uphold the Shabbat. Also, if you are serious, keep *kashrut* (kosher) and do *mitzvot (good deeds)*. Get involved with the Jewish community. You don't need such a thing as Kabbalah"

"But I know it is what I've been searching for Rabbi." I responded in desperation. "I tried your approach. It's not enough for me. It's repetitive and goes in circles. I want, and I need a direct line with G-d. I want to "know" G-d the way Abraham, Isaac, Joseph knew G-d, on a personal basis."

"I can not help you with this." he said sadly. "What you are pursuing is very dangerous. I strongly suggest you forget such ideas and do as I advise. It also troubles me that you are involved in another religion. There is only one G-d, and that is the G-d of Abraham. Don't pursue idol worship. Don't do it. It's a very, very dangerous thing."

"Rabbi, I'm no idol worshipper. In fact, it's G-d I'm pursuing. I know Kabbalah holds the solution to my quest. But if I can't learn Kabbalistic methods of meditation then the only avenue left is to learn meditation wherever I can. In this case, Buddhism offers this opportunity." I said in resolve and frustration.

I knew I was on the right path, but no one would help me to pursue it. I talked to several other Rabbis when I visited my family on the mainland, but their response was pretty much the same as the Rabbi in Hawaii. It was there, in Judaism. Some Rabbis knew about Kabbalah, some denied knowing anything about it, but it all boiled down to the same thing. I ended up with nothing. It was at this juncture that I decided that I must pursue Buddhist meditation, as doing meditation within a Jewish context appeared to be impossible in the Jewish community of today. It saddened me, but at least I knew what I had to do.

However, I didn't give up my search for more information on Kabbalah. One day while browsing through the Religion and Philosophy section in a local bookstore, I came across a book title that stopped me dead in my tracks. It was <u>Meditation and the Bible</u>, by Aryeh Kaplan. I had never heard of Aryeh Kaplan, but over the years I would read many of his books.

This book made the connection I had always known existed in Judaism. Here was a scholar who knew Kabbalah and who was an authority in his own right, but who was willing to share what he knew. As it stated in the inside flap of his book, "One of the greatest mysteries of the Bible involves the methods used by the prophets to attain their unique states of consciousness." Aryeh Kaplan went even further, in order " . . .to demonstrate how meditation played a key role in the methods of the prophets."

This was it! I could hardly contain my excitement. I practically ran up to the check out to purchase this wonderful book. I started reading it as soon as I walked out of the double doors of the bookstore. Driving back home was an agony as I couldn't drive and read at the same time.

What I was reading amazed me. I take the liberty of quoting directly from Aryeh Kaplan on page 17 of his book, Meditation and the Bible.

" . . . it is evident that the concept of meditation was well known among the Judaic philosophers and Kabbalists, and that the term most often used to express this concept is *Hitabodedut*. While philosophers often speak of unstructured meditation involving God and His creation, the Kabbalistic schools advocated more formal, structured ways of meditation. The goal of meditation, especially as described by Kabbalistic masters, is to attain enlightenment. In Hebrew, the word most often used to describe such enlightenment is *Ruach HaKodesh*, which can literally be translated as 'Holy Spirit.' It is a term that is consistently used by all Hebrew writers."

Enlightenment? Up until this moment I had only seen that term used within a Buddhist context. Here I was discovering it in a Judaic context. He then went on to explain how the spiritual realm consisted of ten levels, or spheres, usually referred to as the *Ten Sefirot*. One must purify all ten levels if one hoped to reach the level of enlightenment or *Ruach*.

In order to purify these ten spheres, one must follow the ten steps prescribed which would lead one to the ultimate crown of *Ruach HaKodesh* (enlightenment). These ten steps were listed in the Talmud (the compilation of the discourses on the Torah or Five Books of Moses) and include:

Study:	Constant study and observance being careful not to break any religious law.
Carefulness:	This is related to diligence in that it is being aware at all times.
Diligence:	Being careful to obey every commandment. Not becoming attached to nonessentials.
Cleanliness:	To lead a clean life both in thought and deed.
Abstention:	Reaching a level where one will avoid even permissible actions if they could possibly lead to evil.
Purity:	Purifying oneself from any evil past or present.
Piety:	Dedicating oneself to God, which goes beyond merely following the law.

Humility:	The negation of ego.
Fear of Sin:	Developing such a strong sense of good, that one actually dreads sin or evil.
Holiness:	The total negation of the physical aspects.

The method used to navigate and progress through these ten levels is meditation. Aryeh Kaplan goes on to explain that it "involves a very high degree of mental quietude." and "The spiritual power and enlightenment that is the most important element of the prophetic experience is not found in the whirlwind or earthquake, but in the 'still small voice' of utter tranquillity. This is a state that is attained through deep meditation."

And what was the method used by these seekers of enlightenment? I still didn't know, but I did find out why it was so difficult to find out. In chapter 8 of Aryeh Kaplan's book he wrote,

"Although the prophetic schools never admitted initiates indiscriminately, after the exile they actually became secret societies. The leaders had seen that the open quest for prophecy and the mystical experience had led many people to engage in idolatry and sorcery. In a large measure, it was this that led to the exile, and the leadership was determined that this would not recur. They therefore 'nullified the lust for idolatry,' restricting all mystical teachings to very limited schools, consisting only of the most spiritually advanced individuals. The entire focus of Judaism was thus altered. Where the quest for prophecy and mystical enlightenment had played a key role in the general life of the populace, it was now regulated to the background. The focus shifted, and now the Oral Law, with all its intricacies, became the focus of national life, reaching its zenith with the compilation of the Talmud. The mystical activity that existed remained the domain of a few small, restricted secret societies. The general rule was, 'One may not teach the secrets to two people at the same time. One may not teach the mysteries of the Chariot (*Merkava*) even to one, unless he is so wise that he can understand by himself. An important ramification of this was found in the area of prayer. During the time of the prophets, there was no real formal worship service, and each person would pray in his own words. If a special prayer was needed to channel a particular level of spiritual energy, such a service could be led by one of the prophets or their disciples, who know how to word the prayer to channel the required forces. It is for this reason that a prayer leader is called a *Chazan*, from the same root as *Chazon*, meaning a prophetic vision. When prophecy ceased, however, this was no longer possible. A formal system of worship, including all of its mystical elements, had to be formulated. This was done by the Great Assembly, under the leader of Ezra, shortly after the return from the Babylonian Exile. It is significant to note that a number of the last prophets took place in compiling these prayers."

This certainly explained why it was so difficult to find out about this subject. It also explained why the Rabbis who were aware of Jewish mysticism, avoided it like the plague and wanted no part in letting their congregations know that it even existed. What Rabbi would want to risk leading fellow Jew's into idolatry or sorcery or worse? This also explained why the Rabbi I had spoken to was so concerned about my following Buddhist practices. To him it was a form of idolatry.

It also explained why Temples and Synagogues held services and why these services were so strictly choreographed. The rigid forms and the repetitiveness also made perfect sense in light of this new information. If you were not allowed to enter the realm of mysticism, then all that was left was formal prayer. Although formal worship fulfilled most people's spiritual needs, unfortunately, it fell very short of meeting mine.

And, obviously, I wasn't the only Jew to feel this way. I had discovered that countless Jew's had gravitated toward eastern religions, including Buddhism, as a means of entering that forbidden area of mysticism which they so sorely lacked and so strongly desired. What a pity. Here Kabbalah, or Jewish mysticism, existed in our own backyard and yet we were forced to look outside to find it.

Hopefully, in time, Rabbi's and other Jewish educators would wake up and realize that spirituality is a very important and necessary component. They would see that our young people needed to know that methods do exist in Judaism and they will offer to teach those who are serious about learning it. I can't say that this awareness, and an offer to teach those Jews who desired it, would prevent all Jews from pursuing other forms such as Buddhism, but it certainly would halt an exodus brought about by ignorance of it's existence in one's own religion.

From reading that first book I went on to read his book <u>Meditation and Kabbalah</u>. <u>Jewish Meditation</u> was devoured next. From Aryeh Kaplan I discovered books by Gershom Scholem. Professor Scholem was Professor of Jewish Mysticism at the Hebrew University in Jerusalem. Considered one of the foremost authorities on Kabbalah, I read every book authored by him that I could find.

As time went by I discovered more and more books about Kabbalah by various authors. An entirely new world appeared before me. Yet, I still could find nothing that would enable me to safely learn the meditation methods employed by the Kabbalists. There appeared to be so much similarity between Buddhism and Kabbalah that I felt the next step should be to see if some sort of integration of the two could be possible.

Chapter 13
Kabbalah and Buddhism

Once again it was Aryeh Kaplan who started my process of integration. As I read his book <u>Meditation and Kabbalah</u>, I came across a section where he quoted a section from <u>The Zohar</u>, a mystical work considered the classical text of Kabbalah. Rabbi Moses de Leon, a Spanish scholar in the 13th century, attributed the work to the famous school of Rabbi Shim'on bar Yohai. It was written in Aramaic, a language used from Egypt to India, and still used today in Jewish legal documents. The Talmud was written in Aramaic and there are even passages in the Bible in Aramaic). It was taken from a dialog spoken by Rabbi Abba in *Zohar 1:99b.*

"One day I came to a city of the people of the East, and they told me some wisdom that they had inherited from ancient times. They also had books explaining this wisdom, and they brought me one such book." It continued,

"I said to them, 'My children, the things in that book are very close to the teachings of the Torah. But you must keep yourselves from these books in order that your hearts not be drawn to their [idolatrous] practices and all the [other] facets mentioned there, and lest you be drawn away from serving the Blessed Holy One.'

All these books can confuse a person. This is because the people of the East were great sages, who inherited this wisdom from Abraham. He had given it to the sons of his concubines, as it is written, 'to the sons of the concubines that Abraham had taken, Abraham gave gifts' (Genesis 25:6). [This was originally true wisdom] but later it was drawn into many [idolatrous] sides."

I had to smile to myself. Here was <u>The Zohar</u>, itself, the classic work of Kabbalah, saying that the wisdom of the East was, in fact, given to them by our very own patriarch, Abraham. Interesting. It also implied that the reason the teachings of the East were to be avoided was because the True Wisdom had been altered (by them) so as to be removed from the Truth as it had been originally taught.

Certainly, I could appreciate how this could be thought. I, too, had read many books on eastern religions and philosophies. Many of them did seem to go over the line in terms of superstition, and serving deities of all kinds. I had been aware of this foible and so had been extremely careful when seeking a school of Buddhism to study to make sure they hadn't deified the Buddha's and *Boddhisattva's* or gotten too wrapped up in superstitious practices and traditions.

What I found most intriguing, however, was the fact that even hundred's of years ago Kabbalist's were aware of the "Wisdom of the East" and how similar the teachings were to their own. Whether this "True Wisdom" originated with Abraham and was brought to the East by the sons of his concubines, or that Abraham had had contact, somehow, with a sage from the East who imparted this "True Wisdom" to him, really didn't seem to matter (although the former theory would certainly have made my integration process easier). Merely the fact that it was agreed that there was a link between the two meant that such integration was, indeed, possible.

There was obvious similarity in the terms they used. For instance, both Buddhism and Kabbalah have a term meaning enlightenment. In Buddhism it is *Nibbana* (Pali) or *Nirvana* (Sanskrit). In Hebrew it is called *Ruach HaKodesh*. Individual enlightenment or being enlightened is called *Devekut* in Hebrew, in Pali it is *Sambodhi*. Meditation is called *Hitbodedut* in Hebrew. No-thing-ness in Hebrew is called *Ayin*. The ultimate no-thing-ness (obtaining enlightenment) is called *Parinibbana* in Pali or *Parinirvana* in Sanskrit. It must be noted that *Parinibbana* refers to the state after the death of a fully enlightened person. In Hebrew it is referred to as *Ein-Sof* the potential of no-thing-ness, which also means Infinite Being (not bound by mortal, finite existence). In Hebrew the term for equanimity is *hishtavvut*. Celestial Beings or Angels? In Pali they are known as *Devas*, in Hebrew they are referred to as *Chayot* or Cherubs.

It would certainly appear that we were working with a similar vocabulary of terms that also held identical meanings. If I were to substitute a Hebrew word for a Pali or Sanskrit word I could be referring to the same experience. This would certainly make it easier for me to draw parallels between the two systems.

In Buddhism there are various meditation methods depending on what sect you are involved in. You may be introduced to meditation by using a Mantra (the repetition of a sound or phrase over and over again), a *mandala* (a picture used in visualization), *Koan* (a nonsensical problem given to someone to meditate on in order to try to derive an answer), *Vipassana* or Insight Meditation (meditating on a specific element of reality such as impermanence, conditioning, and ego-less-ness), *Za-zen* or Tranquillity Meditation (the meditation method of No-Thought*)*.

In the Kabbalistic tradition they also used various meditation methods. One method was to repeat a number of Divine Names 112 times (a form of Mantra). Another approach was for the Kabbalist to contemplate on the *Tetragrammaton* (a diagram of G-d's name-- Hebrew letters of *yod, hay, vav, hay*). This system is very similar to the Buddhist use of a *mandala*. Another method of the Kabbalists was to meditate " . . . on thoughts, feelings or mental images that arise spontaneously in the mind." (Taken from p.12, <u>Meditation and Kabbalah</u>, by Aryeh Kaplan). That method sounds very similar to most forms of Buddhist meditation based on insight and tranquillity techniques.

Naturally, both systems have other methods which depend on the sect one is dealing with and what the Buddhist Master or Kabbalist Adept felt was appropriate for the student at a specific time. However, the list certainly shows an uncanny similarity between the two systems. And, the lofty objective in both systems was to reach the stage of Enlightenment, a state of non-attachment, non-ego, compassion, loving-kindness, and equanimity. Being free from all greed, hatred, and delusion. I certainly won't attempt to describe that which can't be described in mere words.

The two even referred to a similar means of moving toward the state of enlightenment. In Kabbalah it was referred to as the "Ten Steps for Purification," in Buddhism it is called the "Seven Stages of Purification."

<u>10 Steps for Purification</u> (Kabbalah)

1. Study (*L'l'mod*)
   (constant study and observance)
2. Carefulness (*Z'herot*)
   (being aware at all times)

3. Diligence (*Harezot*)
   (not attaching to non-essentials)
4. Cleanliness (*Nikayon*)
   (in both thought and deed)
5. Abstention (*P'reshut*)
   (avoiding even permissible actions if it could possibly lead to evil)
6. Purity (*Tohar*)
   (purifying oneself from any evil past or present)
7. Piety (Yey'at Shamayem)
   (dedicating oneself to God which goes beyond the law)
8. Humility (*Anavah or An'v'tanot*)
   (the negation of ego)
9. Fear of Sin *(Yer'at Chataem or Pa'al Chata'at)*
   (developing such a strong sense of good that one dreads, and automatically avoids sin and evil)
10. Holiness *(K'dushah)*
    (total negation of the physical)

7 Stages of Purification (Buddhism)

Note: The number(s) in ( ) are similar equivalents as listed above for the "10 Steps for Purification" in Kabbalah

1. Purity of Morality (*Sila-Visuddhi*) **(5, 6)**
   (right speech, action, and livelihood)
2. Purity of Mind (*Citta-Visuddhi*) **(2, 4)**
   (Exerting right effort, right concentration, and right awareness)
3. Purity of View (*Ditthi-Visuddhi*) **(1, 2, 8)**
   (Overcoming the false idea of self)
4. Purity by Overcoming Doubt (*Kankhavitarana-Visuddhi*) **(1, 9)**
   (Regarding cause and effect/ *karma* or *kamma*)
5. Purity by Knowledge (insight) and Vision (*Maggamagg ananadassana-Visuddhi)*
   (Awareness of what is the path and not the path)
6. Purity by Knowledge and Vision of the Way (*Patipada nanadassana-Visuddhi*)
   (Eight insight knowledges of the coarse of practice/object and awareness)
7. Purity by Knowledge (insight) and Vision (*Nanadassana Visuddhi*) **(10)**
   (Four Stages of Enlightenment: to realize the cessation of all

processes and conditioning/profound knowledge)

An entire book could be written about the similarities, which is way beyond my scope. Let me end my comparison with a quote, again, from Aryeh Kaplan's book, Kabbalah and Meditation, where on page 227 he wrote, "One should avoid idle chatter, although not as serious as the five things mentioned above [pride, anger, temper, frivolity, and malicious gossip]." Then there is the 4th training rule or precept in Buddhism, which states, "I undertake the precept to refrain from false speech [telling lies]." Sounds very similar in intent.

At this juncture I felt as if both paths were leading me to the same goal, so to speak. One method, Buddhist meditation, was readily available to me to learn and practice. The other, Kabbalah, the meditation techniques are not easily found out, rarely taught, and difficult to learn. Add to that, a warning often given by Kabbalists, that to delve in Kabbalah can be extremely dangerous, and to enter the higher realms could prove fatal. Obviously not a technique one would want to pursue on ones own without the help of a competent, qualified and adept teacher. Finding such a Master proved next to impossible for me.

Consequently, I decided to continue my meditation practice using the method from the "Wisdom of the East," as taught by the Buddha. Hopefully, this path would lead me to the Oneness I had been so long driven toward all my life. This didn't, however, preclude my searching for answers from within my own traditions that originated in the Middle East. I would travel to the Holy Land of the ancient Hebrews to further discover and see those places that my distant ancestors had sojourned and settled in. I would come away from the experience with some profound inner awareness of this One G-d who made Him/Herself known to these nomadic peoples of the desert so many thousands of years ago.

Chapter 14
Disillusionment

After 13 years of marriage Evan and I were now divorced. Problems had manifested themselves early on in our marriage, but neither of us was willing to end a relationship that had been so difficult to initiate and sustain. We had both struggled to establish our commitment to one another in spite of the pressure from both of our families to end it. An interracial relationship is always difficult at best.

But we were young and in love. We felt that love would conquer all and that in the end our families would come to accept us as a couple. Surprisingly, my parents bowed to the inevitable early on and accepted Evan as part of the family. My paternal grandparents, however, never could. Even when I was pregnant with Teleia they questioned my relationship with Evan.

Evan had his own family to deal with. At first he was extremely anxious about even telling anyone about me. Once we were engaged, he had to tell his father. Much to our mutual amazement and relief, he appeared to be open-minded about the arrangement. We knew it was acceptable when my soon-to-be father-in-law asked for the date and time of my birth so that he could consult with a *feng-shui* (a diviner) to determine the best time for our marriage to take place. Imagine our feelings when a letter arrived advising Evan that the most auspicious month would be August or May, but definitely not in June or July.

Soon after our marriage we arranged a trip to Taiwan so that I could meet my father-in-law. Although I spoke no Chinese and he spoke no English, we had no difficulty communicating. I served him a cup of hot tea, a Chinese custom showing my new family that I wished to be accepted by them. My acceptance into Evan's family was assured once this patriarch took the cup of tea from my hands, sipped the hot liquid and smiled.

Religion was never a problem in our relationship. As stated before, we each held fast to our own beliefs and raised Teleia within the tenets of Buddhism. The dissolution of our relationship was slow and insidious. Contrary to what many people may have thought, it wasn't due to religious or national differences.

After years of more tears than laughter, marriage counseling, individual counseling, and even a marriage encounter weekend (initiated by Evan), it was time to call it a day. I walked into my lawyer's office already feeling defeated. I sat in a state of numbness as I was advised as to the steps we would have to take in the divorce process. Pertinent information was gathered, documents were filled out, and I was told that the request for a divorce would be hand delivered to Evan by the following day.

Once I had signed the document on the dotted line, I was legally separated from the man I had loved for so many years. The reality of the situation hit me in full force. The hopelessness of continuing in this relationship left me feeling frustrated and disillusioned. How could this be happening? Anger surged up from somewhere deep within me. Did I blame Evan for our relationship's demise? Yes. But I also blamed my self and I started to cry. My attorney handed me a tissue from a tissue box he kept on his desk. Obviously, this was not an uncommon event in his office. Gratefully I accepted the tissue offering and quietly sobbed into my hands.

As I gained some self-control I lowered my hands into my lap. I looked down and saw the engagement ring and wedding band still on my finger. It took me a few minutes to fully comprehend that it was over. I slowly removed both rings from my finger, wrapped them in the tissue I had just used to wipe my tears, and put them away in my shoulder bag.

Dazed, I left the lawyer's office. It was a bright and sunny day. Much too nice for the way I was feeling. I sat down on a bench outside the office building and tried to stop crying.

I had tried to talk to Evan earlier, but he was into his second week of giving me the silent treatment. I had told him that if he didn't talk to me I was going to file for a divorce. He hadn't believed me and so the silent treatment continued. I had had enough. I called for an appointment with a lawyer listed with a legal plan I had subscribed to. Defeated, I stood up from the bench I was sitting on and walked slowly to my parked car. I didn't remember driving home that afternoon.

Evan was already home when I returned. I walked up to him and said the words I never expected to ever be saying. I told him I had applied for a divorce and that he would be served the papers by the next day. He didn't believe me, and the silence continued. I decided to stay away from home the next day. I didn't want to be there when the dreaded document arrived.

And so the yearlong process was over and I was now a "free" woman. Free to pay all the bills, do the chores and errands, to care for my little girl all by myself. Free to wonder what had happened. Free to wallow in my hurt and disillusionment. Free to wonder why I was so miserable. Free to be free.

Evan and I had planned to take a trip to China. I still had my airline benefits and originally decided to go to China on my own. Feeling so adrift I reconsidered and decided that going to China would not be a good idea since it would only continuously remind me of Evan. The end result? I changed my mind and made plans to visit the homeland of my people instead. I would travel to the Holy Land, to Israel.

Chapter 15
Getting to the Holy Land

had started my journey from Boston's Logan International Airport at a very early hour. First there was the short flight to New York's Kennedy airport where I would try to get on an El Al flight to Tel Aviv. Since I worked for a major airline I had a reduced rate pass to travel standby on El Al. I was happy it was a non-stop flight so that I wouldn't have to worry about being bumped off in some other foreign country along the way. The difficult part was to get on.

When traveling on a standby basis one never knew if you'd be on the flight when it left the gate or whether you would be standing there watching the plane you wanted to be on leaving without you. Not a very pleasant feeling especially if you were in an intermediate place and had nowhere to go while waiting, sometimes days, for the next departure.

I figured things weren't going so well when I arrived at one terminal and found out that El Al departed from another terminal quite a distance away. I picked up my suitcase (I only traveled with whatever I could fit under the seat or in the overhead racks) and started in the direction of the International terminal. It was an overcast morning and from time to time it rained. After walking some twenty minutes I came to the terminal I had been directed to and started looking for El Al's check-in area. I couldn't find it. Finally, I stopped someone on the sidewalk whom appeared to know what he was doing and asked for directions. He pointed back to a place I had already passed three times. I thanked him and turned back in that direction.

It was virtually a vault. No wonder I had passed it so many times without realizing it was where I wanted to go. It was all concrete, no windows and had only one entrance/exit. I walked toward the automatic doors and it opened for me. In I went. Although I had worked in an airport for over ten years I had never seen a check-in area quite like this before. It was obvious that security was the name of the game. Some may feel intimidated by this, but I felt amazingly comforted by it. No hijackings would take place on this airline, I thought.

I found the check-in counter and walked over with suitcase in hand. The El Al agent was a tall brunette with a no-nonsense expression on her face. No lighthearted airline banter with this one, I thought. I smiled and handed her my El AL standby ticket, my airline ID, and my passport. While she looked through all this I carefully placed my bag on the stand next to her.

"I have you listed on the non-stop flight to Tel Aviv," she advised me, "but I don't know if you will make it on. Israeli soldiers are being recalled to Israel and they take priority on our flights. Is that your only luggage?"

"Yes." I replied feeling a little let down.

"Did you pack your bag yourself? Did you have it in your possession at all times? Did anyone ask you to take anything? Any presents? Are all items in the suitcase yours?" she asked me in a steady stream.

Now it is the usual line of questioning at US airports, but back then it was very unusual. I felt very uneasy as if I were under suspicion for something but I didn't know what. Then she asked my maiden name. I gave it to her and she asked if I were a Jew. It startled me. It wasn't a question I was usually asked out of the blue. I said yes. Immediately her demeanor changed.

She smiled and said, "Shalom. Do you have a Hebrew name?"

"Yes, it's Chilya Rochel." I answered.

"Ah, Rochel. A very good name." she nodded her head approvingly. "You have a good trip to Israel."

With this she put a cabin tag on my bag, handed me my standby pass, airline ID and passport and told me to be at the gate 45 minutes prior to flight time. I thanked her and walked to the lobby area deciding to look for the assigned gate, find something to eat and, perhaps, change some US currency into Shekels. After all, I had over 6 hours to wait.

As I made my way down the long, wide corridor a young Hasidic Jew started walking along side me. I had heard of the Hasidim, had seen pictures, but although I was Jewish I had never seen

69

one in person and this close to me. He was a mass of black. His black felt hat placed on the center of his head sat straight up, his black ear locks hanging down the sides of his head touched the black collar of his long black overcoat. He was holding some sort of book open in his hands and was talking so quickly I could hardly understand a word he said.

As he spoke he kept pointing at the Hebrew in the book he was holding. He wanted to know my Hebrew name and all I could make out was something about purchasing a Hebrew letter that was to some how protect and bless me at the same time. I'm not superstitious, but I took $10 out of my wallet and handed it to him. He thanked me and asked me for my address that he might mail the paper with my sacred Hebrew letter on it. I told him it wasn't necessary. He smiled, said he understood, handed me a small paper inserted into a piece of plastic and walked away. I looked down at the paper. It was all in Hebrew. Unfortunately, I could neither read nor understand Hebrew. I placed it in my wallet and continued on my way thinking it was a very strange beginning to my journey to the Holy Land.

I had never seen so many people in a gate area before. I just couldn't believe they were all passengers or passenger hopefuls. But with their security no guests were allowed in the gate area. My heart sank. It certainly didn't look good. I started to have serious doubts that I would get a seat on this flight. Many of the young men waiting were obviously Israeli soldiers trying to get back home.

The boarding announcements were called. A steady stream of passengers who already had their assigned boarding passes walked through the jet way to their seats. Time passed. At last the gate agent started to process the standby passengers. One by one they would be called by name. The individual would step up to the desk, collect their boarding card and hurry on to the aircraft. I still hadn't been called and it was only minutes until flight departure time.

One more person was called up. I continued to wait. I was hesitant to go up to the counter as I knew how stressful it was to process a flight and I didn't want to antagonize these agents. Especially as they controlled whether I would get on or not. So, I just stood nearby and resigned myself to the very real prospect of having to find a place in New York to spend the night.

Suddenly, my name was called. I raced up to the desk.

"Follow me," the gate agent directed as he grabbed my paperwork and headed for the jet way entrance. "I don't know if there is a seat for you, but if so you will have it. The other agent is checking the seats on the aircraft now and thinks there may be an open one."

I ran after him as he hurriedly ran down the jet way. At the aircraft door he told me to wait and he ducked inside. I held my breath. To be so close and to be turned away would be awfully disappointing. I felt as if time had stood still.

Suddenly, he reappeared and told me to go inside, that the flight attendant would show me to my seat. Stepping inside, the flight attendant pointed to the first row on the right. I quickly sat down in the middle seat between two men. The aircraft door was secured and the plane immediately started to back off. I was on!

The gentleman on my right seemed friendly, but the gentleman next to the window was almost glaring. I determined I would just read and sleep, but I figured it was going to be a very long flight. I was wrong. Once introductions where made, both gentlemen were very nice and we kept a running conversation going for the entire flight. A lesson: that appearances are not always reality. The gentleman occupying the aisle seat was a returning businessman who owned a diamond shop. The gentleman by the window was a returning soldier.

Some time during the flight I remembered the small piece of paper the Hasid had given me. I asked my seat-companions if they would take a look at it and tell me what it was. They readily agreed. I took it out of my wallet and handed it to the businessman.

"Ah," he exclaimed, "He has given you the Jewish Traveler's Prayer."

The Israeli soldier nodded and looked back out the window at the approaching sunset. Suddenly I became aware of excessive movement in the aisles. I turned to see all the observant men standing in the aisles facing east, praying. It was evening service on an aircraft 40,000 plus miles above the ground, traveling at over 400 mph. The impression was one of surprise and disbelief. The image will never leave me. Truly, G-d is everywhere.

The sun rose a couple of hours prior to our scheduled landing at Ben Gurion Airport in Tel Aviv. Once again the observant rose from their seats, found a place in the narrow aisles, faced east, and began praying the morning service. Shortly after, a small breakfast was served and the landing announcement was made.

My excitement was almost visible. It was my first time to Israel, and to a Jew it is a very emotional moment. I knew there was a special prayer I should be saying at this time but I didn't know how to say it so I thought to myself, "Thank you, G-d, for bringing me to Israel safely." As the plane flew over the Mediterranean Sea, past the coastline of Israel I sat transfixed looking out the aircraft window. It was my first view of the Holy Land. I couldn't talk. I was unexpectedly overcome.

As I settled into my hotel room in Tel Aviv fatigue overtook me. It was morning, but I was exhausted. I hadn't slept at all on the flight and now I was to pay the price by suffering extreme jet lag. I decided to go out and explore some of the city streets. It was a beautiful, brightly sunlit morning. The city looked clean and crisp and the Mediterranean was a crystal, cool blue.

I strolled along the boulevards, past shops selling everything from jewelry to junk. I purchased a couple of cotton T-shirts and felt stupid as I spoke no Hebrew. As I slowly walked and looked around I came to one cafe after another, each with outdoor tables. Deciding a cup of coffee might be a good idea I sat down at a table for two under the shade of a scrawny tree that had obviously been planted in the large pot just for that purpose. It was the best coffee I had ever tasted. Slowly I sipped the hot brew as I people watched. A kaleidoscope of colors as every ethnic type walked by. They were all Jews, like me. Here, I was part of the majority. The sights, the sounds and the smells of this land enraptured me. I felt at home.

I was booked on a tour of Israel that would commence the following morning. I was hopeful that I would be over my jet lag so that I could fully enjoy all I was about to experience and see. Israel is timeless, ancient and modern both at the same time. I was to confront my history, my heritage at every turn. The Torah was to become alive for me in a richly unique way. I was actually seeing, with my own eyes, the places I had read about. It was, indeed, real! The events had really happened.

A cheerful tour guide by the name Zvi picked me up at the hotel. He was to take five other tourists, including myself, to all the historic sites described in the travel brochure. He was dressed casually wearing a soft off-white cap on his head which I was to later learn was a typical kibbutz hat. His shirt was pale blue and hung loosely over his creme colored pants. His sandals were made of the same dark brown leather I would see on Israeli's through out the country. I took my place in the oversized car we would call our tour van and joined the others who would be my companions for the next five days.

There were two sisters from the New York area who were in their late teens or early twenties. They dressed similar to the Orthodox ladies I had seen: long conservative skirts, long sleeved blouses, stockings and head covering. It didn't matter if it were 100 degrees Fahrenheit outside, the costume never varied. The elder sister was rather large, had shoulder length light brown hair and hazel eyes. The younger sister was slightly shorter then her sibling, but almost as large and shared her sister's coloring. Then there were the grandparents who were accompanying their granddaughter. This young lady had just become a Bat Mitzvah (a daughter of the covenant) and this trip and tour of the Holy Land was their gift to her. She was a thin, quiet twelve-year old with long brown hair and large, deep brown eyes.

First we drove north to Haifa. The drive was unimpressive, but the view of Haifa harbor from up in the hillside was quite lovely. We ate at an outdoor restaurant surrounded by pine trees (or at least they looked like pine to me), listening to the constant breeze, smelling the scent of flowers, and catching an occasional glimpse of the harbor as the tree limbs moved aside in the wind.

In Haifa we made a brief visit to the Baha'i Temple. The gardens were absolutely beautiful and I enjoyed walking the grounds and listening to the bird songs carried on the warm breezes. I strolled along the wide, white stone pathways surrounded by green hedges, multicolored flowers with unknown names, tall cedar trees and an occasional lantern, statue or fountain. In the midst of this tranquil garden setting was the Baha'i Temple, itself, with its white stone central tower with elongated, arched open windows, and dome of gold.

Of that entire experience, however, it is the garden that stands out in my memory most. It was a garden conducive to meditation. If I hadn't been part of a group, I would have found myself a shady spot under one of those tall trees and I would have sat. I would have crossed my legs as the Buddha had done when he sat under the Bodhi tree, and meditated. The scents of unknown flowers and the singing of sweet songbirds would flow around me like a soft current. And I would "just sit."

From there we drove on to the Akko (Acco) Fortress or rather the remains of what was once the Akko Fortress. Built during the time of the crusades it resurrected the haunting memory of thousands of Jewish men, women and children who chose to be martyred by the crusader's sword rather then to convert to Christianity. Of coarse, some weren't even given that opportunity to save them selves, but murdered outright. To Christians of that time the Crusader's were counted as heroes, their mission was to save the Holy City of Jerusalem from the infidels. To the Jewish people, however, it was a time of terror and darkness. Even the Jews in the Holy Land weren't exempt from the horror. Many hundreds of Jews were killed along side their Muslim neighbors, by the invading crusaders.

I walked along the walls still standing at the sea's edge and watched the waves as they broke along the ruins. Some rather large chunks of the fortress were still standing within the cradle of the sea, odd shaped brick structures with open sections that must have been part of the battlements, and I could easily imagine how it must have appeared during the time before its aging and deterioration. It sent shivers up my spine. Yet, all that remained was this skeleton of a fortress. We are still here, but the crusaders are no more. Time is funny that way. Ah, another example of impermanence.

Yet, some would argue that it is also an example of permanence. After all, the Hebrews (Jewish people) still exist as a distinct group, upholding their belief in the one G-d. They haven't disappeared into the deep oblivion, as have their former neighbors the Hittites, the Romans, the Babylonians, and the ancient Egyptians. Isn't this proof of permanence? No!

Indeed, can there be permanence in a world of impermanence? As individuals we will pass away into the mist of time just like everyone before us has. Will there ever come a time when the Jewish people, as a whole, also disappear? As a group, the Jews have been persecuted throughout recorded history. In some cases, such as the Holocaust, extinction was the goal. So far, none have succeeded. The Jews still exist and still practice their faith.

Does this mean they don't have to worry about disappearing from the face of the earth? Are the Jewish people destined to be permanent residents of the planet earth? After surviving as a distinct group for thousands of years, many would say, "yes." Yet, some say that the Jews, themselves, will enact their own extinction by becoming totally secular and through intermarriage. Only time will tell. But we must remember that all that exists eventually disappears.

Chapter 16
Safed

From Akko (Acco) we headed further north toward Safed (Zfat). We passed groves of olive trees their old gnarled branches speaking volumes of this ancient land's history. Our tour van steadily made its way up the hills and our ears popped more then once. The air became cool. As we reached a higher part of the hilltop we could see, in the distance, the vague outline of beautiful Lake Kinneret (Galilee).

At the summit Zvi pulled the van over to the right side of the curb and stopped the vehicle. We were advised that we would have a couple of hours to explore this mystical town. First, Zvi gave us a brief history of Safed. He directed us to the small Joseph Caro Synagogue (named after the author of the <u>Shulchan Aruch,</u> a book considered the authoritative code of Jewish Law). He told us how to reach the artist colony down below and then sent us on our way with a promise to be back at the designated location at the appointed time.

I started my exploration at the synagogue, as it was close by. Slowly I walked up the few stone steps. The building was unassuming. The entrance was merely a small arched, stone passageway to the left of a hand drawn sign in the shape of a rectangle, painted in white against the pale blue of the surrounding front wall. The entire Synagogue was built of white stone. There was a two-foot high wall perpendicular to the stairs on which had been placed plants potted in old metal food tins.

As I entered the sanctuary I was immediately impressed with the stillness and unimposing decor. Here, too, the walls were painted that same pale blue. The area of focus was obviously the ark where the Torah scrolls were kept. The traditional curtain (*Parochet*), also in blue, covered the wood panel doors of the ark (*Aron Ha-Kodesh*). A wrought iron grid just behind the wood panels, lent further protection to the Torah scrolls lined up on the narrow shelf inside the ark.

Two columns, located on each side of the ark, stretched up into an arch over the ark. These columns were ornately colored in a zigzag pattern in silver, gold, blue, and Indian red. The arch over the ark connecting the two columns continued the same zigzag pattern, but only in gold. Above the ark, in front of the arch, were the white stone tablets of the Ten Commandments, the Hebrew lettering was again in gold. Surrounding the tablets above the ark was an embellishment of gold filigree with a grape cluster and fig leaf motif.

"Would you like to see the Torah scrolls?" a man asked as I looked at the stone tablets and beautiful columns of the ark.

I turned and found myself facing a short, elderly man with silver gray hair that bushed out from the sides of his black *kippah* or circular head covering. His gray mustache curled up at the edges as he smiled at me and I can still remember those soft, friendly eyes. He wore a long sleeved white dress shirt, brown tie, and a gray knit vest even though it was extremely hot outside. His brown slacks were a little baggy and hung loosely over his gray socks and brown leather sandals. He leaned on his brown cane while holding on to its light colored wood, curved handle.

"Yes, thank you," I replied, "I'd very much like that if it wouldn't be too much trouble."

"No trouble." he said and he immediately set about opening the iron grate that separated him from the scrolls and carefully picked one of them up to show me.

It was obvious he was very proud of the Torah scrolls in his keeping. They were very old. The oldest was over 400 years old and the youngest between 100 and 200 years of age. I was duly impressed. I thought, here was another example, of the long history of the Jewish people. They weren't covered in a velvet mantle as most scrolls in the United States are, but in ornately carved metal cases that opened from the middle. The scrolls and the parchment, however, were the same.

The old man gently opened the silver case and showed me the painstakingly, hand scribed words of the Torah. A labor of love. From the hand of a scribe who patiently wrote down each word letter-by-letter. He was careful not to make any errors. Saying blessings each time the name of G-d was to be written. To this day I am impressed whenever I see a Torah scroll. Not only because of what it says, but also because of the patiently detailed effort it took to hand write it.

Picture 16.1: Rabbi Moshe Benshemon

As I continued to wander about the small synagogue I came to find out that I had been speaking with Rabbi Moshe Benshemon. The Rabbi had been the caretaker of this small house of worship for many years and even at 87 years of age he still cared for this holy place.

We spoke before I had to leave and he astonished me with his insight. At one point in our brief conversation he mentioned my being unhappy, but that it would soon improve. I was surprised at his comment. I didn't think I'd been acting unhappily at all. He patted me on the cheek, said he hoped I would visit again, and then accompanied me to the passageway outside.

Some ten years later I was to return to Safed and to visit the Joseph Caro Synagogue again. I wanted to see the Rabbi, but alas, when I inquired from a young man where he might be, I was told that he had just passed away several months before. The young man I was talking to was the new rabbi and he was Rabbi Benshemon's son. I was deeply grieved and told his son how wonderful his father had been and what an impression he had left on me. He agreed with me, thanked me and I left. Somehow the place didn't seem the same after that.

From the Synagogue I walked down narrow steps and lanes through the town. I saw various artisans at work at their crafts and looked in shop windows at the beautiful artwork produced by these artists. As I turned down the quaint lanes, passed the old stone dwellings, and looked out over the rooftops toward the valley, I could understand why these artists had gravitated to this spot. I also knew why the Kabbalists, the Jewish mystics, had come to this place as well, making it the Kabbalistic center of the Middle East. Up in this beautiful hillside, one felt close to G-d.

Rabbi Moshe Cordevero, also known as "the Ramak," was one of the greatest theoretical Kabbalists. He was born in Safed in 1522 and died in 1570. He was known to have been actively involved in a form of Kabbalah meditation known as *Gerushin* or "Divorce." The exact method, however, is not known.

Rabbi Chaim Vital, once a disciple of the Ari, also resided in this mystic town of Safed. He was an expert in all the forms of Kabbalistic meditations. He wrote one of the few books about meditative Kabbalah, <u>Shaarey Kedushah</u> (Gates of Holiness). Although he was born in Safed (in 1543), he was to move to Damascus in 1594 where he would eventually die in the year 1620.

Rabbi Isaac Luria was known as "the Ari," or the Lion. His fellow Kabbalists called him the "Holy Ari" or the Holy Lion. The Ari was born in Jerusalem in 1534, where he gained a reputation as a Talmudic prodigy by the age of eight. The Talmud is a collection of discourses/discussions/debates of rabbis from the academies in Israel and Babylonia some 1500 years ago. It contains two parts. One is called *Halachah* that concerns that portion dealing specifically with legal matters. The second part is called the *Aggadah* that literally means, "story." It is not specifically legal, but includes discussions, legends, and anecdote showing how one can behave righteously. It consists of some twelve to forty very large volumes. Given the size and content of the Talmud, its study is considered to take a lifetime.

After his father's death, he moved to Egypt with his mother, where he was to discover the Zohar at the age of seventeen then spent the next fifteen years practicing meditation. According to lore, it is said that after he had spent two years meditating, alone, in a hut near the Nile River he was ordered to go to the Holy Land. The Ari arrived in Safed in 1570. It is thought that the first meeting between Rabbi Chaim Vital and the Ari occurred in 1571. Soon after that meeting, Rabbi Vital asked to become the Ari's disciple.

The Ari died on July 15, 1572, less then two years after his arrival in Safed. Rabbi Vital wrote down many of Rabbi Luria's works. These works included the <u>Tree of Life</u> (Etz Chaim), <u>Fruit of the Tree of Life</u> (Pri Etz Chaim), and the <u>Eight Gates</u>. The eight-volume, <u>Eight Gates,</u> not only dealt with Bible commentary, but also with the subject of divine inspiration, and reincarnation.

Picture 16.2: Hasidem at Gravesite of Isaac Luria (The ARI) in Safed, Israel

Picture 16.3: Gravesite of Joseph Caro in Safed, Israel

Chapter 17
To Jerusalem

From Safed we traveled through Tiberias. We visited the oasis of Ein Gedi, and saw the caves at Qumram. A solitary shepherd boy had discovered the Dead Sea Scrolls in these caves. We climbed Masada and then stood in awe at the edge of the Dead Sea. An extremely still body of water, hot and steamy, surrounded by odd shaped pillars of salt. Some of us went into the Dead Sea and experienced the penetrating heat and the strange sensation of not being able to sink.

We passed through the arid desert of Arad. We saw Bedouin at a water hole very much as it must have been during the time of Abraham over 4,000 years ago, and the fortress of Arad that was once a Philistine stronghold during the time of Moses and Joshua some 3,000 years before. We passed by the southern end of the Dead Sea, the location of the infamous towns of Sodom and Gemmorah. I couldn't help but wonder why anyone would want to live at such a location: barren, hot, and oppressive.

The desert was just as I had imagined it to be: long stretches of gravel, stone and rock, some areas rising into hills and mountains of rock, hot, desolate, drawn in the muted colors of white, gray and brown. I could well imagine how the prophets of old had gone out into the desert alone. How they had sojourned there amid the desolation and absolute stillness. How they carefully walked on a landscape which was harsh and which rarely changed. The only change in the stones hue came from the muted changes in light as dictated by the suns rising and setting.

I tried to imagine myself wandering alone in such a place. Would the landscape harden me or humble me? -or both? Would I be able to survive? Would I eventually loose my mind to the deep well of silence this place manifested or would I eventually come to know the

Picture 17.1: Ein Gedi, Israel

face of G-d? Obviously, solitude and silence are a prerequisite to contemplation and meditation. Had the ancients known this? Had they gone into the desert and up these steep slopes in their search for G-d? Was this how one could find G-d?

Most of my young life I had been frustrated by this not knowing. I had been frustrated by the repetition of ritual, custom and tradition. I had been frustrated by the answers given to me by learned rabbis who continued to stress study and observance to the exclusion of actual mystical or spiritual experience. I had wanted to know G-d for myself: not through Bible stories, not by the repetition of the annual holiday traditions, not through just upholding the *mitzvot* imposed from without in the hope that one day it would become an internal influence.

Yes, I was aware that by "acting" in a certain way, eventually habits would develop which would help lead one to a better life. By consciously taking on the *mitzvot,* behaving as one is instructed to do, one should eventually come closer to the ideal of living an ethical, "human" existence. But how much of this outward manifestation actually initiates real inward change? Outward manifestation without a real inward change portrays merely empty form. Wouldn't it be more productive, more real, if one were to work on changing inwardly, which would then become manifest in a change in one's outward behavior? The question that begs asking is how, or by what process, could some one initiate inward change? The obvious answer would be by looking within using the process of meditation.

I have seen too many people "acting" according to expectations. Living by the rules. They attended synagogue or church regularly. Said their prayers. But their everyday actions belied the sincerity of their outward appearances. I would rather do the hard work of looking within, of working on myself, which would eventually change the way I live my life, how I interact with the people and world around me.

The more I had read the Torah the more I intuitively knew, just knew, that some individuals had actually experienced the oneness of G-d. These individuals lived in a certain way within a high moral standard, not because the law imposed it upon them, but because from their intimate experience, from within, there was no other way they could behave. Their actions were wholly correct because they came from an intimate knowledge, a first hand knowledge, a firsthand "knowing" of G-d.

The rules and morals applied to us from the outside were the same as those lived by the patriarchs, prophets and mystics of ancient time, but with one great difference. The "enlightened" individuals acted from inner conviction, from a first hand knowing of the Truth. The rest of humanity only acted in this way by having rules and laws imposed on them from an outside authority for they hadn't experienced it for themselves as yet.

Of course, it was always hoped that by living correctly and morally that eventually this "knowing" would become internalized, but did it? Scratch the surface of most civilized people and you find a fierce, untamed animal. Is their veneer of civilization and moral correctness truly a manifestation of inner knowing, or only a reflection of their ability to uphold the rules society has imposed on them so as to avoid suffering the punishment that would be inflicted on them if they were to disobey those laws?

The law tells us that we should not murder. To the "enlightened" being it would be a useless rule. An "enlightened" being would not murder because s/he would know from an inner conviction, an inner knowing that to harm another living thing was wrong. That in harming another you also harmed yourself. To the rest of us, we don't murder because we fear the punishment society would impose on us if we were to be caught and found guilty. The former acts out of inner knowing of the Truth, the later from fear of punishment. The former individual, knowing the Truth, would not allow his/her anger to overwhelm him/her so as to ever act on an impulse to do harm. To the latter, if the anger becomes stronger than the fear of punishment, a murder will take place.

However, while pursuing the spiritual path the outward practice of morality (via rules and laws), even if not fully understood at the time, is critical to spiritual development. Morality is required in Buddhism (s*ila*) and in Judaism as a prerequisite toward establishing the state of mind necessary for spiritual growth. While I was deep in such thoughts, Zvi continued to drive.

From there we drove toward the hills of Jerusalem. As we drew nearer, the excitement rose. It was as if we all knew we were only a few short miles away. We all grew quiet and the silence seemed to fit the desert setting we were driving through. The sun was slowly descending as Zvi drove his van up the winding road toward Jerusalem. As he turned a tight curve we received our first glimpse of the golden pink city.

The buildings in Jerusalem are built of Jerusalem stone, a rosy, sandy colored stone taken from the Judean Mountains. The glow of the setting sun falling on these softly colored stones creates an unearthly aura that suffuses the Holy City with a wondrously luminous, golden light. Watching the transition of day into night in this way, I was struck by the magic and mystery. This was truly King David's city.

Zvi, our untiring tour guide, had us up bright and early to begin our tour of the Old City of Jerusalem. We would pass through David's Gate where it is said that King David entered Jerusalem in triumph after his victory in battle. We walked through Arab Bazaars viewing countless trinkets, beautiful textiles and trying halvah (a rich, ground sesame seed candy).

We strolled down the legendary "Via Dolorosa," the narrow, cobble stone street that Jesus was said to have walked while carrying on his shoulders the heavy wood cross on which the Romans would later crucify him. Even as a Jew it left a vivid impression on me. I slowly walked the path in silence, imagining the tormented Jesus struggling under his heavy cross, knowing it was to his death, while some of the crowd jeered at him and others cried in anguish. No one should ever have to suffer in that way. That a peace-loving, compassionate rabbi should meet his end like that sickened me. Yes, I do not believe Jesus was the messiah, but one doesn't have to believe in Jesus in that way to realize he was a compassionate human being teaching the virtue of loving-kindness by word and deed.

Jews of all ages had been blamed for his death. This was a great sadness on two counts. First, because Jesus himself was a Jew. Second, any Biblical scholar and historian knew that death by crucifixion was a Roman invention. The most brutal methods of inflicting death on a person in ancient Israel was either by stoning or by fire. Israelites/Jews would never hang anyone on a cross. Add to that, that no Jew was ever killed simply for disagreeing with a priest or rabbi and the absurdity is even more vivid.

In Leviticus 24:15 it states, "And to the Israelite people speak thus: Anyone who blasphemes his G-d shall bear this quilt; if he also pronounces the name LORD, he shall be put to death. The whole community shall stone him; stranger or citizen, if he has thus pronounced the Name, he shall be put to death." Clearly, merely disagreeing with someone or about something isn't enough to enact the death penalty.

Blasphemy would incur public censure or, the most severe punishment in this case, excommunication (being cut off from your people). Usually, it was public sanction. If however, some one pronounced the sacred name of G-d that was punishable by death, a death by public stoning.

Depending on what was said, what belief you held, if found to be counter to mainstream Jewish theology, you could be exiled from the Jewish community, but never killed. For even idolatry, a most severe breach in Judaism was only punishable by excommunication from the group, not by death. The only exception is to be seen in Leviticus 20:1-2, "And the Lord spoke to Moses: Say further to the Israelite people: Any man among the Israelites, or among the strangers residing in Israel, who gives any of his offspring to Molech, shall be put to death; the people of the land shall pelt him with stones."

Jesus was not an idol worshipper, he never had any children and certainly would never have offered any of his offspring to a pagan god, and he most assuredly didn't blasphemy. Clearly, Jews did not have anything to do with the murder of Jesus.

Zvi took us up to the Dome of the Rock, the holy Muslim Mosque, built around the rock that was said to be the same one that Abraham was ordered by G-d to sacrifice his only beloved son, Isaac, on. I decided to go in. I left my few belongings outside, took off my sandals and the followed others into the Mosque. It was an expansive stone chamber with many columns. It appeared to be constructed of marble. My feet felt cool on the stone floor and I could hear the echo of whispers.

I followed a small group toward a short wall near the center of the large room. As I walked around the wall I came across an opening. I peered in and saw the huge, black rock worn smooth by the gentle caresses of the hands of many people, worshippers and tourists alike. I, too, extended my hand and rubbed the smooth, cool surface of the rock. And I, too, believed that this was the historic site of the awesome test that G-d had enacted on Abraham.

From there we walked through the Jewish Quarter of the old city and then started our decent down a long row of winding, stone steps to a large plaza. At the far end of the plaza stood the great Western Wall. No one had to tell me what I was approaching. I knew.

Chapter 18
Touching the Wall

Earlier, Zvi had advised me that it would not be appropriate to enter the Mosque or to visit the Wall dressed in shorts. While wandering through the narrow lanes of the Arab Quarter I had purchased a long piece of cloth that I could wrap around my waist as a long skirt as the occasion required. It was semi-sheer cotton, in oranges, reds, and gold thread. I quickly wrapped it around my waist as we made our way down the steep steps toward the plaza.

Once on the plaza floor I slowly walked toward the Wall. I didn't hear anything except for the melodious chanting of the Jewish men praying. If Zvi was telling our small group anything I didn't hear it. My feet just continued toward the sound of chanting. As I got closer I saw the white lattice partition extending from the Western Wall out toward the plaza. It was there to separate the men from the women as they both approached the Wall and prayed.

In Orthodox Judaism men and women don't pray together. Even in the Synagogue, the men pray near the *bimah* (the raised platform in a synagogue that is usually located at the front, like a stage, where one stands to read the Torah.). The women pray either in a partitioned section toward the back, or in a gallery above the main floor of the sanctuary. This is the usual practice as it is felt that having women in such close proximity to men would distract the men from their prayers as well as possibly leading their thoughts astray into the lower realms.

On the men's side of the partition I could see old, gray bearded men swaying back and forth as they prayed. I could see other men placing their *tallitot* or prayer shawls over their shoulders getting ready to pray while others, who had finished their praying, were carefully removing their *tallitot*. I watched, as the older men seemed to be instructing younger men and young boys. I smiled as I saw the younger boys imitating their elders.

On the women's side of the partition some women where at the wall with their heads covered, also praying. Some had small pieces of paper they were carefully pushing into the cracks and fissures of the large, white bricks of the Western Wall. Later I was to do the same thing. Other women were discretely watching the men on the other side of the partition as they prayed, while mothers held the small hands of their young children.

I made my way into the women's section and slowly walked toward the Wall. It was much larger then I had ever imagined and I was overcome by the size of each individual stone. Some sort of green plant grew in the cracks of these stones and in many places the plants had grown large and bushy. I was later told that they were caper plants. My eyes were transfixed in front of me, staring at the Wall, while my ears filled with the chanting of prayers.

As I drew nearer to the Wall I became aware of a strange sensation within me. It would be very hard to express the feeling I was experiencing. It was a feeling of coming home, of having been here before (although it was the first time I had ever been to this place). A feeling of wonder and awe at realizing how grand the Temple of Jerusalem must have been if its outer, protective wall was so tall and majestic, and this piece was only a small section of the wall built on the western side of the Temple. What awe the Temple must have inspired in the Israelites who came to Jerusalem in ancient times.

Finally, I made it to within arms-length of the Wall. Emotion overpowered me and as I carefully lifted my hand and touched the Wall I became aware of tears streaming down my cheeks. My eyes burned and I started to cry. I remembered the terrible destruction of the Temple in 587 BCE by the Babylonians and, again, in 70 BCE by the Romans. I cried for the loss as if I, personally, had been there when it had happened. My tears joined those of countless other Jews across history who had, in anguished torment, mourned the destruction of the Great Temple in Jerusalem, the focal point of every Jew no matter where on the earth they resided. Now I understood why this wall was also referred to as the Wailing Wall.

I prayed to my G-d, the G-d of my ancestors, of Abraham, Isaac, Joseph and Moses. I prayed in thanks and I prayed in awe. I prayed for peace among all nations and especially between the Jewish

Picture 18.1: The Western Wall

and Arab nations. I prayed for strength and loving-kindness and compassion. I prayed for my parents, my daughter, my friends and my enemies. I prayed for myself. As my tears mixed with my prayers I was unaware of the other people around me. I was alone with G-d among all his people.

I don't know how long I was standing there at the wall. It could have been minutes or hours. Time had stood still for me then. As I regained some of my composure I searched for some paper and something to write with from my purse. I retrieved a piece of paper and tore it into three sections. On one I wrote a request for my mother's wellbeing, on the second a request for my daughter's happiness, and on the third a request for me.

My request seemed odd, even to myself. I was asking G-d for his help in selecting a mate for me. I hadn't been conscious of even thinking about remarriage, but here I was writing on a small slip of paper, asking for His help to find a suitable husband and father. I wrote that I had not chosen wisely and that I desired G-d's help in this matter. I would leave the choice, if I was to remarry, in G-d's hand and He would also choose the man.

I felt a strange sense of calmness and inner peace. I had let go and I had reclaimed something although I wasn't too clear what it was. I mindfully folded each piece of paper and placed each one in a small crevice in the stone in front of me. Shutting my eyes I leaned toward the wall and gently kissed it while my two hands pressed against its cool surface.

Turning around and wiping my eyes, I made my way back to the others. They, too, where making their way toward the left side of the plaza. I was tired and drawn and yet strangely alert and awake. I was aware of everyone around me, again, and heard bits and pieces of conversations being carried out in various languages. I didn't feel like talking to anyone. I only wanted to remain still and silent.

I walked slightly behind the others in our group as we walked away from the Wall and toward Zvi's tour van that would shortly bring us back to our hotel. I was relieved that the tour was over for the day. When I entered my room I walked to the window and stood there until sunset watching as the stones of the Old City turned golden pink in the rays of the setting sun.

Chapter 19
Returning Home

On the long flight back home I had plenty of time to think about all I had experienced in Israel. Of all the places I had seen and experienced the two that had left the most dramatic impression on me were Safed and the Western Wall. Those two experiences had changed me inside. Yet, if asked to explain these subtle changes, I'd be unable to do so. The former involved a more tangible link with the mysticism of the Kabbalists. The recognition of the reality of the spiritual component of this religion I had been raised in. The latter, a deep connection with Jewish history and the Jewish experience. These ancient people from the past were my people. The Jews of today were my family.

I stopped in Boston on my way back home and picked up my daughter, Teleia, who had been staying with my parents while I was visiting the Middle East. I had purchased a Torah book and a Prayer Book when visiting the Mea Shearim area of Jerusalem. It is an ultra-orthodox community of Jews and I had dressed and acted accordingly. I had gone into one of the many bookshops and had purchased these two books because of the beautiful stone-embellished silver work on the covers. I had given my daughter the books to see and read.

She had been delighted with the books and very impressed with the unusual covering. As she turned the pages of the English/Hebrew Torah she discovered the beautiful pictures illustrating the various biblical stories. From that point on she read from that book exclusively during the remainder of her summer vacation. At the end of summer she came to me and asked if she might become a Bat Mitzvah or daughter of the Covenant.

I was surprised and pleased at the same time. Evan and I had brought her up as a Buddhist although we would answer any questions she asked us concerning our own beliefs. Although I practiced meditation and had taken the precepts of a practicing Buddhist, I also observed the Jewish holidays. Many times Teleia had seen me lighting Hanukkah candles or fasting on Yom Kippur and had asked what I was doing and why. I always patiently answered her. Whenever she would visit with my parents, who were open about their Jewish beliefs, she would often be exposed to Jewish practices, too.

Seeing how sincere Teleia was in her request to become a Bat Mitzvah, I immediately set about trying to find a suitable Jewish temple to affiliate with so that she may begin studying Judaism and Hebrew toward fulfilling the requirements necessary to become a Daughter of the Covenant. After returning home to Hawaii, I located the Aloha Jewish Chapel in Pearl Harbor and Teleia and I began to attend Friday night services together. Fortunately, since I had been granted sole custody of Teleia, this decision never became an issue involving Evan.

The Aloha Jewish Chapel is part of the Pearl Harbor Navy complex but at the time I hadn't realized that as, back then, you didn't have to go through any gates with guards to get there. All I knew was that it was much closer to our home then the Reform Temple located on the Pali Highway and that they accepted us there. Being a single parent, finances were tight, and they never asked me for a dime. I am still grateful for that and the opportunity it afforded both my daughter and myself.

The summer was drawing to a close and Teleia was entering fifth grade. I still worked for the airlines and every Friday night Teleia and I went to services at the Aloha Jewish Chapel. Meanwhile, I had come to a decision. After much thought and consideration I had decided to make *aliyah* to Israel. What that means is that I would immigrate to Israel under the right of return afforded to all Jews. *Aliyah* literally means "going up."

I had felt at home there, and wanted to make it my home. My visit, as short as it was, had awakened feelings of affinity, and pride, in my Jewish heritage. Feelings I had never felt before. I would return to Israel with my daughter. I would make it our home. We would connect to our Jewish roots. I would come closer to experiencing G-d by residing in the Holy Land and continuing my meditation practice. I would delve deeper into Jewish mysticism as well as Buddhism.

I never thought my decision would enact such a negative response in my parents, but it did. They were shocked that I would even consider moving to Israel. How could I even think of moving to an area of such unrest? How could I even entertain the thought of bringing my daughter to such an environment to live? Had I taken leave of my senses? Did I realize that Teleia would have to serve in the Israeli army when she turned eighteen?

Then there was the financial concern. I wouldn't have a job and finding one would be that much more difficult since I didn't know Hebrew. And what about Teleia? She was in middle school. She would have to leave all of her friends. She would have difficulties of her own trying to adjust and she didn't know Hebrew either.

This was not to be an easy decision or an easy road to follow. I had to take my daughter's interests into account, not just my own desire. My parent's concerns were very real and were worthy of serious consideration. I tossed and turned, I debated with myself, I made inquiries concerning the pluses and minus's of moving to Israel. My parents were so adamantly against it, that I even consulted a rabbi concerning the ramifications (according to Jewish law) of going against my parent's refusal to accept my aliyah in terms of the commandment to honor one's father and mother.

The later was the easiest part. According to the rabbi, to make aliyah was considered to be one of the greatest mitzvot in Judaism. It was a mitzvah felt to be even more serious than the commandment to honor one's parents. In such a case it was not only allowed, but one was encouraged to do so. Parents who tried to discourage aliyah were, in effect, not to be listened to. The parents were behaving selfishly and so had to be educated as to the importance of returning to Israel.

Once I made up my mind I applied with the local *Shaliach*, or Israeli emissary, who would help me with paperwork and with the application process. I had many things to settle before I could leave the islands. I would have to sell my house, my car, and any unwanted possessions. I'd have to get permission to take Teleia with me. All of this would take time.

As the months went by I finished the application process and I was assigned to an absorption center outside of Tel Aviv called Rananah. The absorption center is a new immigrant's first home. There they learn Hebrew, visit different areas of the country, prepare for a job and wait to be assigned living quarters. Teleia would be assigned with me. She would go to a local school and learn Hebrew, too. I could leave any time now, but my affairs were still not in order. The *Sheliach* was anxious for me to go, but I told him I could not leave until my home was sold. I didn't want to have to tend to that over such a long distance.

Meanwhile, I had decided I wouldn't wait until I arrived in Israel at the absorption center before starting to learn Hebrew. I tried to enroll with the Berlitz Language School but found out it was much too expensive for me. I bought a Hebrew language book and a cassette tape and tried to learn on my own. I wasn't too successful using that approach.

One evening, after Friday night services, a young woman came over to me and introduced herself. Her name was Tzipporah. She was in the Air Force and was also planning *aliyah* with her husband once they left the service. She had heard about my plans from the Rabbi and how I had wanted to learn some Hebrew. She advised me that, although she was no expert in Hebrew, she did know some of the language and asked if I would like to take a class she was invited to teach at the chapel. I told her I didn't have money to pay for classes, but she told me that the classes would be free. I'd only have to pay for the textbooks. I eagerly accepted her offer and so would start studying Hebrew the following month in October.

That fall was a landmark for both my daughter and myself. She started Sunday school learning about Jewish history, holidays, rituals and the Hebrew language toward becoming a Bat Mitzvah at the age of twelve. I began my Hebrew classes with Tzipporah, in preparation to move to Israel as soon as my affairs were in order. Our future seemed to be well planned and in the process of becoming reality.

Chapter 20
Hebrew Class

In mid-October, I left work early and drove to the Aloha Jewish Chapel. Since I worked at the Honolulu International Airport at that time, it didn't take very long to drive to Pearl Harbor. I arrived early. As I entered the foyer another student entered. He was a tall, slim man with short, dark brown hair, a mustache and beautiful hazel eyes. He wore a short sleeved, pale orange polo shirt and casual, tan slacks. As he closed the door behind him he smiled and asked if I were also attending Tzippora's class.

"Yes, and you?" I asked in return.

"Well," he stammered, "I'm attending the class but not really as a serious student. I already know some Hebrew. I'm here to lend moral support to my friend who should be arriving any moment. I'm Matt, and your name?"

"I'm Karen. Nice to meet you." I replied.

At that instant the door opened and in walked a tall, slim woman with flowing, long, blond hair. She quickly made her way over to Matt and they quietly talked to one side. So much for that, I thought to myself. Slowly a few more men and women arrived and then, to my relief, Tzipporah walked in loaded down with textbooks and papers.

"Shalom," she announced. "Let's go to the classroom over there, shall we?"

We quietly followed her into a small classroom to the right of the foyer.

The class was small and she arranged us around a large, round table. Only two of her students were men, the rest were woman. Except for Matt, the rest of us were totally ignorant concerning the Hebrew language. I have great difficulty learning a foreign language, but I was motivated given my pending *aliyah* to Israel and I was determined to do my best.

Every week I attended this Hebrew class and every week I struggled with my Hebrew, but I wouldn't give up. Matt would come to class every week, also, but what astounded me was that he seemed to be accompanying a different woman each week. I had to shake my head. I looked at him as some sort of Jewish gigolo and decided I didn't want any part of a person like that.

Matt, however, didn't know this. So, when he started to come early to class in order to make certain he was able to sit next to me I was a little surprised. When, several weeks later he started offering me coffee or tea, and cookies during our mid-class break, I was more than a little surprised. Several classes later I felt his foot rubbing on my own and I was just plain shocked. Who was this person?

I enjoyed his banter and he would kindly whisper an answer to me when I was struggling for a response to one of Tzipporah's questions. But, he seemed to be a womanizer. I was still nursing my wounds from my first marriage, I had a young daughter to care for, and I didn't need the potential for further hurt that this man would probably introduce into my life. I remained friendly, but didn't encourage his advances.

Several months went by. Hebrew class went as usual with an interesting twist. Somehow the class started watching the television series Hill Street Blues after our learning session was over. We would either watch on the chapel's television or Tzipporah would invite everyone over to her home to watch. One evening we were at Tzipporah's watching and I decided to sit in her large, comfortable rocking chair. During a commercial break Matt crawled over to me through the other students sitting on the floor and sat down on the floor next to my feet.

"Karen, can I ask you something?" he asked.

"Sure. What is it?" I replied, looking down at him.

"Would it be okay if I asked Tzipporah for your phone number?" he blurted out.

I almost started to laugh, as I quickly responded, "Why don't you just ask me yourself?"

I thought it a rather odd and archaic way of asking a lady for her phone number. He had taken me by surprise and so, although reluctantly, I had given him my number. He called me the very next morning.

From the time when Matt had first told me he loved me the

subject of my making aliyah to Israel had been a major topic of discussion. I still wanted to emigrate. I wanted him to join us. I tried to convince him. I wanted it all. I wanted Matt. I also wanted to live in Israel. My emotions were in turmoil. Matt refused to even consider aliyah. He was a United States Naval Officer and intended to stay.

Once the subject of marriage came up I realized I had to make a decision. I couldn't have both. If I stuck with my plan to immigrate to Israel I would have to end my relationship with Matt. If I decided to marry Matt, I'd have to give up the idea of moving to Israel.

It was obvious that Teleia liked Matt very much. It was also obvious that she much preferred to stay in Hawaii. As much as she was excited about learning about Judaism and the Hebrew language, she wasn't as enthusiastic as I was about moving to Israel. I had written it off as just a little girl being afraid of the unknown. Besides, what did she really know? Now I had to seriously reconsider my motives for wanting to move to Israel as well as my possible motive in wanting to marry Matt.

Did I really want to move to Israel just to escape from my present situation? To get away from the places and people that reminded me of my failed marriage to Evan? Was it for the shear desire for adventure and change? And why had I put myself in this situation with Matt in the first place? Did I really want to marry Matt? And if so, did I want to marry him just to make my life easier? Did I subconsciously not want to make aliyah and so this could be my excuse to opt out? What did I really want to do? What would really be the best thing to do for both my daughter and myself?

These were tough questions that required serious soul searching. These were questions I could only look to myself to find the answers. Any decision I made would alter the future for all of us. I sat alone and pondered the ramifications. I sat alone and weighted the pros and cons. I sat alone and tried to analyze my feelings toward Matt. I sat alone and came to my decision. I would marry Matt and abort my plans for making aliyah.

G-d certainly works in mysterious ways. Not only had He decided I was to remarry, He found me a nice Jewish guy within two months from the time I had placed my small piece of paper into that crevice in the Western Wall in Jerusalem. It doesn't sound like much of a miracle, but you must realize that the Jewish population in Hawaii is very small. Add to that the fact that Matt was a Naval Officer running in social circles that airline personnel never cross into and you can see why it was amazing.

Ours had been a whirlwind courtship. We went out on our first date the following week. Two weeks later he told me he loved me. Two months after that we were engaged and four months from our engagement we were married at the very same place where we first met- the Aloha Jewish Chapel.

My parents were in shock. They were convinced that I would either not remarry or I would marry another Oriental guy. My mother had even accused me, once, of being prejudiced against my own kind. They were relieved. Their daughter had finally come to her senses and aliyah had been just a temporary notion. Now, they thought, Karen will practice Judaism exclusively and give up this Buddhist business. Meanwhile, I continued to attend meditation at the Waipahu Soto Temple on most Sunday mornings, while attending Friday night services at the Jewish chapel.

The *Schaliach*, who had made all my arrangements for my *aliyah*, was also in shock. Especially since the first thing Matt said to him when I had introduced them was, "She's not going to Israel." I would be moving to San Diego instead.

Chapter 21
San Diego

Matt and I were married on July 3rd, at the Aloha Jewish Chapel. Our guests were very eclectic. It seemed as if all groups were represented. There were airline personnel, Navy, Army, and Marine officers and enlisted personnel, regular civilians and relatives. And it was a rainbow of Caucasians, Black Americans, Japanese, Chinese, Filipinos, and those of mixed race. Even all the main religions were represented. I had even invited a friend of mine who was a Buddhist Priest at the Mililani Hongwanji and his wife.

A mere six months later we moved to San Diego on military orders. We arrived during Teleia's winter break in school so that we would have time to get settled a bit in our new home before she would start at her new school. It was an adjustment for all of us. Matt had to get used to being a husband and instant father to a ten-year old. I had to adjust to living on the mainland, again, after over a decade and a half living in Hawaii. Teleia had the most to adjust to; a new father, a new home, living on the mainland, a new school, new friends, and having to wear shoes when she went to school instead of her usual flip-flops.

The transition may have been easier if Matt were with us more, but being assigned to a ship he was rarely home. When his ship was on deployment, out at sea, we didn't see him at all. When his ship was dry docked in Long Beach, we saw him during the weekends. Not an easy lifestyle to adjust to.

Meanwhile, I set about putting my network together. I had to find doctors, dentists, drug stores, supermarkets, etc. I had to get Teleia settled into a new routine. I wanted to meet my new neighbors and, hopefully, make a couple of friends. Matt and I decided to join the Conservative Synagogue in the area and we enrolled Teleia in their

Hebrew school, as she still desired to become a Bat Mitzvah.

I decided to become actively involved in this new Synagogue. I volunteered to do office work and had an opportunity to meet some very nice people. It was during this interval that the Rabbi and Cantor told me about a *Bnai Mitzvah* class they were giving to adults who had never been Bar or Bat Mitzvah so that they could do so. I was invited to attend. Not having been a Bat Mitzvah, I eagerly enrolled even though several classes had already been conducted.

It was a yearlong course of study. They assumed you knew very little and started from the very beginning. Jewish history and other subjects taught in English were easy for me, but as usual the Hebrew required a lot of work on my part. Matt was out on the ship and so I didn't have him to help me. However, Teleia watched as her mom struggled and I truly believe it encouraged her in her own studies. She, too, was starting late as most children began their studies in kindergarten and began their Hebrew studies in third grade. She was now a sixth grader trying hard to catch up with her classmates.

It wasn't to be an easy time for her. Being that she was half Chinese, she hadn't look like the others. Having a last name that was not Jewish sounding added to the problem. Her fellow students, unfortunately, were not very kind to this new girl in their class. Erroneously assuming that she wasn't a Jew, they steadily began to harass her. They would not befriend her and they made fun of her, or put her down whenever an opportunity arose. Being young and unused to such treatment, she was hurt, confused, and extremely lonely. As this unkind treatment escalated I spoke to her teacher in order to try to remedy the situation. When that didn't seem to work I requested an opportunity to speak briefly to the class myself.

Naturally, Teleia was extremely nervous and not just a little upset that her mother was going to religious school with her this particular Sunday. Telling her it couldn't possibly get any worse and that I was going to attempt to make it better, we drove to the synagogue. I didn't tell Teleia that if it did, indeed, get worse that I planned to remove her from this particular synagogue school.

"This is Mrs. Cohen and she would like to take a few moments to speak with all of you. Please give her your kind attention," the teacher said in the way of introduction. I stood up in front of the class, took a deep breath and began.

"Let me ask you a question, okay?" I started. "What makes a person a Jew? How do you know you are, in fact, really Jewish?"

One little girl raised her hand and replied, "Because my mother told me I was."

"That's getting close." I answered, "But can you tell me how your mother knew that you were Jewish?"

A pause and then she continued, "Because my mother is Jewish?"

"Absolutely correct." I responded happily. This was exactly the direction I wanted this to go in.

"So, if your mom is Jewish, then you are Jewish. Right?" I asked the class.

"Yes!" the class responded, almost in unison.

"Okay." I continued. "I'm a Jew. My mother is Jewish, as was my grandmother and great-grandmother, and her mother before her all the way back to Sarah, Abraham's wife. Would that make my children Jewish?"

"Yeah." a young boy sitting in the front row volunteered, "So, what?"

"That's why I'm here this morning." I went on. "It appears that some people in this class don't think that my daughter is Jewish. Anyway, I really can't imagine anyone sending someone who isn't a Jew to a Jewish religious school (some giggling from the class). To make it even sadder, because these people don't think she's really Jewish, they haven't been treating her very nicely. In fact they have been very mean to her."

The class became extremely silent. I could sense a change in the air. I looked across at my daughter who was obviously very tense as she concentrated very hard on looking at the desktop in front of her. I prayed I was doing the right thing.

"I'm Teleia's mom, she's my daughter." I looked into every child's eyes as I spoke. "I'm Jewish, so she's Jewish."

Everyone was silent. I noticed some of the children turning around in their seats to look at Teleia. Others looked down at their desktops. I decided to just stand there for a while and give them some time to process all of this and think. Finally, one young man raised his hand to speak.

"I think I'm one of those not so nice kids." he volunteered. He turned to face Teleia and said, "I'm sorry, Teleia. I didn't know."

Suddenly, other kids were apologizing to my daughter and Teleia raised her head to look at her classmates. She was smiling. The tension had eased quite a bit and I was relieved to be able to turn the class back over to their teacher.

"Thank you, Mrs. Cohen, for coming in this morning." she said to me as I gathered my things to leave.

Before leaving the room, I turned to the class and said, "Thank you."

Things weren't perfect after that, but at least it was a lot less abusive for my daughter. She no longer dreaded going to religious school, and she was progressing very well in her studies of Judaic history and Hebrew.

On June 8th, 1984, almost 10 years since I had taken the Precepts and had become a lay Buddhist, I became a Daughter of the Covenant, a Bat Mitzvah, at the age of 35. I wore my husband's *tallit* (prayer shawl) and read my portion of the *Haftorah* while my one friend in San Diego, and my daughter looked on. I only wished that my husband could have been there, but he was out at sea. Now I really felt like a Buddhist-Jew.

Rabbi Irving Golden was the spiritual head of Tifereth Israel Synagogue. He was a very intense, middle-aged man. He had come from a Hasidic background and so his methods reflected some of his mystical training. I was in awe of this man. I was impressed by his candor, his humane-ness, and scholarship. Most of all I was impressed by his familiarity with Jewish Mysticism. I asked him about it and he recommended certain books. I very much enjoyed listening to him and discussing thoughts with him.

Unfortunately, he was a very busy rabbi. I started to attend the weekly men's club meetings held every Sunday morning while Teleia attended religious school. It was a Men's club, but I went anyway. I wanted to be near this rabbi and to hear him speak. Although I'm sure the men in the group must have thought it very strange, they never turned me away. In fact, they would invite me to join them for their bagel breakfast before the rabbi came in, and always made me feel welcome.

I would take my bagel and cup of coffee and sit with the others at a long table. I would eat and listen to the others. I would listen intently to anything Rabbi Golden of Tefereth Israel would say. I wanted to be a disciple of this man, but the rabbis I knew didn't take disciples. He wistfully complained to me one afternoon, that he wished he had more time to devote to study and Kabbalah. I wished he had more time, too, but for selfish reasons. I wanted him to be my teacher. But, alas, he was a mystic buried in paperwork.

I eagerly purchased or borrowed the books on Jewish Mysticism that he would suggest and I would read them cover-to-cover. I saw many parallels between Jewish Mysticism and Buddhism. I noticed that if you were to substitute the Aramaic word for the Pali or Sanskrit word, you were describing the same things. Were there more connections and similarities between the two? Were they really the same, only using a different language? The thought intrigued me.

How did one "practice" Kabbalah? How did Kabbalists meditate? What method or methods did they use? Would I be able to discover what these methods were? Would I be able to practice them myself? I continued to read, to learn, and to ask, but no one could or would help me. I was against a wall of book learning. I could read about what the mystics did, but no book or person could advise me as to how I, myself, could learn these techniques. Once again I was frustrated. Once again I turned to *Za-zen* as a means to that mystical end, as a way of experiencing G-d.

Chapter 22
The Holy Land Revisited

Less then a year later, in fact that following summer, my husband's ship was to change its homeport from San Diego to Yokosuka, Japan. We would have to move again. I decided that Teleia and I should visit my parents in Boston. I didn't know if we'd be able to see them again until we returned from our two-year stay in Japan. Since Teleia was to become a Bat Mitzvah while we were overseas, I also thought it would be a good time to take her for a visit to Israel. This idea was especially appealing as I was still with the airline and would be able to plan this trip using my extensive airline discounts.

My father decided, since he had never been to the Holy Land, that he would come along with us. I thought it a wonderful idea. So, while Matt was on his ship sailing from San Diego to Yokosuka, Teleia, my father, and I went to Israel. We were all on standby and so it wasn't an easy trip. On the first flight there was only one seat available so I made my dad take it. He would get there first and check in to our hotel.

Seven long hours later, Teleia and I made the next flight to Tel Aviv. Unfortunately, the seats were not together. But, I was sure that once we got on we would be able to work something out so that we could be together during the long flight. I was sure no one would really want to be seated next to an eleven-year old for over ten hours. After the doors were closed I asked the flight attendant for her assistance. Once we were airborne and at cruising altitude, the flight attendant told me I should follow her. A seat was available next to my daughter thanks to another passenger who agreed to move.

When Teleia saw me she was visibly happy and relieved. She insisted that I take the middle seat between her and a young Hasidic gentleman who appeared to be trying to squeeze into the porthole on his left. It was obvious that he didn't feel comfortable sitting next to a woman and her child with no husband in sight. I focused on making my daughter comfortable and did my best to appear as if I hardly noticed him.

This gentleman on my left was extremely difficult to ignore. His discomfort at sitting next to me was apparent in every movement he made. He constantly fidgeted and whenever he did so he exaggerated the care he took so as not to come into any physical or eye contact with me. It made me extremely uncomfortable and nervous.

We had been airborne for over an hour and the flight attendants were now pulling their carts carefully down the aisles serving what appeared to be dinner. We were instructed to pull down our tray tables, which we did. The gentleman to my left, however, appeared to become even more anxious, if that were at all possible given the state he was already in.

The flight attendant passed the trays of food to each of us and I painstakingly made sure I didn't touch the tray meant for him or come into contact with him in any way. As the man received his tray he started an animated discussion with the attendant. He must have asked the flight attendant if the food was kosher as she assured him that all food served on El Al was kosher. This statement didn't seem to satisfy him and, finally, the flight attendant just shook her head and continued down the aisle to the next row of passengers waiting to be served their food.

From the corner of my eye I couldn't help but notice how the man inspected the sealed food items on his tray. Even my daughter, who was obviously intimidated by him, couldn't help but look. Suddenly he wanted to leave his seat. Now anyone who has ever traveled on a cramped airplane during the meal time ritual knows that it's next to impossible to leave your seat once food is on the tray tables, especially if you are seated next to the window with two other passengers between you and the aisle.

Teleia and I looked at each other wondering what we should do. We had nowhere to place our trays so that we could rise and it was obvious that he urgently desired to get up. At first we thought he had to use the rest room and wondered why he had waited until now to attempt it. We tried to figure out a way to accommodate this gentleman's needs. Suddenly he picked up his tray with one hand, returned the tray table to its upright position with the other, jumped on top of his seat and propelled himself over the back of it to the aisle behind him. It was lucky there were no seats behind us or we wouldn't have been the only people in shock. I was dumbfounded. Teleia just looked across the aisle at his retreating figure and uttered, "Cool."

Later, he returned with an older gentleman, also a Hasid, who appeared to be some sort of authority figure to this man. An animated discussion ensued, followed by a quick blessing. Meanwhile, Teleia and I were trying to eat our meager meal. The first thing I noticed was how quiet it was. I looked up to see this young man looking imploringly at his vacant seat. With much juggling of trays, Teleia and I were able to get up from our seats to allow him to return to his own.

All of this had just been too much for me. I had to summon all my willpower not to break out into uncontrollable laughter at the absurdity of it all.

I turned toward the man and inquired politely, "Is there something wrong with the food?"

At first he just stared at me in pure disbelief. Then he replied, "No, nothing wrong. I had to make certain from my Rebbe that the food was *glatt* kosher. Must be careful. Not all kosher foods are really kosher."

"Oh," I acknowledged, "are you able to eat then?"

"Yes, thank you." he nodded, "but I will only eat the fruits and vegetables."

"In that case," I offered, "take my fruits and vegetables, too. I will eat the rest. Otherwise, I'm afraid, it won't be enough for you to eat."

"No, no, I couldn't do that." he responded in amazement at my suggestion.

"It's not a problem," I reassured him, "I have already eaten before boarding the plane and I'm really not very hungry. Here."

I carefully placed the saran wrapped apple and salad on his tray. Then I quietly returned to eating with my daughter.

Perhaps my speaking to him broke the ice a little as I noticed that he no longer tried so hard to plaster himself against the left side of the aircraft wall while he sat reading. He was having some difficulty, though, trying to read while wearing a pair of broken eyeglasses. The right lens was badly cracked which interfered with his vision.

I was no longer intimidated by this most humorous man and decided to try and strike up a conversation with him. Of coarse, my daughter thought I was nuts.

"That can't be good for your eyes." I commented, "You should really get a new pair or repair those."

"Yes," he answered slowly, "I try, but I just don't have the time to take away from my studies."

"Perhaps," I ventured," your wife could do the errand for you."

"I don't have a wife." he replied.

"I'm sorry, " I replied, "Perhaps you should think about getting married. Then you would have someone to care for you while you studied. Someone who would make sure your glasses are repaired and that you eat properly."

I was starting to have fun with this. Slowly he turned his head toward me and actually looked at me, not around me or through me, but straight at me. He nodded.

"Yes," he agreed, "that would be the wise thing to do. I just haven't had time to arrange such a matter as that. Too much to study."

"I can see that." I agreed with him. "What are you studying?"

"Ah, you wouldn't understand," he answered, losing some of his shyness, "it has to do with the teachings of the Baal Shem Tov and The Zohar."

"So, you are a student of Kabbalah?" I ventured.

He looked at me in pure disbelief and replied, "You know about Kabbalah?"

"Well," I struggled to formulate a response, "I know a little about Kabbalah. Actually, I'm interested in learning about 'how' the Kabbalists practiced, how they did their meditation on the ten *Sefirot* and *Tetragrammaton*, etc."

It was plain to see from the look of surprise on this Hasid's face that this was not something he ever expected to hear coming from a mere woman. And especially not from an American woman who was clearly not Orthodox. When he regained his composure he once again spoke to me.

"How did you come to this study of Kabbalah?" he asked, "How did you find out about this subject?"

I briefly told him how I had been searching for a way to connect with G-d as some of our ancestors had done. I explained how I had been unable to find a means to do so within Judaism (as it was practiced by the congregations I grew up in, and was currently involved in). I explained how I had studied about Buddhism and learned how to meditate according to their methods. I went on to

107

explain how I had discovered the existence of Jewish Mysticism a.k.a. Kabbalah quite by accident while reading James Michener's novel, The Source. How this discovery had triggered a sense of hope, and a new course of study for me. How I felt Buddhism and Kabbalism were very similar in many ways.

By the time I had finished he was totally captivated. We engaged in philosophical and religious discussions concerning my knowledge of Judaism and Kabbalah. He expressed his concern about my getting involved with a belief such as Buddhism and didn't seem convinced that Buddha was only an ordinary man who struggled and found a way to become fully awake and aware, in other words, enlightened. He was afraid that I was proceeding dangerously close to idol worship and it distressed him.

Our discussions were, at times, amusing, and at other times very intense, but at all times educational. He was very comfortable now and even talked to Teleia from time to time. As our flight landed at Ben Gurion airport, my seat companion tore a piece of paper from his small notebook and scribbled a note.

"Here is the address of where our group is meeting our Rebbe. He is a very learned and spiritual man. I think you should speak with him. All of us will be there. If you can, please come. It will be unusual for a woman to come to such an event, but I'm sure he will understand. It is near Jerusalem." He handed me the note and hurriedly disembarked from the plane.

Once my daughter and I had arrived at our hotel and were settled in our rooms with my father, I took the note from my pocket and looked at it. It was written in Hebrew. I handed it to my father who can read Hebrew phonetically, but doesn't understand the language. I told him about the young Hasid who had given me that scrap of paper. It amused him.

I wasn't exactly sure what school of Hasidism this gentleman was involved with, but generally they are very pietistic and against rabbinical scholasticism as such. The Hasidim usually saw the study of Talmud as actually creating a barrier between man and G-d. What they desired was a direct union with G-d. This feeling, of coarse, is one I could relate to.

They would use fasting, dancing, the joys of nature and fellowship between one another, as well as, esthetic prayer as a means of trying to establish this union. Following their *zaddik* (a holy man or village saint) who later became more like a rabbinical sage, their life would revolve around the teachings of this sage and their closed community.

The original founder of the Hasidic movement was Israel ben Eliezer, also known as the Baal Shem Tov (1698-1760). "Baal Shem" is a title that literally meant "master of the Name" and appeared to be used for those Kabbalists who knew how to make use of the Divine Names during Kabbalistic practice. Although there were many well-known Kabbalists in Eastern Europe during that time, they were primarily concerned with theoretical Kabbalah (Kabbalah as a reasoned philosophy). The Baal Shem Tov moved it into the realm of practical Kabbalah by actually stressing its mystical and meditative aspects.

A major part of his teachings involved *Hitbodedut* meditation. *Hitbodedut* means "solitude" and refers to a process of being alone with God. He was known for going into seclusion for long periods of time in forests, in mountains and even in a special cave he used for that purpose. Later, he would spend much time in his special "Meditation Room" (*Bet Hitbodedut*) in his home.

He stressed to his followers the importance of constantly meditating on the Divine Presence, even if it were to take you away from your sacred study of Torah. He would, however, caution that one must never meditate alone as it could place the meditator in great danger. Consequently, one person should meditate while the other stayed close at hand to make sure the meditator was staying on the right track and didn't fall into any dangerous situations.

Hasidism was a social movement that gave poor and unlearned Jews the opportunity to engage in an authentic spiritual activity. This particular component rubbed the non-Hasidic Jewish communities the wrong way. After all, they contended, only those who spent the appropriate amount of time reading and studying the Torah and Talmud, etc., could hope to reach those lofty heights of understanding and spirituality.

I could have asked some one at the hotel to translate the note for me, but I never did. Some how I felt it would have been inappropriate and extremely disruptive if I were to show up amidst an entire group of Hasidic men waiting to learn from their beloved Rebbe. It would not have been a place for a woman to venture. I was concerned that my reception would not have been a positive one.

I asked my father what he thought I should do? He couldn't believe I would even consider meeting a group I knew nothing about.

It didn't make him feel any more comfortable knowing it would be a group of men. And, must he remind me that I was in another country? This may be our homeland, he insisted, but we certainly weren't at home in it yet. My daughter was extremely anxious. She was still afraid of those strange men in their strange cloths. She held onto my hand and told me she didn't want me to go.

And so I gave in to my own anxiety and the anxiety of my father and daughter. Wistfully I looked once again at the note and placed it in the waste paper basket. If I was to learn more about Kabbalah it was not to be in this way. Perhaps if I had been traveling alone I would have talked myself into going. I would have had the note translated, gotten directions, and made my way to the meeting. But, at this time it would have to be no. Not in this way.

And so I continue to wonder, even to this day, what would have happened if I had taken my enigmatic airplane companion's suggestion and gone to meet his Rebbe. Would I have had the rare opportunity of learning some thing of Kabbalah and Kabbalistic practice firsthand from a practicing Kabbalist himself? Now I'll never know.

Chapter 23
Japan

Shortly after my father, my daughter and I returned to Boston from our ten-day visit to Israel it was time for Teleia and I to fly to San Diego to join the rest of the families being relocated to Yokosuka, Japan. The aircraft chartered by the US Navy would take us from San Diego to Tokyo's Narita airport. We were excited about the prospect of living overseas, but we were also apprehensive.

Some of the families we met at the check-in area had traveled this route before. They were confident about meeting the challenges that would confront them as they had already lived overseas. Those families had a "been there, done that" attitude. But although I had done a lot of overseas traveling while working for an airline, I had never actually lived overseas. I didn't even know if my husband would be waiting for us at Narita. It depended on whether his ship was out to sea or not.

Little did I realize how far away Narita airport was from the Yokosuka Naval Base. After a very long flight, waiting in extremely slow lines for processing through customs and immigration, we finally walked through the automatic doors and into a crowd of Navy personnel waving and shouting trying to find their families. I was relieved to see Matt pushing forward toward us. We were herded into waiting buses and driven south on an over 3 hour-long journey to our temporary home at the Navy Lodge.

Being exhausted from the long flight, clearing government protocol, and the endless bus ride to the base, I was in a mental fog. I hardly remembered the grueling journey. All I could recall was being assigned a room at the Navy Lodge and being a little frustrated and upset that Teleia was expected to be in the same room with my husband and I. Being that she was 11 years old it didn't seem appropriate. Add to the fact that Matt and I hadn't seen each other for several months and I think you get the general idea.

Approximately a week prior to Matt's next deployment we were fortunate enough to find a lovely one level, Japanese home on the other side of the peninsula from the Naval Base. It was located on a hill in a somewhat secluded development. It had two Western style bedrooms, one traditional *tatami* mat bedroom, a Japanese shower room with *O-fudo* (Japanese soaking, hot tub), separate toilet room, small kitchen off a moderate sized living area, adjoining with a good sized *tatami* matted dining area complete with shoji screen doors and altar alcove. A traditional entranceway, a couple of steps lower than the main living area with plenty of wall space to place our shoes, completed the floor plan.

I was extremely happy with our living quarters. I was never comfortable with the military. In fact, I could have been considered anti-military but I kept my opinions to myself. Living off base was a relief for me. I was willing to test for a temporary Japanese driver's license and to go through the initial stress of having to drive on the left side of Japan's narrow roads and lanes. It was a small price to pay, I felt, to be allowed to live as far as I could from a military base and to live among the locals.

Of coarse, not knowing the Japanese language did make it more difficult to find ones way, especially since the Japanese don't usually have street signs and any signage they did have was written in Kanji (a more streamlined version of Japanese characters). I found myself memorizing my routes as well as key Kanji symbols so as to be able to find my way around. Teleia didn't seem to have any trouble, however. She would take the buses and trains and rarely got lost.

It took me quite some time to realize how safe it was to travel around in Japan. My daughter had no fear for her safety on any forms of public transportation. The Japanese people universally love children and are very protective of them. Whenever Teleia found herself lost or in need of help someone would inevitably come forward and offer assistance.

Matt would be away on deployments anywhere from several weeks to several months or longer. Once I had set up the house, found out what bills I'd have to pay and where (most bills were paid at the local post office), and what resources I could avail myself of, I decided to explore this new country in which I now resided. The first trip was to Tokyo where I was to see my first Buddhist monk at the famous

Ginza (shopping area).

Teleia and I were strolling down the rather immense boulevard, window-shopping. We tried to guess what stores sold what, and halfheartedly tried to decide on a place to eat lunch by scrutinizing the plastic food in the display windows, when we both noticed the monk slowly making his way in the crowd. He had a wide, conical shaped, straw hat on his bowed head. He wore the traditional robes of a monk, what looked like straw sandals on his feet, and he carried a brown wood, begging bowl cupped in his two hands. He walked at a very slow, tiny step by tiny step, pace. He never seemed to lift his head or eyes, but seemed to be slowly drifting over the pavement. Whenever someone would place some money in his bowl, he would quietly stop, raise the bowl slightly to his forehead, bow in thanks and gratitude, and then resume his slow pace down the middle of the sidewalk.

Teleia watched in fascination and quickly decided she wanted to donate something, too. I rummaged through my pocketbook and took out some 500-yen notes and handed it to her. She unselfconsciously walked up to the monk, carefully placed the yen notes in his bowl, and stepped aside. Just as we had seen him do several times before, he stopped in place, raised his bowl, bowed in thanks and gratitude, than continued his snail-paced walk seemingly oblivious to the crowds around him. He appeared to me as a serene island of peacefulness and calm amidst the hustle and bustle of this large metropolis. Even now, in my mind's eye, I can see him quietly and slowly walking, bowing, walking, bowing, walking his way down the *Ginza* strip.

Chapter 24
Kyoto and Nara

I decided to try to look up Reverend Fujii who had been the Buddhist monk who had first directed me in my meditation practice at the Soto Zen Mission in Honolulu. He had only been at the Soto Mission a couple of years and was then sent back to Japan. I was told he was residing at Sojiji, the main Soto Temple, located in Yokohama. I found a pay telephone and called Sojiji. I was lucky that the monk who answered understood English. Unfortunately, Rev. Fujii was not there during that time. I was unable to locate him.

Although I wasn't able to find Rev. Fujii, I decided to make a pilgrimage to Kyoto and Nara. These twin cities play host to countless Buddhist Temples and Shinto Shrines. So, during the following cherry blossom season in mid-April, Teleia and I made our way by tour bus to those world-renowned cities.

We left the Naval Base early in the morning. It was bright, clear, and sunny so we only needed to bring along a sweater for the cooler times of the day. As our bus made its way south we passed world famous Mt. Fuji, known as Fuji-san. Its white crown of snow sparkled in the sunlight. The gentle morning breeze caused wisps of feathery clouds to caress the snow-topped mountain as they moved across the baby blue sky. Passing Hakone, we continued southward.

Our first stop was to the East Great Temple, Todai-Ji, famous for being the largest wooden structure in the world. Todai-Ji had been built by Emperor Shomu in 745, to be the headquarters for all the temples in the entire country of Japan. It's Great Buddha Hall, known as *Daibutsu-den*, is home to the worlds largest Bronze statue, *Dainichi-Nyorai*, the Great Sun Buddha. This temple's *Kaidan-in* or ordainment platform is the oldest and most famous in Japan. Behind the *Daibutsu-den*, in a fenced in park, is the Imperial Repository of the Emperor

Picture 24.1: Mount Fuji, Japan

Shomu, called the *Sho-so-in*. Located in Nara, Todai-Ji is the principle temple of the Kegon sect of Buddhism.

Next we went to the Deer Park. The park is located between Todai-Ji and the Kasuga-Taisha or Shrine of 3,000 Lanterns. Kasuga's Shrine's tame deer are believed to be divine messengers. That may have been true, but all we knew for sure was that these deer enjoyed eating. If they saw you with anything in hand that could be construed as edible, they would relentlessly follow you until they were able to grab the item in question away from your grip and run off with it.

Teleia found out the hard way just how devious these deer could be. As she slowly ate *arare* (rice) crackers from a bag, two deer converged on her. One grabbed the entire bag and ran off with it while the other quickly followed. We decided that eating in the Deer Park was foolhardy and so gave up the idea. Meanwhile, other tame deer would come up to us to be petted and one young doe followed Teleia around until we left the park.

The best approach to the Shrine of the 3,000 Lanterns was to go through the *Sanjo-dori* (two vermilion *torii* arches within the Deer Park), continue up the long gravel avenue lined with thousands of stone lanterns, and then cross a large stone portico to the shrine, itself. It is said that there are some 1,780 stone lanterns and 1,012 bronze lanterns lining this beautiful avenue to the shrine. As impressive as the lanterns were, I found the landscape even more so. The balance of trees, flowers, water, the many lanterns, and the gentle curves of the walkway, was outstanding.

Approaching the *Kasuga* Shrine we passed through two gates. These were no ordinary gates. They looked like buildings in their own right, the second one even larger than the first. This was a Shinto shrine. Shinto or "the way of the gods" is Japan's indigenous religion, which originated in prehistoric times, based on ancestor and nature worship.

Worship involved a vast array of spirits called *kami* that personified the various elements of the natural world such as the sky, mountains, the earth, heavenly bodies, etc. The rites performed in Shintoism usually involved prayer, offerings, and rituals performed to produce absolutionary purification.

Buddhism, however, rapidly overshadowed Shinto and Buddhist priests eventually took over the Shinto Shrines. Now the Shinto gods were looked upon as being previous manifestations of Buddha in His other existences. Shinto priests, on the other hand, became known as fortune-tellers and magicians.

Later, in the 18th century, Shintoism experienced a revival. However, it emerged in two different forms. One form was sponsored by the State, meaning the Imperial Court supported it. The other was Sectarian, meaning it was founded and supported by private persons. After World War II and during the American occupation of Japan, the State sponsored form of Shintoism was banned by order of General Douglas MacArthur.

Today only "Sectarian" Shinto remains as a major religion, holding the same status as Christianity and Buddhism. There are currently five main sects of Sectarian Shinto; those emphasizing Confucian ethics, those devoted to faith healing, those that worship mountains, those that devote themselves primarily to rites of purification, and those that continue to practice the traditions and forms of ancient Shinto. It is interesting to note, however, that the majority of Shintoists are also Buddhist.

From there we went out from the South Gate of Todai-ji Temple to the gardens of Isui-En Shrine. We were to learn that these gardens were landscaped in the *Shakkei* Style, in which the surroundings of the garden are incorporated into the total effect. It was in these gardens that we were to see our first cherry blossoms.

Leisurely, we made our way along the curved pathways. We passed tranquil ponds surrounded by rolling hillsides covered in green shrubs and trees. Some of these ponds had round stepping-stones across them leading to a teahouse, of which there were two. We watched as a snapping turtle lazily stretched and dropped itself into the cool, still water of the pond.

Many cherry trees lined the path, covered in their own kimono of delicate pink/white blossoms. The sweet fragrance of these blooms infused the air. With so much beauty around us we were hard put to know where to look first. No one could walk these paths quickly. The fragrant breezes, the tinkling sound of water, and the chirping of birds hidden in the multi-green hued plant life all contributed to making you feel one with the environment you were walking in. Sense of time disappeared as we blended with the surroundings.

Now it was time for us to board our bus for the short ride to Kyoto. It was difficult to leave. Our destination was the *Sanju-Sangendo*, the Hall of thirty-three Bays. The Rengyoin Temple was founded in 1164 and was rebuilt in 1266 after the original Temple burned down in a fire. The present building is approximately 393 feet long and is designated as a National Treasure. Inside sits its chief image, also a National Treasure, the 1,000 armed Kannon (in China known as Kwan-Yin, the goddess of Mercy). This statue was flanked by 1,000 smaller, gold gilded, standing images of Kannon, along with twenty-eight similarly gilded images of her disciples.

Once again we boarded the bus for our brief journey to the *Kujomizu-Dera*, the Clear Spring Temple, founded in 1633. We were dropped off at the head of a narrow street leading to *Kujomizu*. This colorful street was lined with shops selling everything from cloisonné and lacquer to salted plum candy and tea. Because it was cherry blossom season, the shops had decorated their storefronts with boughs of cherry blossom branches.

This street inclined upward toward the Temple and it was made more difficult to walk given the great number of people who were also there to view the famous blossoms. Add to this the constant temptation to step inside the shops and you can well imagine how relieved we were to finally reach the steep stairs leading up to the Temple platform. I was pregnant during this time and so moved quite slowly up those steps.

It was worth the effort. At the top of the famous twenty-five meter high platform, one had a spectacular view of the gorge and the city of Kyoto in the background. It is a very popular spot for cherry blossom viewing and the temple, itself, shows off the ornate design of the *Momoyama* period.

Once on the platform we immediately came to a large temple bell surrounded in cherry blossoms. Ringing the bell is considered to be a means of increasing ones merit. Teleia stood firm as she pulled back the large, heavy mallet and pushed it on its twisted rope toward the bell. Its ring was low and melodious, and the sound of its vibration continued for what seemed to be an extraordinarily long period of time.

Following the others down a steep flight of stairs we found ourselves in another courtyard. To the left was a pavilion where people were lined up taking turns catching water from three waterfalls with a bamboo ladle and sipping from it. I was told that each waterfall symbolized one trait. One waterfall was for wisdom, one for long life and the third for love. Although Teleia wanted to drink from the waterfalls, the line was so long that we decided to forego that experience.

From *Kujomizu-Dera* we went to visit *Heian-Jingu*, a Shinto Shrine built in 1895, in commemoration of Kyoto's 1,100th anniversary. This is the Temple that enshrines Emperors Kammu, who established the city of Kyoto, and Komei, the father of Emperor Meiji. The building, itself, is a replica on a smaller scale of the first Imperial Palace built in 794.

In it's large sand courtyard there stood a rock fountain in the shape of a hexagon. Inside the fountain was a sculpture that appeared to me to look like a bear climbing on a rock. There were two bamboo ladles resting on the lip of the fountain. Teleia immediately went up to the fountain, picked up the ladle and gracefully scooped up some of the water flowing out of the rock formation. Serenely, she stood there, sipping from the ladle. Her long black hair fell across her shoulders as she tipped her head forward.

As if this building of red, white and gold filigree wasn't impressive enough, the Okazaki Park that surrounds it was absolutely breathtaking. This was a garden that embodied, for me anyway, everything a Japanese garden was supposed to be. Every rock, every tree, every plant, everything, was perfectly placed in harmony with everything else around it. But what impressed me the most were the cherry blossoms.

Yes, I had seen cherry blossoms in Nara and in other places in Kyoto, but this was entirely different. Arbors had been built throughout the cherry tree groves. The branches, heavy with pinkish/white cherry blossoms, fell gracefully downward across the arbors. So many of the blossoms had fallen that they covered the ground and pathways in a cloud of soft pink. I felt as if I was walking in a fairy tale land, someplace mystical and magical. Surrounded in fragrant cherry blossom petals.

Teleia and I walked in silence, only whispering if we had an absolutely pressing need to communicate. We felt as if we were walking within some sacred precinct. Slowly we made our way around the curving pathway that was to lead us through this beautiful garden. We passed ponds surrounded in greenery with large millstones set in place as steps across the water. We walked over gently curved, red bridges and passed strategically placed teahouses, their white paper lanterns moving slightly in the breeze. We marveled at rock and bamboo water fountains that provided the tinkling of a waterfall for us to listen to.

I didn't want to leave that place. It was so peaceful. If I had been alone and able to stay for as long as I wished, I would have sat under one of the cherry trees next to a serene pond, and meditated for awhile. But that wasn't possible. However, as I walked slowly through the garden I fell into walking meditation. Silently taking in the moment as well as the aromatic cherry blossom perfume that enveloped me.

All too soon it was time to move on to the next sight on our tour. In contrast to what we had just left behind, we came to the famous Golden Pavilion called *Kinkakuji*. It wasn't difficult to see why it was called the Golden Pavilion. Sitting in the middle of a lake surrounded by gently rolling hillside it's gold color stood out against the green foliage around it. Its three tiers seemed to come up from the waters and it's perfect reflection on the lake's calm surface only heightened the impact.

The third Ashikaga Shogun, Yoshimitsu (1358-1408), retired here. The original pavilion had been built in 1397. After Yoshimitsu's death this pavilion, which had been his villa, was turned into a Zen Temple. In 1950, one of the Zen priests deliberately burned the structure to the ground. In 1955, a replica of the original was built. Although the Golden Pavilion holds many fine paintings and statues, almost no one ever bothers to look at them. Instead, people stand transfixed at the opposite edge of the lake, only moving long enough to take a snapshot of this impressive pavilion with their cameras.

Onward we went to our next objective, the *Ryoanji* or "Temple of the Peaceful Dragon" and its famous rock garden. Although the Temple interested me, the rock garden, with its fifteen stones arranged in clusters of 5, 2, 3, 2, 3, mesmerized me. The gravel surrounding the rock groupings had been racked into ripples and waves. It was as if the water lapping around these silent rock islands had been frozen in time. How patiently the person who had done this must have racked those stones. I sat down and looked at the garden until Teleia eventually came over to retrieve me.

Picture 24.2: Ryoan-ji Garden

Our last stop was Nijo Castle, built in 1603, as the residence of the first Shogun of the Tokugawa family. The immensity of this black and gold structure was as awe inspiring as it was beautiful. The opulence it displayed was very indicative of the Momoyama Period. At the beginning of the Meiji era, this had been the seat of government in Japan. However, on April 6, 1868, Emperor Meiji issued an edict that abolished the *shogunate*.

As the bus left Kyoto for the return trip home, I felt a poignant sadness. It wasn't the Japanese landscape, but the Buddhist Temples that made me feel this way. The people I saw in these Temples chanted in Sanskrit or Japanese. They looked differently than me, and in many cases dressed differently than I did, but they lit the incense sticks the same way as I did, they paid homage to the Buddha, *Dharma*, and *Sangha* just as I did, and they were Buddhists just as I was Buddhist. On some very deep level I had felt comfortable there.

Chapter 25
Being Jewish in Japan

Teleia was still serious about becoming a Bat Mitzvah on her 12th birthday. The closest Jewish facility in Japan for us was on the Naval Base. I would attend Friday night services with Teleia in order to have some where to go (especially when Matt was on deployment), to go some where familiar, and, possibly to make some friends. I met the Rabbi and his family. Soon it was arranged that Teleia, and Sara, the Rabbi's daughter, would be instructed by the Rabbi, himself.

It seemed that Teleia and Sara were the only two Jewish school age children on the base. Fortunately, both of them were in the same grade and only a couple of months apart in their birth dates. Teleia's Bat Mitzvah would be the first. Her birthday was in December. Both girls got along well and it seemed a perfect way for Teleia to prepare for her entry into adult Jewish life.

It should have been a relatively stress free year for Teleia, but it wasn't meant to be. The first sign of trouble started in her new school. On the base they had grades 7 through 12 in one school building. Mixing 11/12 year olds with 15 to 18-year olds wasn't a very wise move given the social considerations of teenagers. Add to this the fact that few households had both parents in attendance as ships were constantly out at sea and you can understand the problem.

It didn't take long for Teleia to start to become involved with some very tough kids. Most were older than her and had a tendency toward bullying the younger children. Teleia was, and still is, a very strong willed person and she would stand up to them and they would usually back down. But occasionally something hurtful would be said, or an implication, made and Teleia would come home from school feeling wounded, helpless, and alone. It was difficult making new friends.

In school there were other problems. Teleia was very involved in learning about and developing her Jewish side. She went to the temple on base after school 2-3 times a week to study with the Rabbi. Add to this her piano lessons and other extra-curricular activities and she was a pretty busy young lady. The school didn't seem to take these things into consideration. Nor did the school take into consideration the fact that many children had to take the bus to and from their homes off base.

I usually waited for Teleia's return by walking to the top of the hill where our Japanese style home was located where I watched for her bus to arrive. This particular afternoon she didn't come off the bus. They didn't have an activity bus that would bring kids home later in the day if they chose to stay for after school activities. If they had to stay after school then the parents had to arrange to pick them up there. I was pregnant and it was no longer easy for me to drive across the peninsula to the base to get Teleia.

I called the school to find out where my child was as she had already been expected to be home. I was informed that the music teacher had decided that his class would have to meet after school in order to practice their singing for chorus. This upset me as no one had informed me of this and no note or other form had been sent to me in order to get my consent. I stopped what I had been doing, got into the car and drove the hour ride to the base to collect my daughter.

I pulled up in front of the main entrance to the school and Teleia jumped into the car. She was obviously upset. On the ride home she told me that she hadn't wanted to stay after school. She was told that if she didn't stay that she would get a poor or failing grade for the class. What was this all for? Her music class was practicing Christmas Carols for an assembly to be held before Winter break. Teleia was hurt and offended. She wasn't Christian and, although she often enjoyed listening to Christmas melodies and certainly didn't begrudge her classmates, she felt it inappropriate for her, as a Jew, to be forced to sing songs about Jesus the Savior. When she told me she was also expected to go on Mondays and Wednesdays when she was supposed to go to the Rabbi for lessons, I was perplexed. Perhaps the music teacher didn't understand our situation.

The following day I left a message for her teacher in order to discuss this. He called me back later in the afternoon and basically told me it was the primary class project for the year and if Teleia didn't participate she would get a failing grade. It didn't matter what I said about the inappropriateness of it or about how an after school activity was, by definition, voluntary. He was insistent. It didn't even appear to bother him that she already had religious school commitments on the two after school days and times he had designated.

I called the principal and arranged a meeting. The three of us sat down in an adjoining room to the principal's office. The principal was a very thin woman with medium length gray hair held back by an abalone shell hair comb on the right side of her head. Her devoted toy poodle would follow her wherever she went and she brought him to school every day. A rather eccentric lady, she would often punctuate her speeches with exaggerated hand gestures.

It was obvious that the music teacher and principal had already decided the outcome of the meeting. Nothing I said had any impact. In fact, no acknowledgment concerning my position was ever mentioned by either of them. This was the way it had always been done for all the years the music teacher had taught at this school. The music teacher was held in high esteem and the case was closed. But it wasn't closed to me.

I called the rabbi and explained the situation, and my frustration at how insensitive and unfair it appeared to me. He agreed and told me he would speak with the principal as soon as possible. Several days later I received a call from the principal. They had decided to exempt Teleia from the chorus, but that she would have to do something else to make up the work she was unwilling to participate in. Both the principal and music teacher thought it only fair that Teleia should do some extra work as her classmates were required to attend this after school function and were being graded on it. I accepted the rational until the terms were explained to me.

Teleia would be required to listen to the music of five different composers. She would then have to research each of these composers and write a separate report on each of them. I was appalled. I didn't mind if Teleia was required to do something comparable, but different. This, however, was blatantly unfair. Writing five reports entailed much more work than singing songs after school with a group. I refused to agree to this. It was obvious that Teleia was going to be punished in this way for not wanting to sing Christmas Carols. Was this an act of bias and prejudice? It certainly appeared to be.

Several days later, and with the Rabbis intervention, it was finally agreed that Teleia would only be required to do one report on two composers. This we could live with. Teleia agreed to do the extra work and I worried that she would be further discriminated against during the remainder of the school year.

December approached and Teleia was excitedly looking forward to being called up to chant her Torah and *Haftarah* portion in the Jewish chapel which would officially mark her entry into the covenant with G-d. She had been practicing her Hebrew diligently, and we were very proud of her. We were also relieved and very happy that Matt would be in port for this special lifecycle event. To add to our joy, my father decided he would fly out to Japan from Massachusetts to see his granddaughter on the *bimah*.

We were to find out that Teleia's Bat Mitzvah was the first such ritual to be celebrated in Japan for over thirty-five years. The Jewish community in Japan is very small and the community in Tokyo is of an older generation. So as my daughter took her place among the men and women of the small congregation in Yokosuka, I couldn't help but be struck by the uniqueness of the event. A young girl in an alien country, involved in a major life cycle event as is the custom of her Hebrew forbears, which all other Jews around the globe do in the same ritual form and fashion, no matter the land they may call home or reside in. Wasn't it this ritual, and the other rituals and customs, that kept Judaism alive? Wasn't it this that kept the Jewish people's identity intact over the centuries and across many lands? Yes, I think so.

Chapter 26
Bris in Japan

Yes, I was pregnant. Being pregnant when your first-born is already eleven-years old is a very strange experience. Diapers and around the clock feedings were a mere memory. I was told that becoming pregnant in Japan was very common. Some even told me it was because of the water. I knew that wasn't true, but looking around me I certainly had to admit there were a lot of pregnant women on base.

Being thirty-five years of age, I was an anomaly at the Yokosuka Naval Hospital. Sitting in the waiting area to be seen by an Obstetrician, I was the oldest pregnant person there. It was obvious to me that they weren't accustomed to dealing with mature mothers-to-be. It was obvious to them that I wasn't accustomed to being treated as a mere military dependent. There was bound to be some conflicts.

My first association with the OB/GYN department was a frustrating one. Having been pregnant before I knew the feeling. When I went in to have a pregnancy test to confirm what I already knew I was told I wasn't pregnant. I returned a week later, after my husband had already left on his next deployment, and was told I was, indeed, pregnant. I had wanted to tell my husband in person that he was to be a daddy soon, but he was now in the Philippines. I broke the news to him late one night when he called me from Subic Bay. Not quite the way I had imagined telling him.

The Corp-persons were used to treating the expectant mom's as herds of cattle. They would snap their fingers at you to get your attention and then direct you to a long line of other pregnant women where you would have your urine tested, height/weight taken, etc. Then you would be placed in a room to undress and wait. After what seemed an eternity a doctor you had never seen before would come in and do the usual examination on you.

This was not what I was about to put up with. When the Corp-woman snapped her fingers at me I just ignored her. When she finally came up to me I told her I had no idea she was trying to get my attention, that I was Mrs. Cohen and she could call on me properly. Then she tried to order me into the lines. I refused to go explaining that I wanted to meet the doctor first before I agreed to anything more. This triggered a round of confusion. It was obvious that no one had ever suggested this before. That a woman may actually want to meet the doctor first was obviously an alien concept. In addition, I insisted that I wanted a Captain or above as I felt anyone with less experience would be inadequate. I told her that I would then decide if that would be the doctor whom I would want to assist me in my pregnancy and delivery. All pandemonium broke out.

Taken by surprise, the Corp-woman stood back, became silent and pensive, and excused herself. A short time later she came up to me, and invited me to follow her to the doctor's office. She told me the doctor was Capt. James and that he would meet with me shortly.

His office was Spartan by civilian doctor standards, but was obviously a physician's office. When Capt. James entered the room he was absolutely charming. He introduced himself and told me he was delighted to meet me. It was not usual for a patient to insist on meeting and selecting a doctor in a Naval Hospital, but he agreed it was a nicer way of doing things. I asked questions, he answered them. I told him I would be delighted if he would be my OB/GYN doctor and he accepted. He told me my child's birth would be the last one in his naval career, as he was to retire that summer.

Being pregnant in Japan while living off base was also a unique experience. A pregnant woman is treated kindly, and with respect. It was expected that after giving birth the new mother would be in the hospital for at least a week being cared for and allowed to rest. In Japanese hospitals, the day prior to being discharged, the new mother and father are treated to a nice dinner alone. Once returned home, it was expected that family members would be staying with the new family for at least a month to help with household chores and cooking so that the new mother could rest and tend to her newborn.

Having a child as an American in a Naval Hospital was totally different. For one thing my hospital stay was only two days in duration. My husband was on a deployment somewhere in the Indian Ocean and off the coast of Oman. There was no send off dinner the evening before my discharge and no relatives would be staying with me for a month to take over the household chores so I could rest, tend to, and play with my new baby.

As it turned out I was over three weeks overdue before my son decided it was time to come into the world. Capt. James had already retired two weeks prior and my labor lasted so long that I went through several shifts of hospital staff. Arik was finally born on the Fourth of July at 10:40 in the morning: A Yankee Doodle baby.

My friend, Ann, had assisted me. She then went to the American Red Cross office to arrange to have a message sent to my husband's ship to advise him of the birth of his son and that both of us were fine. The following morning I received a message in return:

"I'm one very proud father and am overjoyed at the news. I send all my love to you and the rest of the Cohen family. Arik picked a fine day to be born. We can all be proud. Send pictures ASAP. Letter to follow. All my love, Matt."

I put the telex message next to the small picture, of Matt I had placed on the table next to my hospital bed. Arik was sleeping in a bassinet next to me.

"Your daddy is happy you are here little boy." I whispered to Arik as he slept.

I remember feeling very sad that my husband wasn't with us. How long would it be before his ship came back and he would be home again? I had no idea.

My Japanese housekeeper was in awe. Not only did she obviously respect me for having given birth to a son, she was shocked that I had only stayed in the hospital for two days and had no one to care for us upon our return home. There was obviously a large cultural gap here and there was no way I was going to be able to explain it to Tomiko-san.

As is the law in Judaism, a newborn boy is to be circumcised on the eighth day after his birth. It is a law G-d gave to Abraham as a sign between G-d and His people that G-d had a covenant with the Hebrew's. It was to be done at home so that the mother and infant would be in comfortable and familiar surroundings and so they wouldn't have to venture outside so soon after birth. The naming of the child was also to take place at the same time.

The circumcision is to be performed by a rabbi referred to as a *Moyel*. This professional does nothing but perform circumcisions according to Jewish Law and so he is very adept and quick. It is often done so quickly that the baby doesn't even realize he was circumcised until it is over. By that time he is being cuddled and nursed by his mother and so no more than a slight whimper is heard from the infant from the ordeal.

Unfortunately, living in Japan made getting a *Moyel* extremely difficult if not impossible. The rabbi advised me that the only way to get a *Moyel* was to try and contact one in California, to pay all the expenses of air travel, accommodations, food, etc., and hope that he would arrive by the eighth day after birth. Time and expense worked against using this avenue and so option two was the usual approach used.

Rabbi Horowitz would ask one of the Pediatric Surgeons at the Naval Base hospital to officiate. This particular pediatrician, I was told, knew how to circumcise according to Jewish Law (which is not how circumcisions are done in the hospital) and that he, the rabbi, would officiate to make certain the ritual was done correctly. The ceremony would be done at the chapel, the rabbi informed me. I was not very happy about that as I was still very weak after giving birth and my son would only be eight days old.

It is the father's responsibility to take care of the planning, etc., for the Bris (circumcision and naming) of his son. This is because it was an edict to the fathers to bestow on their sons, plus it was to spare the mother having to be part of something she would, obviously, be upset about. In ancient times, fathers were expected to perform the circumcisions on their sons. As time went on, however, fathers were allowed to assign a surrogate who would perform the deed for him. This was better for all concerned. The father would be spared having to perform some thing on his son that he would, obviously, not feel very comfortable with or be skilled at. The child would be spared the very real possibility of his father botching the job or taking an unusually long time in doing the deed, itself, that would cause unnecessary pain and discomfort. Unfortunately, Matt was out to sea and so the Rabbi took over the responsibility. He insisted we had to do this at the chapel as it helped to justify having a Jewish chapel on base. No matter my protests, it was to be done at the chapel, not at home.

It was now the eighth day since the birth of my son and time for the ritual circumcision that would bring him into the covenant with the G-d of Abraham, Isaac, and Jacob. It was also the time for his official naming. My husband and I had decided prior to his birth that we were going to give our child an English name that would also be his Hebrew name. It is the custom among American Jews of *Ashkenazic* (East European) background to name their baby after a deceased relative who is admired for his/her virtue. It is usually a deceased relative who the parents wish to honor and remember by naming their child after him or her. It is a further custom amongst American Jews, after selecting the Hebrew name of the deceased relative to be so honored, to select an English name using the first letter of the Hebrew name. For example, my husband is named after Menachem Mendel, his paternal great grandfather. Using the "M" from the first Hebrew name, his English name was selected as Matthew. So, he is then considered named after his great grandfather Menachem even thought he is called Matthew except during certain occasion in the Synagogue when his Hebrew name is used.

It was decided that our son's name should be Arik David in both English and Hebrew. David was in honor of his paternal great-grandfather, also named David. Arik is the shortened version of Aryeh. Aryeh meaning in Hebrew, "lion of G-d," and Arik meaning, "little lion." Since David means "beloved friend" we thought our son's new name to be perfect.

The naming was the easy part. Not so the circumcision. I handed my little boy to the doctor and watched in horror as he carefully strapped my son onto a body shaped board. His little arms and legs were strapped so as to render him immobile, but it also frightened him into fits of crying. The rabbi's wife led me to the rear of the sanctuary into a small room where I was to wait until the ceremony was over. My daughter would remain out front with some friends from the base to observe the ritual. As the rabbi soaked a small piece of cloth in deep red, sweet, kosher wine and gently placed it on my sons lips to suck on (in the hope of dulling the pain), the door was closed and I was directed to sit on a small, blue padded chair.

At first I only heard an occasional cry and at times peoples voices. Then I heard terrified screams coming from my newborn. Minutes seemed like hours. Suddenly, my daughter ran into the room. Her face was red, tears were falling from her eyes and she was obviously extremely upset. She did something she hadn't done in years. She crawled up into my lap and continued to cry. I found this quite alarming especially while hearing the high-pitched wails of my son.

The doctor, it seemed, was having an awful time performing the circumcision. He was unused to the method required and he was doing it extremely slowly. The rabbi tried to coax Arik to suck on the wine saturated piece of gauze, but Arik was too terrified and too much in pain to do so. As the rabbi and guests looked on helplessly, the doctor continued his gruesome task, and Arik continued to wail loudly while squirming relentlessly on the board he was secured to.

I could take it no longer. Even in a separate room with the door closed I could hear my son's screaming. Add to that my daughter's distraught weeping into my shoulder while curled up in my lap and it was just too much for me. I gently pushed her off my lap, grabbed her left hand and quickly made my way to my distraught baby. As I came up to the *bimah* (the front portion of the synagogue) and to the table my son was being tortured on, I was quickly reassured that Arik was all right and that the procedure was over. Tears fell down my checks and I openly wept into my daughter's long black hair as the doctor cleaned the wound, added ointment and wrapped it in gauze.

As soon as my son was removed from the board he had been strapped to, I quickly snatched him up and ran back to the room I had been sequestered to earlier. I cooed to him, rocked him, tried to nurse him. His cries became less intense. He tried to catch his breath and cried softly and whimpered. Slowly he started to calm down. Then, from sheer exhaustion, he fell asleep. Meanwhile, I was a wreck. I had completely forgotten about "equanimity" and trying to maintain calm through meditation.

And so I learned a valuable lesson. If you're Jewish and plan to have a child while living overseas, especially in the Orient, don't, unless you have the money and can arrange for a *Moyel* to be flown in to do the circumcision on time. What a difference it would have made. I have attended other ritual circumcisions after I returned to the States and I was greatly impressed with how quick a *Moyel* can perform his task. The baby, the parents, and none of the guests had to go through any undue stress. It was, literally, over almost as soon as it began. How I had wished I could have done that for my own little boy.

Matt returned home over four months after the birth of his new son. It was to be a homecoming never to be forgotten. Arik cried when his daddy picked him up and talked to him for the first time. There are few men on the naval base when the ships are out and Arik was not used to the touch or the deep sounding voices of men. Matt, on the other hand, had never had a baby before. He was amazed at how tiny Arik was although he had since doubled his birth weight.

We were a united family once again. Matt wanted to celebrate in some way so he decided we should take a trip up to Tokyo. The train ride was quick and without mishap. The new father, however, was overcome by how much equipment had to be dragged along for the use of his infant son. Matt just couldn't believe a small baby would need so much stuff; extra clothing, diapers, stroller, water bottles, medications (just in case), baby blankets, special toilet articles.

One afternoon after sightseeing in different parts of the city, Matt asked Teleia to watch her brother while he took me out for a short walk alone. As we strolled outside he took me up to a jewelry shop that specialized in pearls. He selected an opera length pearl necklace with a beautiful gold double ball clasp. He had me try it on just to see what it looked like. When I declared how beautiful it was he told the sales person we would take it. I think both of us were surprised. I was shocked because I hadn't really taken this excursion seriously and these were very expensive pearls. The Japanese salesperson was surprised, as she really hadn't had to work too hard to make this sale.

She placed the pearl necklace in its rich, blue velvet lined box. After wrapping the box in gold and white paper, she accepted my husband's American Express card. When she saw the last name on the card she became very excited. She told us that her last name was the same. This was a woman who was obviously pure Japanese and we were more than a little skeptical that she should have the last name Cohen. She went on to explain that her husband was Jewish and that she had become Jewish just before having children.

Naturally, we were interested in this, to us anyway, unique story. She lived in Tokyo with her family and they were members of the Jewish Community Center there. She asked if we had ever gone to this center. We advised her that we hadn't. She then told us that Emperor Hirohito's daughter was going to be visiting the center in two weeks and asked if we'd be interested. My husband was scheduled to go back out on deployment, but I would be home. She excused herself and disappeared into the back room. Some minutes later she returned with a formal invitation in her hand.

"Please," she pressed, "take this invitation and please come. It would be a good thing. Please do try."

"Thank you," I responded as she placed the invitation in my hand, "I am very grateful to you and will try to come."

She smiled, thanked us for coming in, and walked us to the

door. As Matt and I made our way back to the wide sidewalk outside, we both started to laugh at the same time. Never had we ever thought we would meet a Japanese Jew and especially not one with the last name Cohen. And to be invited to a Jewish Community Center in Tokyo to meet the Emperor's daughter, it was just too much.

Chapter 27
Life and Death in the Big Apple

Matt received his new orders. He was to report to DCASMA (Defense Contract Administration Services Management Area), in Garden City, Long Island, New York. He was very excited about this assignment as it meant going back to Long Island where he had grown up. His parents were ecstatic as they lived in Manhattan and would now be able to see their son and grandchildren much more often. I wasn't so thrilled. After living so many years in Hawaii, I had no desire to live in the cold environs of the Northeast. But, the needs of the Navy came first and so we went. Fortunately, we arrived in May. Spring was definitely in the air.

During the first two months, Matt had to attend classes in Athens, Georgia, so Arik and I stayed with his parents in Manhattan. Teleia, meanwhile, flew up to Boston to stay with my mother and to attend a local Middle School in order to complete her school year. I was concerned that she might be behind academically coming from a DOD (Department of Defense) school. I was much relieved to find out that she was right up to speed. Once we purchased and settled into our new home Teleia would return to us and attend school in New York.

My husband was in Georgia, my daughter was in Boston, and my in-laws worked during the day. Arik and I soon developed a routine. One of which included daily walks around the neighborhood and sharing a chocolate Italian ice from an Italian Pizza Place around the corner. Soon they came to know us and so even if there were a line of patrons waiting to order lunch, they would wave us to the front and give us our usual chocolate ice.

I had found the city intimidating. It was so large, so busy, so no-nonsense, and most of the people seemed to be in such a hurry and oftentimes very rude. However, as time went by I realized how New

York, as large as it is, is broken up into unofficial neighborhoods where everyone gets to know who is a part of the area and who isn't. After a while I started to feel at home in that section of the city. The blocks surrounding my in-laws apartment became my neighborhood and I enjoyed walking along the sidewalks and saying "Hello" to familiar faces. I was no longer so intimidated when someone acted rudely although the pseudo-politeness of the Japanese, that I had become accustomed to, still caused me to be surprised when it occurred.

It was during this time that an event occurred that was to alter my view of life in many profound ways. I was in the apartment talking to my mother on the phone. We were discussing how Teleia was doing. Arik was playing in the adjoining room and I was waiting for his baby-sitter to arrive so I could have two hours to myself to catch up on errands. As I was talking I was looking down at that day's newspaper. I wasn't reading it, just scanning the page as I talked.

Suddenly I noticed that something wasn't quite right.

"Mom," I said, "something is wrong. Letters are missing at random across the page of print I'm looking at."

"What do you mean?" my mother asked.

"The letters aren't right. Something is wrong with my eyes." I replied anxiously.

"Blink." she advised me. "Sometimes you just have to re-focus."

I tried what she said, but nothing changed. Letters throughout the page of newspaper print where still randomly missing. It was as if someone with white out had eliminated letters across the page. I heard the doorbell ring. It was the baby-sitter.

"Mom," I exclaimed, "the baby-sitter is at the door. I have to go."

I hung up and quickly went to the door and let Cindy in. I was more then relieved that she had arrived. My vision was still abnormal and I was starting to feel strangely. I didn't know what was happening and I was glad someone was here to look out for Arik. I invited her in and started to explain to her what was happening to me.

At that moment my speech became garbled. I knew what I wanted to say, but when I said it, it came out all garbled. What terrified me was that I heard the garbled speech and knew that something was very, very wrong. I fell to my knees and continued trying to communicate. I wanted her to watch out for Arik. I wanted her to contact my mother-in-law, Harriet, at her work. I wanted her to know that I desired to be sent to Mt. Sinai Hospital, in the event I should need to be hospitalized. I tried to tell her all these things, but nothing but a garbled mess came out of my mouth.

Amazingly enough some words must have come through intact. Cindy went to the phone and immediately contacted Harriet at the school she taught at in Brooklyn. She then told me to lie still, that Harriet was on her way home, and that she would take care of Arik. I was relieved that I could still understand what was being said to me and that someone was here to help. I closed my eyes and prayed that Harriet would come soon.

As soon as Harriet came through the door I felt calmer. She spoke with Cindy, called the doctor, and immediately had me in a taxi. Because we didn't know what it was she had decided to take me to her ophthalmologist as my eyes had been affected. The worst had been over after only a few minutes but my eyes and speech still weren't normal. I felt extremely tired and I was starting to get a terrific headache.

Dr. Latif was very kind and examined me thoroughly. He determined that a blood clot must have passed behind my eyes causing the vision abnormality. What caused the speech problem? He didn't have a clue. He immediately contacted a neurologist. I was to see Dr. Bransen and was scheduled to have a MRI of my brain as soon as possible.

After the MRI, Dr. Bransen viewed them and told me he wanted me to have a CAT scan, with dye, of the area. He wanted a closer and better look. I was more then a little afraid. I showed up for the CAT scan in the morning. Unlike the MRI I wasn't to be confined in a long, noisy tube, but I was to be injected with an active isotope while my head was placed in a donut looking contraption. The CAT was much faster than the MRI, but the injection was extremely uncomfortable. I felt hot and dizzy.

Later, in the neurologist's office, I was shown all the pictures of my brain (which meant little to me) and was told that I had something called an Angioma Venous Malformation in the cerebellum portion of my brain. Was it a brain tumor, I asked? All I had been thinking about was the possibility of a brain tumor, cancer in the brain.

The answer was "No." I was extremely relieved. I shouldn't have been.

"You see that shadow over here?" Dr. Bransen pointed to an

insignificant looking dark spot on the plastic picture of my brain.

I stepped closer to the wall where the x-ray looking sheet hung over the square light and looked carefully at the picture. I really couldn't make out anything that made any sense to me. I fixed my gaze to where Dr. Bransen was pointing and nodded my head.

"Well, that's what we call an AVM, an Arterial Venous Malformation. Can't tell if you were born with it or if it just recently developed, but there it is." Dr. Bransen stepped aside and turned to face me.

"I'm sorry," I stammered, "but I don't know what an AVM is."

The doctor went on to explain it to me. Unfortunately, with all the medical jargon I had an extremely difficult time following him. Finally I interrupted and asked, "Could you go over this in layman terms please?"

"Of coarse, I apologize. My intent certainly isn't to confuse you" he responded.

Basically, from what I understood, the Arterio Venous Malformation involved the vessels and arteries in my brain. Specifically, those vessels in the left cerebella hemisphere, that section toward the back of the brain that controls balance and movement. It's the coordination center for motor control. Since it also coordinates the muscles of the tongue and face, damage to that area of the brain can also alter speech articulation. The cerebellum is an enfolded structure that sits above the brain stem.

As for the AVM, itself, it would be easier to explain what is normal first.
Normally the pressure from an artery is broken when the blood is passed to the veins, then in turn to smaller vessels, which in turn, flow into the capillaries. In an AVM there are no vessels between the artery and the smaller vessels and/or capillaries it feeds into and so these smaller vessels look like a mixed up blob of spaghetti. Consequently, the extreme blood pressure that the artery exerts in order to move the blood throughout the circulatory system isn't lessened at all before the blood charges into the smaller vessels or capillaries. The threat was the great possibility of leakage at that vulnerable point.

Any brain hemorrhage is serious and this was no exception. If it is a small leak, as it was assumed that I had experienced, then minor abnormalities are manifested. In my case my vision was temporarily impaired and my speech was altered. I also suffered a pretty bad headache afterwards as well. If the leak were large enough then a major brain hemorrhage would be the result, causing unbelievable damage to the surrounding brain tissue.

"So where does that leave me now?" I asked Dr. Bransen.

"Well," he began to explain, "You will just have to modify your lifestyle somewhat. No heavy lifting or doing anything that would put any stress on your vascular system. That means you shouldn't go to high altitudes, fly only in pressurized planes, no deep-sea scuba diving, and no mountain climbing. Don't lift anything over ten pounds . . ."

"Okay," I replied, "I can do that. Arik weights over 10 pounds, though, which will make it difficult for me, but, yes, I can do this. If I do these things will I be okay?"

Dr. Bransen was silent for a few moments. It was obvious he was trying to select his words with care. "It will help, " he advised me, "but it doesn't mean this episode won't happen again. It only means it could lessen the likelihood. The only real 'cure' would be surgery but that isn't possible given its location in your brain."

The solution, in most cases, is surgery. The neurosurgeon goes inside the brain affected, finds the artery and vessels it feeds into, and then cauterizes the vessels involved so as to prevent them from leaking. Unfortunately, in my case the AVM was located so deep inside the cerebellum that the surgeon would have to cut through too much healthy brain tissue to reach it. Because of this, if I were to opt for surgery the risk would be extremely high. As much as we know about the brain today, it is still mostly a mystery. What side effects would I experience? No clear-cut answer was available. I could become paralyzed or, at least, substantially lose my ability to move.

"So, what does this mean? Will I be okay?" I asked him again.

"Let's put it this way, " he began, "we really don't know. You could live with this until old age. You may have more episodes just as you experienced before. Or, if the artery ruptures you could suffer a brain hemorrhage."

"What happens to me if that should occur?" I inquired apprehensively.

"One of two things could occur." He went on to explain. "You could be dead as soon as you hit the ground or you would be in a coma. If you were to recover you would probably be brain damaged."

So, I was being told that it could stabilize, as it is now with no further problems or, at worst, a replay of similar symptoms if any small leakage's occurred. Or, I could experience a massive brain hemorrhage. If the later occurred one of two outcomes could be expected. Either I would end up in a coma from which it would be doubtful I would recover, or I would die instantly.

"When could this possibly happen?" I asked him numbly.

"I can't answer that," he returned. "You could live the remainder of your days to a ripe old age with no incident, or you could walk out my door and collapse."

I was only in my thirties. I had a daughter going to High School in the fall and a baby who was just going to turn a year old. I was too young to be facing the prospect of death. I was afraid. I was angry. I was frustrated. I was confused. I wanted my husband. I wanted there to be something pro-active I could do. I didn't like feeling helpless.

I went through all the various stages of grieving although, at the time, I was unaware of such stages. I spoke to my husband on the phone. I felt as if I were talking about someone else, not myself. I was emotionless. I was in denial. Later on I found myself making unofficial deals with G-d. If I did such and such or this and that, would He allow me to see my children grow up, be married, have children of their own? I became angry easily. Not at my children, but at life in general. What was the sense of it? Why bother? I became depressed. I didn't feel motivated to get involved in anything. What was the point? Then one morning I decided to climb out of bed and do something.

I couldn't "cure" the AVM and I couldn't predict the possible consequences, but I could get back into life. Perhaps by doing something to try and understand death, to get rid of the fear associated with death, would allow me to feel alive again. I decided I would do something about it. As I scanned the Sunday newspaper my eyes were attracted to an advertisement for a volunteer position with Hospice of the South Shore. I was vaguely familiar with the hospice concept that was to help those who were terminally ill. On some impulse I decided to give them a call.

The phone rang several times before I was connected to a message asking me to give them my name and phone number and that they would contact me shortly. I did so. The following day I received a call from Mary Jane, the volunteer coordinator for the Hospice of the South Shore. We talked, she asked me questions, told me about the program, advised me as to what areas I could volunteer for, what training would be involved and when, and generally made me aware of what it was all about. Since some of the positions involved lifting I decided I'd better tell Mary Jane about my situation. I was fearful that she would no longer want me as a volunteer, but I felt it was best to be honest about it.

I briefly explained to her about my AVM and what it meant in terms of my possible performance. She seemed very interested in all I had said. I told her I would understand if she decided not to pursue my becoming an Hospice volunteer in light of all of this but she said she would be delighted if I would come to the next training session which was to begin the following week. Her voice had sounded accepting, but a little confused and/or amazed. It made me feel slightly uncomfortable all though I couldn't explain why.

The following Tuesday, with a neatly printed piece of paper with the directions to the church where the training was to take place written on it, I drove to the designated location. I parked my car in the church lot and made my way to the main entrance where I hoped to get directions as to where I should go from there. I saw several ladies waiting outside and approached them.

"Hello. Are you Karen?" asked a heavyset lady dressed in a long, wool, gray shirt over an oversized navy blue, short winter jacket.

"Yes," I replied smiling, "but how did you know?"

"Just a good guess, " she said smiling back at me. "I'm Mary Jane. We spoke on the phone last week."

I extended my right hand, "It's wonderful to meet you in person. " I acknowledged, "Will you be conducting the training?"

"Some of it." Mary Jane answered. "There will be a lot of speakers. Come and follow us." She opened one side panel of the heavy, carved wooden doors of the church and stepped inside. I followed along with the others who had come and were waiting to enter. We walked down a flight of stairs, turned left, and entered a rather large and brightly lit room, set up with rows of chairs. I took a seat and looked around.

Across the back of the room some long tables had been set up. Food items and an assortment of beverages including hot coffee, tea, and cocoa were neatly arranged along with small paper plates, plastic ware, and napkins. Obviously, we would be having at least one break.

Training was to cover many subjects. First we were told about the Hospice alternative. Then a Hospice nurse discussed the process of death and dying. Another speaker told us how this process affected family dynamics and especially how it affected children. How to approach the management of a patient with a terminal or end stage disease was next on the agenda. Following this topic a nun spoke on the issue of spirituality and care giving. Jane then came up to tell us about the responsibilities and work of the Hospice volunteer. Another speaker touched on the subject of effective communication and then some current volunteers spoke to us about their own experiences.

During the break period, Mary Jane came over to me. It was obvious by her expression that she very much wanted to talk with me. I smiled and waited.

"May I speak with you?" she asked.

"Of coarse" I replied.

We finished filling our plates with goodies and carefully carried our food and drink to a small table against the far wall of the room. It was removed from the main food tables and so afforded us a little bit of privacy in that open training room.

"Let me say how surprised I am that you are still alive." she expressed suddenly.

"What do you mean?" I asked in amazement. I had never expected to hear a statement such as that from anyone.

"Let me tell you why I was so interested in speaking with you after we had spoken on the phone. This is very emotional for me."

I sat and listened as she relayed a story I will never forget. She had a little grandson who she adored. One afternoon they had brought him to see a movie at a local movie theater. They were just leaving when the little boy collapsed on the sidewalk for no apparent reason. After being rushed to the hospital he had died. Naturally, the entire family was shocked and grieved. It had been so unexpected. They were all perplexed. What had happened? He was fine one minute and dead the next.

Upon investigation it was determined that her grandson had had an AVM, just as I had. It had ruptured and he had died shortly afterward. The doctors had told them that it was probably a blessing in disguise as he probably would have been severely brain damaged had he survived. They had been told that most people with this condition die early in life. That was why she had been so struck by my story. I was not old by any means, but she was enormously surprised that I was still alive and, apparently well, at thirty-seven years of age. Since her grandson was only four or five years old when he died of the same condition I had, I could understand her feelings.

As much as I empathized with her loss, it also created an unnerving terror within my own being. It had happened to her

141

grandson just as Dr. Bransen had described the possibility to me. The realization that it could happen to me had now been made vivid. Although I had thought about my mortality, I really hadn't accepted it in this way. I was terrified. I was afraid of the uncertainty of it, the suddenness in which it could happen, and the void it would leave in its wake for my entire family.

The reality that I probably wouldn't even have time to say good-bye to those I loved made me feel helpless and frightened. Starting that very moment I would speak to all of those closest and dearest to me to express my love for them, my hopes and dreams for them. I wanted to leave nothing unsaid. Who knew if I would be around long enough to say whatever I felt I had to say to those I loved?

As it turned out, one of the first exercises we had to complete for our next training class was to write a couple of pages on what we would do and/or say if we were to be told that we only had 6 months to live. It was an exercise to help the potential volunteer's to get in touch with the feelings the individuals they would be assisting would be dealing with. For me, however, it was to be much more than just a mere exercise in empathy.

I sat down the next morning to complete the assignment. Sipping my coffee and looking out the window at the winter landscape of barren trees and white snowdrifts, I started to write:

If I Had Six Months to Live

Sitting quietly at my kitchen table, surrounded in silence, and looking out my window at the snow-covered landscape of my backyard, I contemplate the very real possibility that I could only have six months to live (or thirty-six or less than a month). For me, the time element is unimportant. If my time should come at this moment than six months is a long life; if in ten years, than six months is extremely short.

My greatest anxiety concerns my children, especially my son who is only two and a half years old. Would he be cared for the way I would wish? Would he remember me, his mommy, at all? Would he be angry with me for leaving him in this way (although it was certainly not my choice to leave at all)? I desperately want to see how he turns out. What will he look like and be like when he's a teenager, a man? My daughter is fifteen. I am at peace when I think of her. She is extremely intelligent, a survivor (like me?) and I know she would remember me, and even tell her brother about "their" mom.

My priorities are shifting. What seemed so important doesn't appear so important anymore (e.g., building a career, earning a lot of money, etc.). Things I put on hold, indefinitely, are more compelling. I'm no longer interested or even motivated to do anything that doesn't mean something to me -or- I don't enjoy. I am becoming selfish. I feel guilty sometimes, especially when my husband and/or daughter get angry at my "attitude problem." They don't understand the motivation behind my selfishness.

But "time's" borders are a reality to me now, and I no longer have the luxury of being able to postpone things for "when the time comes," or "later." The time may not come. "Later" may not exist. There is a new sense of urgency and, yet, I also sense a growing calm. I hope I am able to live life to the fullest for whatever time I am allotted. I want to stay in contact with other people, to be surrounded by family and friends, to enjoy the beauty of nature (I feel closer to nature now - although I'm not sure why).

It bothers me, and concerns me, too, that my husband is unable to accept this reality. As far as he's concerned everything is fine and nothing is going to happen. It is a curse, sometimes, that an AVM is hidden from view inside ones brain. No one can see it when they look at me. My appearance is normal, and I am in good health. It's easy to delude yourself into thinking there is nothing wrong. I am guilty of this myself.

Only on those occasions when I have a seizure, when my vision gets screwed up and my speech becomes garbled, does the reality of the situation sink in. I experience no pain except after the seizure. Then I get a headache that sometimes feels as if my skull is going to blow off. At that moment in time, when I must lie perfectly flat on my back until the headache is gone (sometimes up to six hours or longer), we realize that everything isn't "okay." But as soon as I am "back to normal" we pretend, once again, that nothing is remiss - mommy is fine. But one time, I know, I will lose consciousness, die immediately or go into a coma and then pass away. I pray that when my time comes that I go quickly. I have no wish to cause my family unnecessary anguish.

I must find a way to break through this denial so we can "be" with each other again. I can no longer pretend nothing is wrong with me, and their denial alienates me. I often feel so alone, and I often become angry with them over trivial things. I want us to live each moment to the fullest. To appreciate each other and love each other every minute of our time together so that there is no need for any of us to say a formal good-bye. For, in all probability, I will depart unannounced and so quickly that I won't have time to say any departing words -or- to hear them.

Chapter 28
Being Buddhist in New York

I pulled my black meditation cushion out from the back of my closet. Tucking it under my left arm I wandered around the house looking for a suitable place to sit. Arik was taking a nap and the house was extremely quiet. Finally, I decided that the fourth bedroom, which I had made into my library, of sorts, was a suitable location. Thousands of books covered most of the wall space on rows of bookshelves from ceiling to floor. There was a computer desk to one side encroaching on what was left of the open floor space. To the left of the doorway, there was just enough space, hopefully, to set something up.

I went into the storage room and pulled out the box that my Buddhist altar and its associated objects were packed in. I dragged it into the library, opened the carton, and carefully unpacked the black, lacquer altar, the Buddhist statuary, a small gong and mallet, candle holders, an incense cup, flower holders, offering cups, and the small duster that came with the altar. Slowly I take the paper wrapping off the incense sticks. Their pungent odor started to scent the air.

I became totally involved in placing the alter on the small table I had prepared for it, dusting it, and painstakingly putting each object in it's correct place. After setting everything up I brought over my meditation cushion and placed it in front of the altar. Kneeling, I lit the incense and placed the three sticks into the fine sand in the incense burner. I decided not to light the candles, but I did bow three times to the Buddha, *Dhamma*, and *Sangha*, rang the little gong, and took my place on the *zafu*.

It had been awhile since I had last sat like this. With everything going on I had kept delaying it. Actually, I was avoiding it. I didn't want to be left alone. I was afraid of what I might encounter. I knew better, but was still fearful. My meditation hadn't been deepened enough. I still had to practice more.

I was restless as I sat motionless with my legs crossed in the half lotus position. My right leg was crossed on top of my left. I placed my right hand, palm up, into the cradle of my left hand. Swaying back and forth I found a balanced, comfortable position and then lowered my eyes toward the floor. The first sensation I became aware of was the smell of incense as its smoke curled toward the ceiling of the room. I couldn't see it, but I could sense it and it helped me to relax.

My thoughts kept slamming into me as I tried to "not think." At first I kept thinking about my little boy sleeping in the room next door. Would he wake up and interrupt my attempt to meditate today? Then, would someone ring the doorbell? Would the phone ring? Eventually, the thoughts slowed down and my breathing came more gently. A brief thought of "I'm doing it" crossed my mind and then disappeared. I sat.

Enveloped in silence and shadow, I sat. The phone didn't ring, no one came to the door, and my son remained fast asleep. I sat. Miami, our pet cat, walked over me, sat down next to me on my right and starred at the altar. I was aware of his presence and saw the vague outline of his black and white fur out of the corner of my eye. He sat so still that my thoughts no longer focused on his being there. Then I heard his deep purring. Miami remained very still, but his purring seemed to be getting louder.

What to do? Now I was thinking again, not meditating. Should I shoo the cat away? Should I stop my attempt to meditate for now? No, that was my ego talking. I decided to just sit. I would just listen to the purring. I would just sit. My thoughts eventually calmed down and seemed to disappear.

I was only aware of the tip of my spine resting on the top of my *zafu* when the first thought, which I had feared, emerged from deep inside. I would be no more. The world and everyone and everything in it would continue without me. I would no longer exist. But everything that is alive, will one-day die. Nothing lasts forever. Even if I could live forever, all other living things would eventually perish. If this were so, why was I so afraid? Why was I suffering so much about something I could do nothing about?

Just because of that. Just because I couldn't do anything about it, and because other living things weren't aware that they would die one day, be gone for good. I didn't think animals anticipated such things and so had no anxiety concerning it. Most people rarely gave their mortality a second thought and if it did arise they would quickly subdue it in other thoughts or distracting outside activities. I felt so alone with this. I was going to die. I didn't know when, but I knew it would happen. I would be non-existent.

Suddenly, I felt anger and frustration. Why me? Then, why not me? The realization that all beings are subject to death bored into me. Was my ego so strong that I could not even conceive of other beings also suffering from their "knowing" of the existence of death and that, one day, they would die? I had seen animals that had been hurt, crying out in pain and fear. Did they not feel some thing? I felt humbled.

I sat. Thoughts would disappear and I would feel peaceful. Another onslaught would follow. I tried to "think" it away, but that method never worked. I realized that to end this I would just have to sit and watch it go by. Not attach anything to whatever came up. Just sit. I started to feel very hot, but I just sat.

All that is subject to birth is subject to illness, old age, and death. All sentient beings are born to suffering. The Buddha realized this and he realized that the only end to this suffering was to end birth. To end birth was to eliminate the attachment and craving that desired life and things, that had wants and desires, preferences and aversions. To eliminate suffering was to eliminate the voice inside that constantly evaluated and compared. That voice could torment with such thoughts as "how unfair," and "why me?" "I want it," or "I want him/her," or "I don't want it/him/her," or "I want more or less." Thoughts which could cause frustration, or jealousy, or anger, or hate. Thoughts that could generate fear or calm. Thoughts came first, judgment second, feeling/emotion about that thought, third. The Buddha knew this.

Everything that is born, that is alive, suffers. Suffering has a cause. Suffering's cause is craving and clinging. By eliminating the craving, you can eliminate the suffering. The way to eliminate craving is to follow the Eight-Fold Noble Path. It made sense to me now. Not just intellectually, but in my inner most being (what ever that was).

My eyes were now looking outward instead of inward. It wasn't just me, me, me. All living things were subject to illness, old age, and death. That's the way it is. That's Reality. If you are born, you are exposed to and experience suffering in some form or other. This is the way it is. To struggle against this truth of that which is, is to embolden the act of clinging and so enhance the suffering. The physical pain may exist, but my mind can be still. My mind is painless, empty and clear. Death is a reality, but my feelings about death are of my own design. Just accept Reality as it is. Stop struggling against Reality.

But this didn't mean that people should just stand there and allow bad things to happen. It didn't mean people should just look on while someone was suffering and not try to do something to lessen the pain or decrease the suffering. It meant being aware that this is the way life is and that to complain about it, or to cling to aspects of it, was futile, pointless, and subjected oneself, and others, to more suffering. Deep compassion and loving-kindness were born.

I realized that I wasn't really alone. At least I was no more alone than any other living thing. If I felt alone, it was my own mental construct. I could reach out to anyone at anytime whenever I felt like it. If I chose not to, it was my own doing. If I felt sorry for myself, it was MY self, feeling sorry for my SELF. Life meant eventual death and the potential for much suffering as well as gratification. To cling to or to try to avoid any of these experiences was sheer folly.

You could live your life with your eyes wide open and still have no control over some of the things you may experience. To be wise was to be able to know when to act, when not to act, when to speak, when to remain silent, when to accept, when to turn away, when to step forward, when to step back. To become wise one had to be still, in order to cultivate that ability to hear the inner voice of wisdom without clouding it with desires, hopes, or fears. To be one with wisdom meant that you listened, and that you opened yourself to the world as it was/is/will be.

I recalled reading in the Bible, Proverbs 3:13-18, which states:

"Happy is the man that findeth wisdom,
And the man that obtaineth understanding.
For the merchandise of it is better than the merchandise of silver,
And the gain thereof than fine gold.
She is more precious than rubies;
And all the things thou canst desire are not to be compared unto her.
Length of days is in her right hand;
In her left hand are riches and honour.
Her ways are ways of pleasantness,

And all her paths are peace.
She is a tree of life to them that lay hold upon her,
And happy is every one that holdeth her fast."

And in Ecclesiastes 3:1-2,

> "To every thing there is a season,
> and a time to every purpose under the heaven:
> A time to be born, and a time to die;"

I heard Arik talking to himself in a language only he could understand. Slowly I moved myself back and forth and loosened my crossed legs. I knelt next to my *zafu* and bowed three times to the image of the man who had discovered these Truths first. The Buddha, the being who had had the compassion to go out into the world in order to teach and share this wisdom with whoever wished to hear it. I reshaped my *zafu*, stood up, and went in to get my boy. He was probably hungry. I smiled.

Chapter 29
I'm a Jew

Since moving to New York I hadn't been working. I was still on an extended leave of absence from my airline position and, realizing that being married to a Naval officer meant moving every couple of years, I was trying to decide what I should do career-wise. Staying with the airlines wasn't very feasible. At least not given the lifestyle we would be living while Matt was in the military.

My private pity party had gradually ended. I had come to terms with the AVM that could quite possibly kill me without notice. I was no longer willing to sit by and do nothing. Whatever length of days G-d allowed me to have I was going to live them to the best of my ability.

I had seen a definite need for good educators when we had lived in Japan and Teleia had been attending the Department of Defense School in Yokosuka. Perhaps I should earn a Masters Degree in education. It would be a much more useful career path. On the other hand, perhaps I should really stick with the airlines. Try to get back to work, perhaps at Laguardia Airport. Maybe I could even stay long enough to take an early retirement with benefits.

I visited various college campuses and discussed what it would take for me to earn my Masters within the limited time we would probably be living in the New York area. At the same time I contacted my airline's headquarters to ask about coming off my leave in the New York area, preferably to Laguardia as it was closer to home. I was hoping that 15 years of service would help me in this request.

As I agonized over the choices (school or work), the decision was made for me. I received a letter from my airline telling me that no positions were available in the New York area and that I would have to relocate to Los Angeles within two weeks time if I desired to keep my position. I wasn't about to leave my family in New York while I went off to Los Angeles, so I decided to give up my airline career. I called Dean Coplin at Dowling College and advised her it was a "go," so long as she could get me enrolled for the coming semester. She told me it would be no problem. I was now a student, again.

Shortly after my graduate classes had begun, I was looking at the Sunday newspaper, when a short notice caught my eye. It was an invitation for interested parties to take a two-year program in Jewish Studies and Hebrew Language that would culminate in a teaching certification in Jewish education. The program was called "Morasha" and classes were to take place just a couple of town's west from where we lived on Long Island.

Not knowing if it was a legitimate certification or not, or even if there was a need for Jewish teachers, I decided to contact someone to find out more information. I looked at the classified ads until I found one looking for elementary teachers for a Jewish supplementary school near my area. I decided to call the principal and to request an opportunity to talk with him or her concerning the information I sought.

When I called, the headmaster, Mr. Witman, was extremely nice. He invited me to visit with him that very afternoon. When I arrived, he personally took me on a tour of the Temple and the classrooms. He took me into some of the classes and introduced me to his staff and students. He told me that the Morasha program was very legitimate. It had been created out of a need for trained and qualified religious-school teachers, as there was currently a shortage. Then he apprised me of his own need for good teachers.

As we entered his office he invited me to take a seat. Suddenly the conversation took an unexpected turn.

"Karen, I think you would be an excellent Judaic's teacher. In fact," Mr. Witman continued, "I would like to offer you a position here at Isaiah."

"Well, Mr. Witman, I'm quite flattered but I wasn't really looking for a job right now. I was primarily interested in finding out if there was a need and if the Morasha program was a good one to pursue." I responded, just a little flustered. "I'm not even at that stage yet. I'm not even trained."

Mr. Witman smiled, looked straight into my eyes and said, "I know that. But I can tell from speaking with you and watching you with the children, that you would be a natural. I have a need for a second grade teacher and a teacher for our special education class of second through sixth graders. I'm offering them to you. I'd very much like to see you here with us."

I was overcome. It was totally unexpected. As I sat there trying to take all of this in, he continued to supply me with information. He told me what my hours would be, what the pay would be, what class rooms I would be using, who my students would be, and what books I'd be using. I became lost in his words. I just couldn't process the information as fast as he was giving it to me.

This was certainly a surprise. I had come down to information gather, figuring I'd look for such a job after I completed the Morasha program if I were accepted into it. Here I was being offered a position, and he was even advising me that he personally knew the director of the Morasha program and that he would speak to her about me. He was actually assuring me that I would definitely be accepted into the program.

"May I have a few minutes to think and make a phone call home?" I asked.

"Of course, take your time." Mr. Witman responded. "You can use my phone." As he got up to leave he said in departing, "Karen, please accept my offer. I'm sure you'd be an asset here. I'll be back in a little while, or you can have me paged when you're ready."

I thanked him and immediately caught my breath as I watched him go. I walked into the outer office and sat down to think. It certainly was flattering. What an ego boost. What was I to do? I decided to call my husband and discuss it with him.

Matt was just as surprised as I had been. He even flattered me more by telling me that he, too, thought I'd be great at doing this. I had wanted some teaching experience, he reminded me, and here was an ideal opportunity. I would only be teaching on Sunday. That would allow me time for my studies. He was right. I would accept the offer and complete the Morasha program as well. Plus, taking the Morasha program would fulfill another longing I had had, which was to learn more about Judaism than I had been taught in my youth. Here was my opportunity.

Mr. Witman was a very happy man. He raced out to tell the secretary that I was to be given whatever I needed. He brought me a pile of books and supplies and excitedly gave me a typed list of the students in both my classes. After processing my paperwork, he returned to advise me that he had contacted the director of the

Morasha program, and he was sure there would be no problem. Before I could even look at the materials he had just handed me he was rushing me off to the main part of the Temple to meet the Rabbi.

A week later the reality hit me. Not only was I currently in graduate school, but I was also accepted into and attending a two year program of Judaic studies, as well as, working part-time as a religious school teacher. Not really bad considering I had only moved to Long Island a couple of months before.

The Morasha program met three times a week and the class lasted from 9am until 4:30pm. Half of the time was spent learning about Jewish history from Biblical times to the present, Torah study, Jewish rituals and beliefs, the various movements within Judaism, holiday observances, symbols, life cycle, ethics, and Jewish law. We learned about the Soviet Jews, *refusniks*, about cults, anti-Semitism, and the Holocaust. Studies went into the Zionist Movement, the World Zionist Organization, Israel, and contemporary issues. We read about famous Jewish personalities, from Einstein to Maimonides. We attended classes on theology, studying about G-d, and we were even exposed to other religions while taking comparative religion classes. Highly qualified educators and guest speakers were invited to teach us, including priests from churches in the area.

The other half of our time was spent learning Hebrew. We were taught the prayers used in liturgy as well as learning Hebrew as it is used as a living language. We learned to read and write. We were also taught teaching methodology and how to integrate music and art into the curriculum, the most effective way to use the library and its resources. We were even required to complete fifteen hours of student teaching along with being observed.

I learned more about Judaism in those two years than I had during the entire period of my life up until then. It excited me as well as saddened me. What I had learned about Judaism was so rich and encompassing and yet I hadn't known even a tiny part of it until now. Why wasn't I exposed to all of this earlier on in my life? Why did it have to take so long? If I hadn't stumbled on to this program, I still would be ignorant of all the facts and facets within Judaism; it's history, its theology.

At the culmination of my two years of intense study, as I accepted my certification, I was overcome with emotion. I had studied more subjects then I could begin to relate. I had learned more than I had ever expected to learn. New areas of exploration were uncovered for me. I realized that one could study for the duration of an entire lifetime and still not get to it all. The tapestry of Judaism was so detailed and so immense.

And I was a part of it. I was a Jew. I was a product of over 4,000 years of history and countless generations of my ancestors. My roots extended far and wide and deep. I was linked to all the Jews on this earth not only by religious belief, but through a shared history as well. All Jews were of one tribe. I realized that I didn't have to be affiliated with a synagogue to belong. I was, and always would be, a member of this tribe.

During the four years we lived in New York, I was also to complete my Masters in Education. I also took twenty-seven credits above a Masters in Reading (Psycholinguistics). I spent half a year student teaching full-time in a fourth grade class in a Long Island elementary school. At the same time I continued to teach Jewish studies. I eventually taught grade levels from second grade up through Hebrew High School level. I taught for three different temples. I was even making a bit of a name for myself in the Jewish community. I had a reputation for being an excellent religious schoolteacher. I was in demand.

Chapter 30
Interview with Rabbi Don

I t had been four years since we had moved to the New York
area from Japan. Teleia was starting college in the fall and
Arik was going into Kindergarten. Matt had just gotten out
of the Navy and was working for a civilian company. I really wasn't
very happy in New York. I found the weather depressing, especially
the cold winters that seemed to last forever. Although the school
system was excellent, I just didn't want to live in such a fast paced
environment. Everything was rush here, rush there. People were often
rude and for no apparent reason.

We found ourselves at a crossroads. Should we stay or should
we move? Up until now the military dictated where we would go and
when. We were now in a position to decide for ourselves and it wasn't
an easy choice to make. Matt found out that the military would pay for
this last move if we decided to leave. That made it much more feasible
to do. We spent many late nights discussing the pros and cons of
moving.

I wanted to move south to a warmer climate. If it were up to
me I would go straight back to Hawaii. Matt wasn't about to go back
to Hawaii. He had suffered "rock fever" and just couldn't envision
living long term on an island. He enjoyed the seasons and missed
seeing the leaves turn bright red, orange, and yellow in the fall. Matt
liked snow and wanted to play in it with his son, as he grew older.
Plus, his family was in New York. He didn't want to live so far away.

Finally we reached a compromise. We would look for
employment in the areas we thought we'd like to move to. Whoever
got a job first would determine where we would move. I had an
undue advantage since I was currently on summer break. Networking
like crazy and perusing the classified ads, I busily sent resumes and
cover letters to any positions I thought I'd enjoy in a location I felt

would be suitable.

One early evening I received a long distance telephone call from the education chairman of a synagogue in North Carolina. They were looking for a full-time education director/principal and were extremely impressed with my credentials. He interviewed me on the phone for almost an hour and then told me he would get back to me in a day or two. The following evening he called to say that the Board wanted to interview me as soon as possible. They would fly me down, arrange for a hotel, and pay for all my meals.

When I told my husband about all of this he was thunderstruck. He never thought I'd find an opportunity so quickly. He was equally impressed with how squared away this synagogue appeared to be. Matt, always the pragmatist, assured me all would be fine at home, to go for it. The following weekend I would fly down to meet with and interview with the board of directors and the rabbi.

Mr. Perlmutter, the Chairman of the Board, picked me up at the airport and, since he had so kindly offered me his home instead of a hotel, I accepted and returned with him. His family had been waiting and I received a very warm welcome from his wife and three children. Although they were extremely kind, I was extremely nervous. Tomorrow was the big day. After some tea and dessert, I took my leave and went to bed.

The next morning I was up bright and early. The trees in North Carolina had overwhelmed me with their height. I stood at the bedroom window and just looked, transfixed, at the forest before me. This was a planned development, but the beautiful trees gave one the feeling of a forest. The window was open and the scent of pine drifted in on the morning breeze.

I met the Perlmutters down stairs in the kitchen where breakfast was being served. I was so nervous my stomach just wouldn't allow me to eat very much. Then off we went to the synagogue with Mr. Perlmutter trying to ease my nerves by talking about "other" things. As he turned into the curved driveway to the parking area on the right of the synagogue, I was immediately impressed with the beauty of the building. It flowed. The stonework reminded me of the Western Wall in Jerusalem. The immense windows gave it air, space, and lots of light.

The inside was equally impressive with its deep beige carpeting, rich blue upholstered chairs, and the polished, light wood accents. The sanctuary was uplifting. As one moved down the center aisle toward the *bimah* the back wall, which housed the Ark of the Covenant, rose to a multi-colored, sheer, pastel silk drape that covered the tall section of glass window that let in the sunlight. The light cascaded through the window, picking up the purple, blue and gold colors from the silk brocade and casting them gently onto the carpet below. The serenity and peacefulness of this sanctuary left me speechless. I knew I could easily meditate here.

From there I was brought downstairs to where the Board was waiting to meet me. They had brought in bagels with cream cheese, coffee and tea, but I just couldn't eat anything. For the next four hours I was to be interviewed by this eclectic group. As nice as they were, it was still stressful. Sometime after 1pm, they ended their interview and asked me to wait for the rabbi. I was emotionally exhausted, but nodded my head.

A little later I was directed to the rabbi's office. It was upstairs off the foyer where I had originally come in. It was well lit with sunshine that came in the window from the left as I stepped inside. The rabbi held out his hand, introduced himself, and invited me to sit down. He seemed incredibly young to me. I had assumed the rabbi would be much older.

I sat down, relieved to be dealing with only one person. I anticipated theological questions, or questions about how well versed I was in the Hebrew language. I waited for him to ask about my background in Judaism.

"So tell me, " Rabbi Don Bernstein began, "do you think you could work well with a younger man?"

In spite of myself I started to laugh. I would have gone over the edge into hysterical laughter if I weren't already worn out. Rabbi Don was obviously confused by my unexpected reaction to his innocent question.

"No," I replied trying to catch my breath, "no problem at all. I'm used to dealing with younger men. In fact, my husband is one of them."

I briefly explained to him how Matt was almost eight years younger than I was, and it was never a problem. Other attributes were much more important such as knowledge, interpersonal skills, beliefs, etc. Looking much more relieved, Rabbi Bernstein pulled up his chair and the interview formally began.

He started out by giving me an overview of his vision for the religious school, what had been done before and what he would like to see happen. He asked me questions about my training with Morasha, and told me I had received glowing recommendations by everyone they had contacted. He asked me how proficient I was in Hebrew and what I hoped to bring to their school. We touched on numerous religious issues as well as the nitty-gritty of directing a supplementary school of their size.

"Well," Rabbi Bernstein sat back, "I think we pretty much covered everything. Do you have anything to add or any questions you'd like to ask me?"

"There is one thing I'd like to discuss with you." I ventured.

"Yes."

"I didn't mention this to the Board, but I think it is important enough for me to mention to you. I'm a Jew, but I'm also a Buddhist."

I noticed that the rabbi was listening intently and wasn't making any move to speak so I went on. I explained how I had come to study Buddhism and how I was attracted to the meditation aspects of it. I told him of some of my frustrations concerning Judaism and how I viewed meditation as a means of "hearing" G-d. I went on to explain about my discovery of Kabbalah and how it was unlikely that I would ever be able to uncover and learn how the Kabbalists of old meditated and experienced the reality of G-d. That the method taught by the Buddha was a solution to my predicament.

"But don't Buddhists pray to a statue of the Buddha and other deities?" the rabbi inquired, "Aren't they idol worshippers?"

I went on to assure him that in no way did I ever give up my belief in the one G-d. That I had been very careful to make sure that whatever I got into would not be in conflict with any of the tenets of Judaism. I explained how the Buddha was not a divine being, but was a human being just like the rest of us. The only difference was that he discovered some very fundamental principles of Life and Reality and so became the Enlightened One. All of us had the potential to become enlightened, if we would just put in the effort. I assured him that I never looked at the Buddha as a god, but as an example of someone who had found the way, a teacher.

Yes, some Buddhist sects did deify the Buddha. Some sects even got into superstitious rites and rituals, but I wasn't involved in any of those. I was extremely careful and I strove to deepen my mediation and use it as the Kabbalists had done. I went on to explain how I had been studying Kabbalah, Jewish mysticism, and how similar it appeared to be to Buddhist practices and beliefs.

"However," I ended by saying, "I will certainly understand if you feel this would disqualify me from the position of education director for your school. Just let me assure you that I would in no way do anything to compromise Judaism."

The rabbi didn't speak for several minutes. He was obviously thinking about all I had just shared with him.

"From what you have just told me," he replied after much thought, "I don't really think your practicing Buddhist meditation would get in the way of your being a very effective principal for our school. I suggest, however, that you don't mention any of this to the Board, or to any one else for that matter."

"Agreed." I replied, as I stood up to shake the rabbi's hand.

He thanked me for coming down to met with the Board and he, himself, walked me to the door, and showed me where to go to met Mr. Perlmutter. I thanked him and told him I looked forward to meeting him again.

I waited in the foyer a few minutes until Mr. Perlmutter arrived. He was all smiles and offered to take me on a drive through the city on a sightseeing tour. As we drove down the streets he told me that the board would be meeting with other candidates over the next week and that I should be contacted within the next two weeks one way or the other. The following day I flew home to Long Island where I was amazed at how short the trees appeared to be.

Returning home I immediately set about staying busy so I wouldn't be thinking about the prospect of being hired by the synagogue in North Carolina and, consequently, having to move down south. I had only seen the area for half a day and here I was on the verge of moving there. I didn't know if I really wanted to be hired or to be turned down. Approximately one and a half weeks later I received a call from Mr. Perlmutter. I sat down prepared for rejection. Instead, he offered me the job telling me that it had been a unanimous decision by the board. He congratulated me and asked how soon I could come down.

"I can't come down until August 1st," I advised him, "but I would like to start working on the curriculum, etc., while I'm still up here. Could the rabbi, or current principal send me the materials I'll need to get started?"

"I'm sure that can all be arranged." he responded. "Meanwhile, during the transition of your move, if there is anything I or my family can do to make it easier for you, please don't hesitate to ask."

And so it was official. Effective August 1st, I would be the new, full-time education director. I had never done this before and so had my work cut out for me. I immediately set about learning as much as I could, getting my resources together, networking with the directors I already knew on Long Island, and generally working full-time before my position even began.

I set up the curriculum for each grade level for Judaic studies and Hebrew. I selected the textbooks to be used, created teacher-training workshops to be held throughout the year. Once I arrived I set up a teacher resource room, ordered books for the religious school library, hired, fired, and trained teachers, and recruited volunteers. I worked out agreements with vendors, updated our educational media equipment, and purchased classroom supplies. All in all, I was extremely busy.

I was currently living alone in a two-bedroom apartment near the synagogue. Teleia was to start her freshman year in college in upstate New York. Matt and Arik would join me once the house sale was complete and our household goods packed up for shipment. It was to be over a month before they would join me, but I was so busy the time seemed to fly by. In fact, I was relieved that I was alone as I was putting in well over forty hours a week.

I labored hard and long to develop a continuous curriculum that would not be too repetitive. I wanted to have each grade level build on the grade that preceded it with as little overlap as possible. I wanted it to be interesting and useful as well as fun. I wanted the children to come away from the experience feeling as if they really learned something and hadn't merely wasted their time.

I wanted the parents to participate in their children's learning and to see the importance of having their children attend up through Hebrew High School. To see that each year was substantially different from the year before and that their children were learning more than just the annual cycle of holidays and prayer Hebrew. As a child moved from one grade level to the next I wanted the material to get more into depth. I also wanted to introduce conversational Hebrew into the Hebrew curriculum, not just the phonetic, prayer based Hebrew currently being taught. This was some thing I wish I had been exposed to when I was attending religious school.

I formally wrote up the curriculum for each grade. When you looked at each year in this manner, you could easily see the progression and the ultimate goal. I carefully selected textbooks for each level that supported the subjects being taught. I instituted teacher workshops so that my staff would have opportunities to see the curriculum in its entirety and so see how their part fit into the whole. It would also afford them the opportunity to actually talk with fellow teachers to get more ideas and insights. I also developed a teacher resource center so that my faculty would have access to supplies, books, and creative ideas to help them with their lesson planning.

With all this effort, as well as the support by the rabbi and the education committee, I felt sure I was on the right track and doing a good job.

Chapter 31
Introducing Jews to Jewish Mysticism

I worked closely with Rabbi Don Bernstein. It was gratifying to have someone I could go to whenever the need arose. We shared a vision and, fortunately for me, he had an open mind. When I approached him concerning the new curriculum I had developed I wasn't sure how he would react. I had decided to introduce Jewish Mysticism, Kabbalah, into the upper grade levels. I also wanted to introduce some basic meditational techniques.

"I just want our children to know what's out there." I implored. "I want them to know that Judaism has a mystical/spiritual side as well. That they don't have to go outside of Judaism to find it, as I had to do."

Rabbi Don was pensive. We had sat together in his office on many occasions discussing Buddhism and Kabbalah. I had shared with him my history in terms of my gravitating toward Buddhism and practicing Buddhist meditation. He had questioned me about Kabbalah. He asked for suggestions on what books he should read about the subject. He admitted to me that they really hadn't touched on the subject of Jewish Mysticism very much in seminary. He, himself, wanted to learn more about it.

"I don't have a problem with introducing upper level students to the existence and basic concepts of Kabbalah, but I think you have to be careful about teaching them how to meditate." he responded.

After more discussion I agreed with him. We would introduce Jewish Mysticism, but I wouldn't get into the meditation techniques. Since I couldn't expect my teachers to be able to teach "meditation" and I certainly couldn't be in every classroom when it would be introduced, it just made sense to leave it alone. I was gratified that I'd be able to include Kabbalah in the curriculum. How I had wished it had been part of my education when I was in religious school.

I wrote a detailed summary of what I envisioned being taught. I put together a resource sheet with lists of the best books I could find on Jewish Mysticism that I felt would help the teachers to understand more about it and how to teach it appropriately. I even created some of my own materials.

The introduction given to the upper level students was still too simplistic to me, but I was gratified to know that, at long last, Jewish students would at least know that such a thing existed. They could choose to explore more deeply if they had the desire to do so. They wouldn't have to look outside to find something their own religion embodied. Unfortunately, I knew it would only be book learning. I knew of no avenue for interested students to find out "how" to practice in this spiritual way. I hadn't even been able to find a teacher to provide that for myself. But, it was a start.

Some months later the rabbi began his plans for a two evening series of adult workshops. Various subjects would be offered and people could sign up for whatever interested them. He approached me with a request.

"Karen," Rabbi Don began, "I know how interested you are in Jewish Mysticism. I also know that it is rarely touched upon and that most Jewish adults aren't even aware that it exists. Would you be agreeable to hold a couple of workshops on Kabbalah? Obviously it would have to be a mere introduction to the subject as you wouldn't have more than an hour to teach it, but it would be a start. What do you think?"

I was speechless. I had never imagined doing such a thing. As much as I was excited about the possibility, I didn't really think I was knowledgeable enough about the subject to be the one to teach it.

"Look," Rabbi Don explained, "how would we ever be able to find a Kabbalist to teach this workshop? Besides, it isn't going to cover everything. In an hour no one could do that. But I certainly think you would be most qualified to teach an introduction to the subject. Give some historical background. Introduce then to some of the more prominent Kabbalists and what they taught. You could even get into some basic philosophical tenants and beliefs that they held."

It sounded less overwhelming to me now. I'd have to create a very compact introduction. I'd create visuals to help make the teaching more understandable. I would even go so far as to introduce the concept of meditation if I had enough time.

"Yes," I replied with enthusiasm, "I think I could do it. I think it would be great. Yes."

That first evening I was very apprehensive. What if no one attended my workshop? After all, there were other more "down to earth" subjects being taught such as "How to Prepare for the Holidays," "Introduction to Hebrew," "Torah Study," "Crafts during the Holidays," and "Conducting your own *Havdalah* (Saturday evening) Service."

At the assigned time I waited in the classroom. I rearranged my materials, again. I could hear the clock ticking behind me. There was movement in the hallway. It was close to the time I was to begin and no one had come in yet. I felt a little letdown. Suddenly, a couple came in and asked if this was the right room for "Jewish Mysticism." I said yes and they sat down. Then more people entered my classroom until all seats were taken and some people were standing at the back of the room.

As I started to go out in search of more chairs, the rabbi stepped into the room. He immediately saw the situation and volunteered to find more chairs for me. Once that was taken care of he pulled up a chair for himself and sat down. He pulled out a legal-size writing pad and a pen from his pack and then looked up at me as if to say, "Well, are we ready yet?" And so I began.

First, I introduced them to Moses de Leon's belief that, as divine speech, the content of the <u>Torah</u> or <u>Five Books of Moses</u> possessed infinite meaning. There was the literal meaning called <u>Peshat</u>. Then there was the allegorical meaning referred to as <u>Remez</u>. Delving deeper you would arrive at the Talmudic and *Aggadic* meaning [as discussed and debated by the Rabbis and Sages] called <u>Derash</u>, and at its deepest level one would find its mystical meaning referred to as <u>Sod</u>.

This system was referred to as *Pardes*, meaning "Paradise." It was believed that entry into this "Paradise" could be achieved by going deeper and deeper into contemplation and ecstasy until one finally entered the level of vision that would include a direct and personal experience of this Oneness. Yet, following this method was considered dangerous for those who were unfit or unprepared.

A story is often related concerning four great sages who attempted to enter the Palace and so reach this *Pardes* or Paradise. Their fate demonstrated how spiritual experiences achieved through meditation and ecstasy could pose a very real danger to those who weren't yet ready to experience it. Simeon ben Azzai died in the attempt, Zen Zoma went insane, Elisha ben Avuyah turned his back on rabbinical Judaism and, it is hinted, became an apostate. Only the great Rabbi Akiva entered and returned in peace.

I showed them a visual:

PaRDeS

/   /   \   \

Reshat Remez Derash Sod

I introduced them to the concept of the *Ten Sefirot*, which represented the "Unified Universe" of God's hidden abode and life. The term "Sefirot" came from the Hebrew "*sappir*," meaning sapphire. For it had been felt that God's radiance was like that of a sapphire. I placed a visual I had created of the *Ten Sefirot* against the blackboard for them to see:

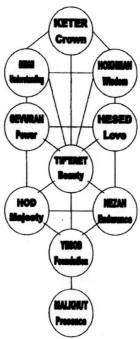

Illustration 31.1: The Ten Sefirot

165

Next I explained how we can only experience God from the viewpoint of creation since we are an aspect of creation and so, limited in that *Ein-Sof* is Absolute where there are no distinctions, no context, and no differentiation. This is where Awareness enters the picture. It is Awareness that allows us to bridge this gap between the Creator and the Created.

Developing Awareness, so as to be able to "know" God (also referred to as *Devekut* or merging with the Divine) is the aim of the meditation methods of Kabbalah. It is also the aim of prayer, which strives for communion with the Supreme Will. Yet prayer must be done with *kavvanah* or (mystical) intention in order for it to be elevated in this way. I shared with them another visual demonstrating the place of *kavvanah* in prayer.

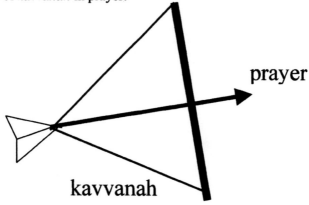

Illustration 31.2: Prayer with Kavvanah

I then touched on the ultimate aim of creation that is *tikkun*, or the process of restoration. *Tikkun* is dependent on mankind to complete. For as Gershom Scholem explained,

> "The object of this human activity, which is designed to complete the world of *tikkun*, is the restoration of the world of *asiyyah* [spiritual world now mingled with the lower world] to its spiritual place, its complete separation from the world of the *kelippot* [evil or the dark side], and the achievement of a permanent, blissful state of communion between every creature and God which the *kelippot* will be unable to disrupt or prevent." (page 143, <u>Kabbalah</u>)

Since mankind had been given freewill, and was made a partner in bringing about *Tikkun Olam* or World Repair, I felt this was the time to introduce the three parts of the soul according to the Kabbalists. Briefly, the three parts of the soul were called *Nefesh, Ruah,* and *Neshamah. Nefesh* was considered the lowest level. It is in every person. It is the animal vitality that is necessary for existence. It is some times considered the "Ignorant" level of the soul, operating solely on instinct without reasoning.

The next level up is called *Ruah.* This is the Developing soul and it is entered when a person succeeds in rising above his/her purely vitalistic (animal) side. This is the stage of development when the ethical power needed to distinguish good from evil begins and grows. It is at this point that a person may decide to pursue a path toward Enlightenment (*Devekut)* as the means to raise the divine sparks back up to *Ein-Sof.*

As a means of doing this there must develop an intent (*kavvanah*) concerning prayer, meditation, and life, itself. Through this continued practice, eventually a level of awareness is developed. This is the beginning of the third, or highest, level of the soul called *Neshamah.* It is during this time that the individual experiences intuitive/cognitive powers, a mystical apprehension of the "God-Head," and an awareness of the divine spark within him/herself. It is here that the person experiences individual enlightenment or bliss.

This enlightened state is called *Devekut.* It is at this level that the divine sparks are elevated high enough for *tikkun* (repair) to occur, when these sparks return to their Divine Source, *Ein-Sof.* There are three different ranks of *Devekut.* The first rank is that of *hishtavvut* or "equanimity." This is a state where the soul is indifferent to either praise or blame. The second rank of *Devekut* is *hitbodedut* or "solitude," as in being alone with God. The highest rank is that of reaching the stage of "Prophecy" or "Insight." This is when one has experienced, first hand, intuitive awareness and Oneness.

The hour was over and yet no one made a move to leave. I told everyone that they were welcome to keep all the handouts, but if they didn't want them to please return them to me. One or two couples left, but the rest stayed and plied me with questions. Some I could readily answer, but others were much too complex for my knowledge base. I apologized for my ignorance and suggested several books on the subject that might help.

"Are you going to be teaching any other classes on Jewish Mysticism?" a middle aged woman asked me before her husband moved to leave the room.

"I really don't know." I replied, smiling.

"I think it would be a wonderful thing if you did." she continued. "I would certainly take the course and I know lots of other people who would like to learn more about this subject, too. Would you teach how to meditate?"

"Well, I don't know if I will be teaching anymore about Kabbalah. It depends on the Board, what Rabbi Bernstein wants, and how much time I could feasibly take from my duties as education director." I responded in surprise.

"But would you be able to teach us about how to meditate?" she persisted.

"I could show you some simple meditation techniques, but not Kabbalistic practices. I don't know any Kabbalistic methods that I could teach. Plus, it would be too dangerous. However, a safe method that I, myself, practice, I could demonstrate."

"That would certainly be a start," she acknowledged. "I sincerely hope you pursue this. I have always wanted to do something like this. It's gratifying to know that Judaism encompasses all of this."

She took her husband's hand and they strolled out of the room together. Several other people came up to tell me how they enjoyed the introduction and how they would very much like to learn more. I was extremely pleased with the positive response.

When the evening of workshops came to an end, the rabbi walked up to me, as I was getting ready to leave.

"Well," he began, "I guess we could say it was a success."

"Yes," I replied grinning, "I guess we could say that."

"I think you did a wonderful job with a very difficult topic." Rabbi Don went on. "I think I'll start studying Kabbalah myself. Can't hurt."

"No, it can't hurt." I agreed.

Rabbi Don smiled at me and we made our way to the double doors leading outside into the parking lot. I chuckled to myself as I started up my car engine and turned on the headlights. Never in a million years did I think I would ever be introducing the subject of Kabbalah. Of coarse, I never thought I'd ever be a principal of a conservative religious school either.

Chapter 32
Trouble in Paradise

So far I haven't discovered a perfect paradise or Garden of Eden. As gratifying and wonderful as I found my work at the synagogue to be, occasionally it also had its downside. Even though I accepted a position as education director for a synagogue school, I must admit I was still rather naïve. I knew there was politics in the public school domain and, naturally, I was fully aware of the intense politics played out in the business world, but I never expected to see it within the context of a religious environment. Why I believed that to be so? I still can't fathom. Yet, I did.

During my first few weeks, everyone in the community seemed very caring and warm. Rabbi Bernstein, as well as the chair of the education committee, and the prior education director went out of their way to introduce me to every one, and to make me feel welcome. People would come up to speak with me and to offer assistance and help. Since my family would not be joining me for another six weeks I was extremely grateful. Consequently, I was even further convinced that I had made the right decision to move down there to work.

It was after the first Shabbat morning service I had attended that I was kindly invited to lunch by one of the synagogue member's and her family. I was touched and gratefully accepted her offer. Janice gave me directions and I followed her to her home.

We sat down in the formal dining room, said a prayer in thanks and gratitude, and commenced eating lunch. Janice had introduced me to her family earlier and we had now moved on to convivial conversation. The food was good and I was feeling quite comfortable. Suddenly the conversation took a turn and I was being asked what my plans were for the religious school now that I was there and settling in.

I decided to keep my answers vague as I had no idea who these people were, really, and I didn't want to get into any problems discussing things that I hadn't yet solidified or even discussed with Rabbi Bernstein. I assured her that I was dedicated to doing the best job I could and that I, too, had a vested interest in the quality of the school since my own son would be attending.

After a brief silence, Janice began to speak. Or rather, she began to pontificate and lecture. I sat for over an hour listening to her ideas on how a religious school should be run and what should be taught there. I was advised that most of the parents involved with the congregation felt exactly as she did and it was hoped that I would "see things her way." Her husband said very little, and I sat uncomfortably in complete silence.

A while later, I had an opportunity to take my leave and I did just that. It was with much relief that I said "thank you," and "goodbye." I quickly walked down the front walkway to my car and drove off. Little did I know then that Janice would continue to make her views known to me on many more occasions.

During the school year it was not uncommon for her to intercept me in the school hallways or anywhere she spotted me, to give me her opinion on the way the school was being run. She had insisted that her son, Joey, be placed in a grade one level lower then his age and knowledge base would dictate and, reluctantly, I had conceded and done so. It caused many problems in that classroom. Because Joey, not his real name, already knew the information being taught he was, naturally, bored. This boredom often translated itself into inappropriate behavior.

I called Janice, explained the situation, and advised her that I felt it would be best to place Joey back in the classroom with his peers. She vehemently refused to hear of it and insisted that I leave Joey in his current class. It took me a while to figure out why she was so insistent. With his peers he was challenged and although did a good job, he certainly wasn't the top in his class. In his current situation, however, he was the star. It finally dawned on me that it wasn't the best interest of her child Janice was concerned with. Rather, it was with how her child could shine at all times even if it meant extreme frustration for Joey to be with a younger group of children having to listen to what he already knew all year long.

Against my better judgement I left Joey alone and asked his teacher to try to give him some enrichment activities to relieve his boredom. This was actually an unfair burden to put on this teacher, as

Joey would have been better served at his own grade level. However, I decided to go along with his mother's wishes. So, we tried to serve the best interest of Joey while also trying to do the best for his younger classmates.

Meanwhile, Janice was still not pleased. She went to the rabbi to complain about the curriculum. The rabbi called me in and we tried to discuss the situation with her in light of the overall goal of the synagogue school. We shared the entire school curriculum, grade by grade, so she would be better able to see how all the pieces fit together. We, again, suggested that Joey be placed with his peers in the next grade level. It was of no use. It was obvious that Janice had her own agenda and would settle for nothing less.

A week later she confronted me, again, while I was waiting my turn to see the rabbi. She insisted that she wanted a "quality" school for her children. I agreed with her and asked her to define what a "quality" school meant to her. Without getting long winded (she went on and on) she felt that the entire school curriculum, the content and way of providing the lessons, should be as she specified. When asked how she had come up with this strategy, she blatantly said it was what would be best for her children.

It was now crystal clear to me what her agenda was and it was a very selfish one indeed. So long as her children's needs were met (as accessed by her desires) she could care less about the other children attending the school. I listened to her carefully, asked her questions for clarification, and when she was finished I carefully responded.

"I can see, Janice, that you are greatly concerned." I began. "Some of your ideas and suggestions I will certainly take into account and see what I can come up with, but please understand that I have over 100 other students who must be entered into the equation."

"They all have the same needs as my own children." she countered, " The other parents feel just as I do in wanting a quality religious education for their children. What I am presenting to you, is what a quality education is all about. Any thing short of that is not quality and, therefore, unacceptable."

"Janice," I replied, "I certainly can't tell you what all of the other parents desire for their children. But I can tell you that I, too, am a parent of a child in this school. I, too, have my own set of ideas on how my child would be best served. I, too, would like nothing more than to have the school rotate around my boy, but I would and could never do that. The only way this would be possible is if a child was privately tutored, so that the lessons could be tailored specifically to that child's needs. In a group setting, such as this, you must have a range of options available. Each child has his, or her, own learning style and comes to class with a unique knowledge base and background. We need to accommodate as many of these needs as we can."

By the expression on her face I knew that I hadn't made a dent in her reasoning. Nor had I made a friend. She made a nasty, closing remark, and quickly left the building.

Going in to see the rabbi, I now had even more to discuss with him. The "Janice dilemma." Rabbi Don agreed with my response, but warned me that Janice was not likely to let the matter drop. As I left his office that late afternoon, I felt a strong sense of foreboding.

Weeks went by and I hadn't seen Janice. I wasn't to see her, but she was to make her presence known. Parents who were usually very friendly suddenly became cool. Board members would call me about problems they had heard about which I could not address. In reality, those problems just didn't exist. I started to hear about things I supposedly did or did not do and comments I had supposedly made, which I had never been involved in or said.

As time went by and the accusations and rumors increased, I realized that some one was making up these horrific stories. It didn't take much investigating to find out it all went back to Janice. She was having a field day "casually" telling whomever would listen, all sorts of misinformation, distortions, and out right lies about my activities and my character. Not being able to get her way directly, she was apparently trying an indirect approach.

I certainly don't want to give the impression that everyone was against me because of Janice. Many parents and synagogue members were quite distressed at hearing these fabrications and came to tell me about them and to offer me support. But I had never seen anyone stage such an orchestrated attempt at character assassination. At first I was at a loss. Then I decided I wanted to confront her face to face.

Once again I went to Rabbi Don for his opinion and help. He suggested a meeting involving the three of us. He would invite Janice to attend and advise her that he would be there to mediate, if necessary. His rational was that given how Janice was behaving it would be foolhardy to have a private meeting with her. All it would accomplish would be to fuel the fire. Janice would manipulate whatever I said and I would have no witness to say otherwise. It would be, once again, her word against mine.

I was doubtful that she would show up. I was wrong. Much to my amazement she not only came to the meeting, but also continued her assault on my character, insisting that she had said nothing untrue about me. As far as I could tell it was a useless attempt at discussion and mutual understanding. I felt like a car going down the road in the wrong direction watching as several lumbering trucks were heading straight for me and I had no where to turn to get out of harms way.

Rabbi Don assured me that nothing of value came easily, that everyone knew what Janice was about and what her true agenda was, and that I wasn't to worry. I was advised to continue to do the wonderful job I was doing and to try not to let the Janice episode get to me. Easier said than done.

First, I tried to bury myself in my work. If I kept busy I wouldn't have time to think about such things as Janice and her fabrications. It wasn't enough. I decided to go back to that which would, hopefully, help me regain my bearings and perspective. I decided to sit in meditation. I hadn't done so formally for quite some time. Especially since I couldn't very well go looking for a Buddhist Temple to attend when I was currently a Jewish education director, and, I had promised to keep that part of myself under wraps. But, I did find a viable alternative.

I was working in a beautiful synagogue. Not only did it have a wonderful main sanctuary it also had a smaller sanctuary. Across the foyer from the main sanctuary was a room decorated in the furnishings from the original synagogue. The benches were of deep, rich wood, as was the ark cabinet that housed the Torah scrolls. Stained glass windows allowed the outside sunlight to gently drift inside, carrying the color pigments across the room and conferring an angelic softness to the atmosphere within this quiet and solitary room. The heavy, blue velvets and dark carpeting lent a further air of other-worldliness.

I loved to "escape" to this sanctuary whenever I felt tense, overworked, or just needed a quiet place to think. I would come inside and sit in the soft light while facing the ark. I would sit silently and watch the *Ner Telmid* (eternal light) hanging above the ark. It's ever burning light would reflect off the dark ceiling and flicker across the room. It was extremely restful. I felt at peace and very close to G-d. I would stay until I felt calmed. Then I would return to work. Now, I decided to actively do meditation in this small sanctuary. No one usually came in here. It would afford me quiet and privacy.

Knowing the schedule of events held in the synagogue made it extremely easy for me to plan my excursions into the small sanctuary to meditate. Knowing I would be left uninterrupted inspired me to go as frequently as I found the need to do so. I would slip into the room, leave the lights turned off, and take a seat on one of the benches. I would usually select a place to seat just to the left of center that was slightly closer to the stained glass windows. I would then sit up straight, align my feet and legs, look slightly downward, and begin mediation.

I decided not to bring a meditation cushion. If some one were to walk in on me, it would cause unnecessary curiosity if they found me sitting on a black, round cushion in the half lotus position. Instead, I sat on one of the benches. This way, if anyone were to see me they would just assume that I wanted to be alone to pray. And, as I had predicted, this had come to pass on several occasions.

The time I spent in this small sanctuary, meditating in the presence of G-d, as I have no doubt G-d is always everywhere, allowed a sense of calm to flow through me. I would clear my mind and just rest in the silence of no-thing-ness. Then I would shift my focus toward watching my reactions, feelings, and perceptions of what was going on in my life and with Janice. I would just watch as the shifting feelings of my anger, frustration, and exasperation swelled and moved through my field of awareness. I tried to see Janice with the insight of compassion.

What a torturous existence she must live in, I thought. Always in conflict, always clinging to her views and never, seemingly, able to let go of her desires. Unable to see another viewpoint, being tortured by wanting things to be a certain way and yet not being able to make reality conform to her perceptions. I worked hard to unlock the gates of understanding and compassion within me so that I could let go of my own defensiveness and frustration.

I could feel the tenseness diminish inside myself. I would feel more at peace with the situation and realized that much of this was out of my control and so there was no sense in my trying to enact an influence where it could never take root in the first place. I had expressed my viewpoint to no avail. I certainly had no power to change another individual. All I could do was change my own reaction. I may not have any say in how someone would behave or act, but I certainly could choose how I would act and/or react. My response, or lack of one, was in my total sphere of influence. I would maintain my inner peace as best I could, and let events take their course. Hopefully, the Truth would prevail and all of this would soon be past history.

Janice wasted no time in staging the next assault. She was now on the education committee and decided to attack using that forum. The majority of the committee knew what she was trying to do and dismissed most of what she said. This continued for the remainder of the year. It made for an extremely uncomfortable environment that, I'm sure, was one of her intentions.

Meanwhile, one school year ended and the next school year began. Things were running much more smoothly then my first year since the teachers were now familiar with the curriculum and the resources they had at their disposal. I was extremely pleased with the teacher workshops and I saw more creative and wonderful learning opportunities happening in the classrooms I sat in on randomly during the year.

I was on a two year contract which would be up the following August. As is the custom, the board would vote on whether or not to renew my contract about nine months before the expiration date. Rabbi Don assured me that it would not be a problem. The school was running well, he endorsed me, teacher retention was extremely high, my record was excellent, and the board was happy. I was told it was merely a formality and I would definitely be offered a new contract.

Except, not if Janice could help it. She decided to wage an all out assault. She became so vocal that the board made a decision that, to this day, I still can't comprehend. The only rational I can come up with is that she was so vicious and vocal that they decided to give her what she wanted in the hope of shutting her up. They would hold a special community board meeting to discuss the renewal of my contract. Naturally, Janice would be there to voice her viewpoint. She then advised everyone on the Board that she intended to bring to that meeting a large group of people who supported her views and her assessment of me.

To say I was extremely surprised and disappointed would have been an understatement. I just couldn't believe the board would condone a public forum, such as this, for the sole purpose of denigrating another individual. I had done nothing to warrant this sort of public humiliation. In fact, all of her allegations were false. I felt like a public lynching was being planned, with Janice acting as the leader of the pack. I voiced my concern and objections, but I was advised that the community meeting would be held regardless. Even the rabbi expressed his concern, but to no avail. We were both appalled.

The infamous evening of the meeting arrived. I had been told that I was not to attend. This frustrated me as I felt I should have the right to confront my accuser. Since I was not to be allowed to attend my husband Matt advised me that he would definitely be there. He arrived on time and was promptly asked to leave.

When he walked into the house I realized what a set up this really was. I was appalled to think that a synagogue, of all institutions, would allow someone to talk about another while, at the same time, not allowing the other person to be present. In Jewish law it runs quite the opposite. An individual has the right to hear what is being said about him/her and to have an opportunity to defend him/herself. One had the right to confront one's distracter.

It was at that moment that I realized that politics was alive and well even here in this synagogue dedicated to G-d. My frustration gave way to hurt, then to anger, which, in turn, gave way to disillusionment. I had done nothing to deserve this. It just wasn't fair. How could this have been allowed to happen? To be allowed to go so far? How could they treat me like this?

Matt sat silently beside me that entire evening. He held my hand and tried to lend me encouragement, but I could see he was equally frustrated and upset. My morale was at a long time low. I felt as if I had no energy left. I didn't even feel like going in to work the following day. How was I going to continue working at this religious school in light of all of this? Especially if they believed anything Janice had fabricated about me and decided not to renew my contract. How would I get through the next seven months?

The telephone rang. It was the chairman of the education committee. My hand was shaking as I took the telephone receiver and placed it to my ear. He told me that the evening had been quite intense, but that I had received a vote of confidence from the Board. My contract was being renewed for an additional three years and I would be given a nice raise if I accepted the offer. With a sigh of relief I hung up the phone. I immediately told my husband what had been told to me. He gave me a hug, but he wasn't smiling.

The following day Rabbi Don asked me to come down to his office. I was relieved to do so. It had been a terrible evening for me and I hadn't slept well. I was having difficulty concentrating and my heart just wasn't into my work. I was glad to have an opportunity to discuss things with Don. I knew it would make me feel a little better. I valued his opinion very much.

As I entered his office he gestured for me to take a seat. I sat down and waited. He wanted to tell me what had transpired at the open meeting the night before. What I was to hear lightened my heart somewhat. In brief, Janice had, indeed, made a strong statement against my character. She insisted that lots of other synagogue members felt the exact same way and would be arriving shortly, but not one person showed up or stood up to agree with her.

In fact, quite the opposite occurred. Many people had come to the meeting, in light of the topic up for discussion, to defend me. One by one they stood up, were recognized by the board, and went about refuting everything Janice had said. Much to my amazement, many of the people who defended me were the very people who Janice had insisted were against me. There were even a few people who stood up to say that Janice had lied about what they had actually said concerning me. That it was untrue, that they were outraged that these things would be said in their name and that Janice was not to be trusted.

Rabbi Don ended by telling me that by the end of the meeting it was quite clear that the general consensus was in my favor and that the majority of people in attendance were against Janice. In fact, he felt that contrary to her intent, Janice had been the one publicly humiliated. He advised me that he was only telling me this to let me know that the congregation was behind me and that they sincerely wanted me to remain as the education director of their religious school.

I was at a loss for words. My mind raced. But what if it had gone the other way? What if Janice had gotten her way? What if the silent majority had remained silent? What could I say after all of this? I remained silent. I left the office feeling flat and dull.

How would I make sense of this? How would I come to terms with it? Would I even want to renew my contract? After all, if the board would hold such a meeting just because one individual became vocal what would stop them from doing it again and again? I didn't want to have to worry about this happening every time someone complained. As far as I was concerned, I was hired to do the job because they knew I had the credentials and the experience to get the job done. If they didn't think I was capable or that I was incompetent, then they shouldn't have hired me in the first place.

Even though the incident was now over, and a very good contract had been offered to me for another additional three years, I was still licking my wounds. I just couldn't seem to get over the fact that the board had allowed Janice to go so far that it had, in essence, developed into a public spectacle. Then, I couldn't get over the fact that I hadn't even been allowed to attend the fiasco in order to confront my attacker and defend myself. Yet, short of actually getting into other people's minds, I would never be able to know what inspired them to make the decisions they made and to do what they did.

I would have to switch my focus. Instead of dwelling on the "wrongs" that I perceived as having been inflicted on me, I would have to remind myself that a lot of people attended for the sole purpose of coming to my assistance, to stand by me and to defend my character. Many people, who would have never stood up in a crowd, did so that night. No matter what "could" have happened, in fact, what did happen was that I came out just fine. I was offered another contract and Janice had been removed from the education committee. Plus, at the same time, Janice decided to quit her synagogue membership and she withdrew her children from the religious school.

And yet, I still felt a deep sadness. Why? During my solitary meditation sessions in that small, peaceful sanctuary I eventually came to terms with what had happened. I certainly couldn't change past events, but I could definitely change my reaction to them. I was even able to go a step further. I came to realize, in a non-verbal way, that Janice was a very unhappy and frustrated woman. She constantly ran up against barriers and conflicts because she refused, or was unable, to see any alternatives. In essence, she was enclosed in an airless, tight, hostile, and lonely prison that she, herself, had created. My awareness of her suffering was what made me feel sadness. She was truly worthy of compassion. How could I wish her any harm? She was inflicting so much misery on to herself. I let it go.

Chapter 33
The Farewell Service

Almost two years had gone by since I started working for the synagogue. With such a small Jewish community, I had become rather well known in the area. It wasn't uncommon for people to come up to me while I was out shopping to say hello or to ask me a question. Even the children would wave and shout a big hello whenever they saw me on the street or at the shopping mall.

I had reviewed the new contract that I had been offered and I had decided that I would accept it and stay an additional three years. The school had been experiencing rapid growth and changes would have to be made to accommodate the greater number of students. I was excited about the increased interest in Jewish Mysticism and I was looking forward to expanding the curriculum for our high school age students.

Meanwhile, my husband was doing very well himself. His job responsibilities had been increasing and he was becoming well known in his field of expertise. All in all things were going fairly well. During the same week that I had planned to renew my contract with the synagogue, Matt came home with some news of his own.

"Karen," he announced excitedly over dinner, "I've been offered a promotion!"

"That's wonderful." I exclaimed in excitement. "Obviously you'll accept. When does it start?"

"Well," Matt hesitated and looked intently at me from the other side of the dinner table, "it would be effective in a couple of months, ah, after we move to Northern Virginia."

I was dumbstruck.

Matt continued, "They want me at corporate headquarters in

Reston, Virginia. The promotion would be to head up the department there. Otherwise, no promotion."

Now a very important decision had to be made.

The rest of the week Matt and I stayed up late discussing the advantages and disadvantages of his accepting the promotion and our relocating to Virginia. Finally, after much deliberation we decided he should accept the offer. I would not be able to accept the new contract and so would notify Rabbi Don and the Board as soon as possible so they would have time to search for a new director before I had to leave.

It was obvious that both the Board and Rabbi Don were disappointed, but they understood the reason for it. The hardest part for me was over once I advised them that I wouldn't be continuing on as their religious school principal. But the difficult job of recruiting someone for my position was just beginning for the board.

I had a couple more months before my current contract would end and we would be moving to Northern Virginia. I busily tried to get all the teachers signed up for the next school year, to order all the materials and books, and to generally make sure everything was in order for the new director when I was gone.

One late afternoon while I was busily updating my files, Rabbi Don came in to speak with me. Since I was the one who usually went down to his office, I was a little startled.

"Hey," I looked up, "What's happening? Is everything all right?"

"Sure. Everything is fine." Rabbi Don replied, "I just have a question I need your expertise on."

"I'm listening." I replied.

"Well, as you know," he explained, "We are trying to upgrade our synagogue library. People have been very good about donating books and the sisterhood has even offered to purchase several sets of Judaic books as well. I thought it would be a great idea to include some books on Kabbalah, possibly a complete set of The Zohar. I have this catalog I wanted you to take a look at."

He opened the catalog to a page where various books on Jewish Mysticism were listed, as well as several different versions of The Zohar.

"I wanted to suggest a complete set of The Zohar, but didn't know which version would be better." he pointed to the various sets offered in the catalog. "Do you think you could recommend a set?"

I looked over the descriptions. "That one." I said pointing to the five-volume set published by the Soncino Press. "If I had my choice, that would be the set I'd want."

"Great." Rabbi Bernstein replied, "Thanks."

This was wonderful. I had inspired him enough to actually want to have the Zohar in the library.

Before I knew it I was down to my last few weeks at the synagogue. I had been so busy getting things organized that time had flown by. The rabbi and board of directors had decided to have a Shabbat service in my honor as a way of saying farewell. Although I was a little embarrassed at the prospect, I went along with it as it was obvious that they very much wanted to do this for me.

When that Friday night arrived, my husband and I sat in one of the front rows along with our son. It was an well-attended service. I was a little nervous since they had asked me to prepare to be "called up" to the *bimah*. I shouldn't have been.

Toward the end of the Friday night service, Rabbi Don came forward and announced the date of my departure from their community. He praised my work with the religious school and generally made me feel lousy that I was leaving. After what seemed like hours of "talk about me" the rabbi stopped and took out a beautifully gift wrapped item from underneath his pulpit. I hadn't even noticed it was there.

"Karen has done much to introduce the concepts of Jewish Mysticism to our community. For those who had the privilege of attending her workshop last year, including myself, you know what I mean." He turned to me, "Karen, this is only a small token of my, and our, appreciation of all you have done during your two year stay with us."

With that he handed me the gift that, to my surprise, weighed much more than I had expected and I almost dropped it on the floor. It was obvious that they wanted me to open it. I carefully untied the ribbon, undid the wrapping paper, and had to stifle a scream of excitement.

I held in my hand a five volume, boxed set of the complete Zohar. In fact, it was the exact set I had recommended to Rabbi Don that he try to purchase for the synagogue library. Then it dawned on me. He had fooled me into divulging what I had wanted most. As I looked up at the rabbi tears were coming into my eyes and I had a difficult time speaking. As I struggled, Rabbi Don commented, "We really did get a set for the library, too."

I had to laugh through my tears. Somehow I managed to thank everyone in the congregation, and, especially the rabbi. I was overcome by the thoughtfulness and generosity of this most precious of all gifts. I had longed for a set of the Zohar. But, given the expense, I never really thought I'd ever have the opportunity to purchase a set of my own. Even the prospect of having a set in the library that I could go to to read had excited me. Owning my own set was just, well, unbelievable to me.

As I stepped down from the *bimah* to rejoin my family, congratulations and well wishes for our future filled the air. I would miss this synagogue and the people I had come to know during my two years living in their community. I would miss Rabbi Don even more.

Chapter 34
Exodus to Northern Virginia

Our home was sold, our household packed up by a large moving company, and both our cars were loaded down with everything we felt we'd need as soon as we arrived at our new location. Matt would drive in front, and I would follow him. Arik and our cat, Miami, would be in the car with me. It was to be a very long drive from Raleigh, North Carolina to Reston, Virginia.

Matt, driving alone, had the radio turned up high and kept the cooler full of drinks and snacks on the seat next to him. I had Arik and the cat, both of which fell fast asleep almost as soon as I backed out of the driveway. In fact, they both slept most of the way up to Reston. Consequently, I drove in almost complete silence. It was at this time that I realized that I could, in fact, hold a meditation state of mind and still remain alert to the driving conditions around me.

We made our exodus in less than six hours, but I was still exhausted. Of coarse, Arik and the cat were wide-awake and ready to play. Much of the next several weeks were a blur, but we did manage to get settled into our new home and unpacked by Labor Day. Arik started first grade and our cat, Miami, spent days exploring his new home and making sure he identified all of his familiar household objects.

The High Holy Days of Rosh Hashanah and Yom Kippur were approaching fast and we realized we had better affiliate with a synagogue soon. Since we felt closer ties to Conservative Judaism we decided to look for a Conservative Synagogue. The closest one we found to our home was Beth Emeth, located in a town called Herndon. It was small in comparison to what I had become used to in Raleigh, but the people seemed friendly. We joined and enrolled Arik in Religious school.

I suppose I was feeling a little let down. Plus, I had been putting in such long hours as education director that I felt I had practically lived in the synagogue. Whatever the reason, I just didn't feel up to getting involved with this new temple. Matt picked up the slack and took the lead in terms of Arik going to religious school and services. He became involved with a car pool arrangement, and started to become friendly with some of the other families. I, however, stayed pretty much to myself.

I can't say it was totally deliberate. My heart, for whatever reason, wasn't in it. I just wasn't motivated to go back to the same rituals done over and over exactly the same year after year. I became easily frustrated with the repetition and still longed for that spiritual "something more." I felt as if I had returned to ground zero, a place where I had been as a child way back then.

I rarely went to services unless it was for something special that Arik should attend. Naturally, I prepared for and celebrated all the Jewish holidays as they came up on the calendar. I cooked the traditional foods, entertained family, and tried to give the event a religious feeling. But my heart wasn't really in it. It was pure repetition. It was familiar. It was automatic. It was expected. It was mindless. Devoid of a spiritual base it was just another elaborate meal with company.

During Passover Matt and I would often try to make it special and meaningful by conducting the Passover Seder in the traditional sequence and using the customary symbolic foods. Seder, which means "order" is conducted in a set sequence while telling the story of how Moses lead the Israelites out of slavery from Egypt back to their homeland in Israel. The miracles performed by G-d were related, and the symbols of the food explained.

But, inevitably, some family members would become impatient and insist that we move on to the meal. It was upsetting to me, as the event then became just another meal. Once again I felt the frustration and emptiness I had felt as a young girl. Where was the substance?

I guess I was something of a borderline Jew when viewed in terms of my participation in synagogue activities. I wasn't interested in services or taking an active roll in the Jewish community. But, I was still very interested in Judaism itself. I was deeply involved in studying about the beliefs, the mystical connotations, and the spirituality behind the ritual, and form. I didn't want to be caught in this net of tradition and repetition, especially the mindless repetition. Again, I was faced with that longing for the experiences I knew the prophets and mystics of old had had when they "found" G-d.

Once again I carefully unpacked my modest, black lacquer alter and set up the small, gold colored image of the Buddha, and the other Buddhist paraphernalia. I found my black *zafu* and placed it carefully along the right side of the altar. How long it had been since I last went to a Buddhist temple, I thought. I reclaimed my meditation cushion and decided to sit for a little while in this quiet house in Northern Virginia, located near the Potomac River, and west of Washington, D.C.

While living on Long Island, I was much too involved in Judaic studies and my graduate work to think too much about Buddhism. I still read, but didn't feel a need to look for some sort of Buddhist affiliation. In Raleigh, it would have been totally unrealistic. I had promised Rabbi Dan not to mention my being a Buddhist to anyone and I had kept that promise. Trying to find a Buddhist Temple in North Carolina would have been foolhardy given my position as principal of a Conservative Jewish religious school. But now I was in Virginia. I was no longer the principal of a Jewish religious school, and no longer bound by my promise to Rabbi Dan.

I tried to sit in meditation at home as often as possible. If I only spent ten minutes doing so I was content. Life had become very hectic. Since I didn't want my son confused, as he was being brought up in the Jewish tradition, I did my Buddhist "thing" privately when I was alone in the house or after everyone had gone to bed for the night.

Several years, and several different work situations, came and went. I was still a peripheral Jew, still doing the holidays as they came up. I continued to meditate on my own but worried that I may have slipped unknowingly into some bad habits. I had no one I could ask to check my sitting posture for me, or to get my questions answered from, or to express my concerns with. I was becoming a bit restless and wanted to find some like-minded people that I would feel comfortable with, be able to talk with, and who would understand what I was talking about. I wanted contact with a Buddhist *Sangha*. A *Sangha* is a group of people who practice the teachings of Gautama Buddha, the Enlightened One. It commonly refers to all Buddhists, but traditionally, it usually meant the Buddhist monks and nuns.

I picked up the phone book and looked in the yellow pages under the heading "Churches." I came across a listing for a Buddhist

Temple in Springfield. I hadn't a clue as to what they practiced in regard to meditation technique, but I picked up the phone anyway. If I could walk in cold to a Soto Buddhist Mission in Honolulu, dialing a phone number would be a piece of cake. No one answered. An answering machine clicked in. To my relief, the message was in English. I left my name, telephone number, and a brief reason for my call. I waited. Days went by, then weeks. No one ever called me back.

Chapter 35
Thai Food

A nother year slipped by and spring was quietly making another appearance. Teleia flew down for a long weekend visit. Her visits are exciting for all of us. She has boundless energy, relishes excitement, and loves to experience new things. Her visits are usually over much too soon and we try to pack as much activity into her stay as we possibly can. This was not to be an exception. She asked if she could have her boyfriend join her this time. We agreed.

The evening prior to her returning to Boston, she asked if we would mind if she and her friend went out to dinner alone. Since we had been running around for the last three days we were actually relieved to have an evening we could spend just relaxing in. We sent them on their way with our blessing.

Later that evening, after dinner, Teleia came upstairs to tell us about her evening out. She loves spicy food and they had discovered a wonderful Thai restaurant near by in Herndon. Teleia couldn't rave about the food more. It appeared that every item they had tried was excellent, as was the service. She told us we would just have to make it a point to try it out. I don't do very well with spicy food and so reminded Teleia that this may not be a wise choice for me. At this point she said that it would be no problem. She had noticed that they prepared the food as requested from a range of mild, to American hot, to Thai hot.

Teleia and her boyfriend left and we pretty much forgot about this Thai restaurant that they had raved about. Matt's parent's had driven down for a short visit and we were busy entertaining, sightseeing, and shopping, again. One evening they suggested taking us out to dinner. Matt recommended we try the Thai place Teleia had enjoyed so much.

"Where is it? Is it far from here?" asked Matt's father.

"No," Matt replied, "in fact, it's just one town over. It's called "A Little Place Called Siam.""

"Let's give it a try then." Matt,s mom, Harriet, suggested.

And so we prepared to eat out. I hurriedly changed my clothes and decided to wear my Buddha pendant necklace that had been purchased for me years ago by a friend of mine who had gone to Thailand for a few weeks vacation. I hadn't worn it in quite a while. It was done as an afterthought, an impulse.

As we entered the restaurant I was immediately taken with the decor. It wasn't a very large restaurant, but it was tastefully decorated and the area, although small, gave a feeling of space and light. We were immediately seated at a long table in the main dining area and handed menus. To my relief, Teleia had been correct. The menu clearly stated that you could select the intensity of spiciness you preferred.

I tried the coconut soup, and had *pad thai* (a traditional Thai rice noodle dish with peanut sauce). The portions were huge and I took half of it home for another meal. I had hot tea and a wonderful dessert of fried plantains (bananas) drizzled with honey sauce. Everyone had to take home leftovers. We were extremely full and content as we stood up to leave the restaurant.

As I followed the others out of the restaurant our waiter came up to me and pointed to my necklace.

"Do you know what that is?" he asked me.

"Yes, I do." I replied in some surprise. "It's Buddha sitting in meditation. It was purchased in Thailand. I'm Buddhist."

Now it was his turn to be surprised. And I couldn't believe I was telling this man that I was Buddhist. He looked closely at the pendant.

"What temple do you go to?" he asked me.

"None right now." I replied a little sadly. "I haven't been able to find one near here."

"I know of one that most of the Thai people go to."

"That's wonderful. Would you mind telling me where it is?" I asked with a little anxiety.

My mother-in-law was watching all of this and I could tell she wasn't particularly pleased. But I was extremely excited. At last I would be able to link up with a Buddhist Temple. Whether it would work out or not, I didn't know. At that point I really didn't care. At least the opportunity was presenting itself. I couldn't believe my good fortune.

The waiter's accent was difficult for me to understand. After several attempts he called one of the hostess's over. A brief discussion in Thai ensued and then a piece of paper and a pen were taken from the counter and the waiter copied a name and address down as the hostess dictated it. The paper was handed to me: Wat Yarnna Rangsee, Fairfax Station, and it included the phone number.

I thanked them profusely and ran out the door to catch up with the rest of my family. Arik wanted to know what I had been doing. When I told him, my mother-in law looked across at me from the back seat of the car and informed me that she didn't think it was such a good idea.

"You are only going to confuse your son." she insisted. "And," she continued, "I don't think it's really a very good idea wearing that necklace. You're Jewish and it's not appropriate."

"But, I'm a Buddhist too." I quickly inserted.

She shook her head and dropped the discussion. I knew she was unhappy with this turn of events, but, as usual, she was smartly withdrawing. I felt saddened by her obvious concern and love. How could I really expect her to understand? Sometimes I found it difficult to understand myself.

Chapter 36
Wat Yarnna Rangsee

I sat at the kitchen table looking at the piece of paper with the name and phone number of the Thai Buddhist Temple printed on it. Slowly I rubbed the right side of the paper's edge with my thumb. Why was I so apprehensive about calling? What was I fearful of? It's not as if I didn't have some idea as to what to expect. I stood up once again and picked up the receiver of the wall phone.

Carefully, I dialed the number. It rang several times and I almost hung up. Someone picked up and a woman answered. Unfortunately, I couldn't understand a word she said.

"Is this Wat Yarnna Rangsee?" I asked, fearful that I may have dialed the wrong number.

"Yes." the woman replied.

"I'm a Buddhist and the Wat's number was given to me by someone at the Thai restaurant in Herndon." I explained.

"Yes," the woman replied.

"I would like to know when I could come to do meditation." I continued.

"Yes," the woman replied.

"When would it be? And could I get some directions? I'm coming from the Sterling area." I asked.

"Yes." the woman replied again.

It finally dawned on me that the woman I was speaking to knew very little, if any, English. I felt very stupid.

"Do you speak English?" I decided to ask her outright.

"One minute." she replied and the phone line went silent.

I waited for several minutes and then someone else came on the line. It was a gentleman this time. Although it was obvious from his accent that English wasn't his native language, at least he had a working knowledge of the language and it soon became apparent to me that I would be able to make myself understood this time. I felt relieved.

It was a very simplistic conversation, but I was able to get directions to the Wat that was located in Fairfax Station. I was also able to arrange a time when I could drop by to talk with one of the monks before I went on to work, as it was located along the way. As I hung up the phone, I felt very proud of myself for making that call. It felt similar to the way I had felt when I had first made contact with the Soto Mission in Honolulu. Although, this time I pretty well knew what I was getting into.

The following day, with directions in hand, I drove south on Fairfax County Parkway on my way to the Wat. The directions were very good. It was further away then I had anticipated, but I found it without difficulty. The driveway was unpaved and made up of pressed stones. It was a modest structure, a small house actually, which was being used as a Buddhist Temple. I parked my car as close to the side of the driveway as I could without getting on the grass, and made my way to the door.

I knocked softly and a saffron robed, bald headed, ageless looking Thai monk opened the door and motioned for me to come inside. As I entered I removed my shoes and left them at the door. I then followed the monk into the main room that I assumed was the *zendo* or meditation hall, as it had an altar with many Buddhist statues and flower arrangements on it.

Along one side of the wall, to the right of the altar as you faced it, was a long platform that came up approximately six inches from the floor. It extended only a couple of feet from the back of the wall and square meditation cushions were lined up in uneven intervals along its length. The monk who had let me in, stepped up to the platform and sat down, cross-legged, on one of the cushions. He motioned for me to sit on the floor in front of him. As I carefully sat down on the floor and assumed the half lotus position, two more monks entered the room and also stepped up on the platform and sat down next to the other monk.

I had come to ask for some feedback regarding my meditation posture. I had also hoped to find out if they held any formal meditation sessions that I could attend. Instead, the monk who had invited me in started to ask me a series of questions. At first they were of the type that anyone would expect. He asked me how I had come to hear of this Wat, my name, etc. Then the more insightful questions were asked such as what my understanding of Buddhism was, how did I do meditation, was I a Buddhist, what were my experiences with Buddhism and meditation, did I know of certain patriarchs in Buddhist history? Between questions the monks consulted with one another in, what I assumed, was Thai. It was obvious that all three monks were asking me these questions even though the monk who spoke English was the only one speaking directly to me.

There was a moment of silence and then the English-speaking monk started to give me a discourse, or lecture, concerning various components of Buddhism. He covered the Four Noble Truths, The Eightfold Path, the Precepts, Insight or *Vipassana* meditation, etc. I was later to learn that he was giving me a *Dharma* talk. In the Mahayanist tradition formal *Dharma* talks were not given quite in this fashion. But I was very familiar with what the monk was telling me and I was grateful for the learning.

After approximately an hour and a half it was obvious that it was time for me to depart. I bowed three times to the monks, as I had noticed others had done, and thanked them. I then asked if they had meditation sessions and if I would be allowed to attend them. I was told that a group met once a week on Tuesdays at 7pm and that I was more than welcome to come. As I was leaving the Wat I noticed stacks of moving boxes lined up along the walls.

"Are you moving?" I asked.

"Yes," the monk nodded. "We hope to move in a couple of weeks to our new location."

Great, I thought to myself. I finally find a Buddhist Temple where I can do meditation with a group and they're leaving.

"Where will you be moving to?" I asked feeling greatly let down. Traveling to Fairfax Station was a long enough journey. I didn't think I'd be able to drive at night anywhere further away.

"We will be going to Sterling." the monk replied. "Do you know where that is?"

When what he had just told me sunk in I was beside myself in relief and happiness.

"Yes, I know where that is." I answered with a smile across my face that must have been from ear to ear. "I live in Sterling!"

As I backed out of their driveway and headed toward my work, I was elated. Not only had I finally found a Buddhist Temple, it was actually moving right next door to me. I couldn't help but think that all of this was meant to happen. It seemed just too much of a coincidence that I should decide to wear a Buddhist necklace out to dinner to a Thai restaurant, where the staff would notice it and put me in contact with a Buddhist Temple, which was, in turn, moving in to my own community.

Chapter 37
The Meditation Group

Several weeks later, at a few minutes before 7 o'clock, I drove up the circular, stone driveway of the Wat Yarnna Rangsee, now located in Sterling. I saw several other cars parked near the building and so figured I was in the right place. Reaching the door I peered inside and saw a young woman with short dark hair sitting on the floor facing the altar. As I slowly and quietly opened the door she looked around, smiled at me and welcomed me inside.

"Hi," she said as she placed the palms of her hands together in front of her and bowed, "I'm Margeuritte. Welcome to the group. Have you done meditation before?"

I introduced myself and advised her that I had, indeed, done meditation before but in the Soto tradition of "no-thought." She didn't seem aware of that particular school, but that didn't bother me, as there are so many differing sects and meditation techniques in Buddhism.

Margeuritte kindly introduced me to the three other people waiting to do meditation and then she lead me over to the Buddhist monk who was sitting on the platform to the left of the altar and made a formal introduction. I watched as she knelt and bowed to him. I lowered my head in a standing bow while placing my hands in front of me, palms together.

She explained that they normally did some yoga exercises prior to sitting, then some chanting if the monk felt it appropriate, and then we would meditate for about 40-45 minutes. At that time there would be 10-15 minutes of walking meditation usually followed by a *Dharma* talk from the monk.

A few moments before we were to do the yoga exercises she asked if I were familiar with Thai protocol. When I advised her that I wasn't, she went into her tote bag and took out a typed page of the most common do's and don'ts. It read:

Dear Friends,
The Mindfulness Meditation Group at Wat Yarnna Rangsee
thought it would be helpful to our new members to know some of the
Thai customs regarding behavior towards Monks and Nuns. We
hope the following will help you feel more comfortable when you visit
us. Thank you for your consideration.

1. Please remove your shoes before entering the building.

2. Please dress, speak and behave modestly. No tank tops, halter tops,
   or shorts should be worn to the temple even on the hottest of days.
   This is in respect to the Monks vow of chastity. When meditating it
   is the Thai custom to wear loose, light colored clothing.

3. The traditional Thai greeting is to place the hands together in front
   of the chest or face to say "hello." The monks refrain from
   touching anyone, they do not shake hands.

4. It is the custom to sit on the floor in the Buddha Hall. It is
   considered "bad form" to point the soles of the feet at the Buddha
   image or towards anyone you should respect. It is appropriate to sit
   cross-legged, on ones feet or to retrieve a chair from the kitchen.

5. To offer something to a Monk, ask if they would like the item
   first. If they would like it they will say so and will place a small
   cloth or piece of paper down for you to set the item on it. Please do
   not offer food at any time other than meal time.

It was now time for yoga. I had never done yoga before, but
she assured me it would be easy to follow. Slowly and mindfully she
went through various yoga postures while everyone followed along.
Some postures proved to be more difficult then the others but she had
been correct in saying it wouldn't be difficult to follow. After
completing the exercises we took our places on the pale yellow carpet
in front of the altar to begin meditation.

My mind had quieted down quite a bit while doing the yoga
and I came to realize the benefit of doing those exercises first. It really
did help to bridge the space between our everyday, work-a-day

monkey mind and the stillness of the meditative mind. Sitting on the floor with legs crossed, Margeuritte handed out Xerox copies of the stanzas we would be chanting. One side was in transliteration in a language as yet unknown to me, the other side in English. She lit the candles on each side of the altar and then carefully lit and placed the three incense sticks in the round incense bowl. After bowing three times to the altar she returned to her place and the chanting began.

As I followed along I was enthralled with the melodious chanting. It felt, somehow, familiar. I could sense my mind becoming still while following the intonations and I found myself saying the unfamiliar sounds to myself. Later I was to find out it was Pali, the ancient language thought to have been spoken by the Buddha, himself. Some stanzas were chanted in unison, some were chanted line by line following the monk's lead. Sometimes a stanza would be repeated in English. Then the chanting ended, the lights dimmed, and the formal meditation began.

I positioned myself on my *zafu* and crossed my legs in the half lotus position. After so many years of sitting facing a wall, it felt odd to be meditating facing the altar. I also noticed that the others closed their eyes completely, whereas I was always instructed to keep my eyes open a little at all times in order to prevent sleepiness. I found a spot some three or so feet in front of me and I lightly focused my eyes there. The silence enveloped me. I watched the shadows that were cast by the candle flame move across the floor and I could smell the pungent smoke from the incense. I felt calm and at home in this place. I was glad to be here and felt fortunate that I had found this Wat. For some reason I felt more comfortable here than I had in the Japanese Soto Mission.

Suddenly the monk started to speak softly to us. He explained about *Vipassana* or Insight meditation and how it differed from some other forms. He gave some brief instructions as to how this meditation should be practiced and told us that it was all right to change position if we felt any discomfort. That we should be patient with our training and it would progress. It was obvious that they felt I was a novice and were fearful that I may become frustrated if I were unable to sit the full session. I sat, and waited for the monk to act as disciplinarian as they had done in the Soto method, but no one moved.

Some time later I became aware of movement and discovered that it was now time for walking meditation. No gong had been struck, as it would have been in the tradition I had become used to. I slowly swayed back and forth, uncrossed my legs, and carefully stood up. Instead of walking one behind the other in a circle, everyone walked in there own way, individually. One had to be aware of the position of the others so as not to bump into them or cross into their path. I also noticed that some people decided to go outside for walking meditation, while others remained indoors.

I was amazed that approximately fifteen minutes later everyone silently came together again in the meditation room and sat down in front of the monk. No gong or mallet had ever been struck to mark the intervals and yet everyone knew when it was time. Little did I know that in a very short time I, too, would come to know how to judge the times passing in this way.

Once we were all settled the monk began to talk. I can't recall the exact content of this night's *Dharma* talk, but I do recall that it touched on the basic tenants and practices of Buddhism. I remember feeling connected, somehow, to this group of strangers, this *Sangha* I'd just met.

After the *Dharma* talk, Margeuritte went into the kitchen. I followed as I really didn't know what else to do. She was making tea for the monk and the others. I offered to help and she kindly allowed me to do so. She then handed me the cup of jasmine tea she had prepared for the monk and asked if I would like to present it to him myself. It was at this point that I was to learn the ritual associated with giving *dana* (an offering) to a monk.

Carefully, so as not to spill any of the tea, I walked over to the monk who had moved to the table in the other room and was sitting down on a western style dining room chair with a very high back. As I came towards him with the tea, he gracefully opened a cloth and placed it in front of him. Realizing I was to place the cup on the cloth, I did so. Margeuritte whispered to me from the kitchen doorway that I should bow. After my bow to the monk, the monk bowed to me and accepted the offering of tea.

Later I was to learn that Theravada monks don't partake of anything unless it is offered first. It is considered a way of earning merit to give to a monk and so the lay people feed, clothe, and shelter the monks. In return, the monks give *Dharma* to the lay people. I was also to discover that they took their main meal prior to 12 noon, after which time they were allowed to drink liquids, but not to eat any solid foods until the next morning. The only exceptions to that were pure chocolate and cheese that were considered a liquid in a solid state and allowed to be eaten in Northern climates as a medicinal used to help them stay warm in the Winter. Often the tea offered to the monks would be accompanied by a small plate of cheese cut into cubes with an even smaller bowl of honey placed next to it for dipping the cheese into.

What sect one belongs to, or what method of meditation one practices is really of a secondary concern. To work on oneself, to try to be a good human being, and to help others is really the bottom line. As I continued to join the Tuesday evening meditation group at the Wat I was to eventually blend the two forms of meditation, tranquillity and insight, into a hybrid form.

Often I would begin my meditation by lowering my eyes and practicing tranquillity meditation. As I relaxed into it, my mind would shift to insight meditation and I would often close my eyes. If I became fatigued and sleepy, I would check my sitting posture and open my eyes slightly. I would then return to *vipassana* and close my eyes. At first I was concerned that perhaps what I was doing was inappropriate in some way. But after a while I came to realize that it is the flow, not the method that was important. And, the blend suited me.

Tuesday evenings were set-aside for meditation. My work and home schedule were arranged to accommodate my going to the Wat. Unless I was ill or someone in my family was ill, I would always attend. Like all voluntary acts, the numbers each week varied depending on the people who decided to come that time. Sometimes I would find myself there alone or with Margeuritte. At other times there would be so many people that it became a challenge to find a spot to sit. Over time I came to recognize the others who came frequently or infrequently.

It was an eclectic group. Some were American. Some were Asian. Some came from the Middle East and others from Europe. A few had been born into a Buddhist family and other's came from an Islamic, Jewish or a Christian background. Some were veterans of meditation having practiced for many years. Others were novices, just starting out and having lots of questions, concerns, and enthusiasm. Yet, we came together as one *Sangha*, meditating on Tuesday evenings.

Chapter 38
Black Robes/Saffron Robes

B
eyond the obvious difference in the color of their robes,
Mahayana monks usually wear black robes and
Theravada monks usually wear saffron robes, they are
really quite similar. In this chapter I will show some of the similarities
and differences that I have experienced in practicing in both traditions.
One must keep in mind, however, that this is a very simplistic, and in
many ways a superficial, comparison.

When I had first decided to go to a Thai Wat in order to do
formal meditation in a Buddha Hall, I have to admit I was concerned
about how I would be able to "do it their way" after doing it the Soto
Zen way for so long. Much to my relief, I found them to be very much
alike. And the differences really didn't make much of a difference.

Dogen-Zenji, a Japanese monk, brought Soto Zen Buddhism to
Japan from China. Soto is part of the Mahayana school of thought,
Mahayana meaning "The Greater Vehicle." The Thai forest tradition
is part of the Theravada school, Theravada meaning "Way of the
Elders." Theravada is much older than Mahayana and is thought to be
more in keeping with the original doctrine, as taught by the Buddha,
himself.

Some of the more obvious differences are, of coarse, on the
physical plane. I noticed right away that whereas Soto monks and
nuns could marry and have children, the monks following the
Theravada form were expected to be celibate. Because of this the
latter would never touch a member of the opposite sex, not even in a
handshake. This is not the case in Soto Zen.

In the Soto sect the monks and nuns could take three meals a
day, but it was usually strictly vegetarian. The Thai monks took their
last meal before 12 Noon, and ate whatever the community offered to
them. After their main meal they were not allowed anything except

liquids or items deemed to be liquid in their natural state (such as pure chocolate, and cheese).

The Mahayana tradition stresses the *Boddhisattva* Ideal. A *Boddhisattva* is someone who wishes to gain enlightenment in order to help others experience it as well. Consequently, they chose to be reborn even though they have developed enough to enter final or *Parinirvana* where the round of rebirth ends forever. The Theravada tradition stresses the ideal of the *Arahat* or *Arahant*. The *Arahat*, or "Noble One" is someone who seeks enlightenment for his benefit alone. At least that is how the Mahayanists portray them. This perception of the *Arahat* is not totally accurate as they do help many other beings while helping themselves. I, too, didn't get the impression that an *Arahat* selfishly worked on helping himself, alone. You will understand why when I touch on their meditational methods.

In Soto, a novice follows the Three Pure Precepts (Cease from evil. Do only good. Do good for others), and the Ten Great Precepts:
1. Do not kill.
2. Do not steal.
3. Do not covet.
4. Do not say that which is not true.
5. Do not sell the wine of delusion.
6. Do not speak against others.
7. Do not be proud of yourself and devalue others.
8. Do not be mean in giving either *Dharma* or wealth.
9. Do not be angry.
10. Do not defame the Three Treasures (Buddha, *Dharma*, *Sangha*).

In Theravada they practice the Eight Precepts:
1. To refrain from taking life.
2. To refrain from stealing.
3. To refrain from sexual intercourse (lay person: illicit sexual activities).
4. To refrain from telling lies (including slander, harsh speech/vulgarity, and frivolous talk/gossip).
5. To refrain from intoxicating liquors and drugs which lead to carelessness.
6. To refrain from eating after twelve-noon and before dawn.

7.   To refrain from dancing, singing, music, watching shows, wearing garlands, beautifying one self with perfumes and cosmetics.

8.   To refrain from high and luxurious seats and beds.

A lay Buddhist in the Theravada tradition is supposed to practice the first five precepts. Novice monks and nuns, as well as lay Buddhist staying at a monastery or attending a retreat, are expected to follow the eight (8) precepts, plus an additional two (2) which include separating the seventh precept into

- (8) To refrain from dancing, singing, listening to music and watching shows.
  And,
- (9) To refrain from wearing garlands, and beautifying oneself with perfumes and cosmetics.

The former eighth precept, to refrain from high and luxurious seats and beds, becomes the ninth precept. To this a tenth precept is added: 10.   To refrain from engaging in business activities, and not accepting, or dealing, with money.

Fully ordained monks and nuns practice two hundred and twenty seven (227) precepts, an additional 217 precepts added to the ten already listed above.

Although there are some differences in the two sets of Precepts, there is also much that is similar. Especially, if one looks beyond the words into the spirit behind them. Then they are quite similar, indeed, as are many of the Buddhist tenets they both ascribe to. For example, both hold that the Buddha is the "Fully Enlightened One," "The Awakened," not a god. They both follow the Four Noble Truths (truth concerning *dukka* or suffering), and the Noble Eightfold Way, and recite the Three Refuges (I take refuge in the Buddha. I take refuge in the *Dharma*. I take refuge in the *Sangha*).

The monks and nuns of both orders have few possessions and depend solely on the Buddhist community of lay people for their support. Both groups follow the practice of moderation, or avoiding both the extreme of asceticism as well as the extreme of indulgence (this is also called the Middle Way).

They both strive toward behaving with loving-kindness and

compassion while fostering a state of equanimity. They both believe in *anatta* or non-self and the reality of impermanence. They value all living beings, not just human beings. Both strongly feel that learning, alone, won't lead to enlightenment but that one must experience it directly. And both groups stress the importance of meditation practice.

There is also a lot that I found to be the same in regard to their meditation practice. Both advocate the same sitting positions (full lotus, half lotus, Burmese style, etc.) and maintaining an upright and comfortable posture, and that a person should seek solitude, (so as not to be interrupted) and should, ideally, meditate in the open or in a well-ventilated room. They both teach that meditation is an activity that is never-ending, even when one reaches the stage of enlightenment (when one is living in a constant meditation state).

Yet, I also experienced differences in how they practiced meditation. In Soto Zen, I was taught to sit facing the wall and to keep my eyes opened slightly during meditation practice in order to prevent falling asleep. In the Thai Temple I was facing the Buddhist altar and was instructed to keep my eyes shut in order to decrease distraction. Meditation was practiced in the *Zendo* or Buddha Hall in Soto Zen, whereas at the Wat meditating outdoors was considered preferable so long as the weather conditions were favorable. If not, then we would sit in the Buddha Hall.

In the Soto meditation hall a meditator would sit on a round, black cushion called a zafu that was placed on top of a large square cushion called a *zabuton*. In the Thai Wat the monks usually sat only on a thin *zabuton* while the lay people would sit on whatever they had whether a rolled up blanket or towel, or a seat cushion. I found it to be much more ritualized in the Soto *zendo*. Meditation in the Wat appeared to me to have a more relaxed atmosphere.

In Soto Buddhism they practiced a form of meditation called *Shamatha*, "calm abiding" or tranquillity meditation. It is a practice that develops focus and used to help free the Mind of all dualistic thought formations. It develops mindfulness and concentration. In *zazen* we would just sit, watching our "thoughts" as they would stream across the screen of our consciousness, without attaching anything to the them. Just watching. Just sitting.

Vipassana or "Insight" meditation was the form practiced in Theravada. It was also referred to as "Higher Vision" meditation. I found this to be a more active form of meditation as one investigated and analyzed all phenomena in order to realize their true nature. It was a means of fostering wisdom and the understanding of Truth. Theravadan's recognized the "Calm Abiding" meditation of the Mahayana, but only as a preliminary practice toward learning how to cultivate and maintain concentration and mindfulness. However, it was felt to be only an initial method that would have to be eventually broadened through practicing the higher form called "Insight" meditation. Tranquillity meditation could only take one so far. In order to experience nirvana one had to go further and actually take a penetrating look into him/herself, the world, and reality as it is.

Metta meditation is also practiced in the Theravada school. For this, one meditates on loving-kindness, perfect benevolence, and compassionate love. By looking deeply into these traits they are developed in one self and so are transformed into the actions reflecting them. Even the merit of the meditator was often dedicated to others. This is why I couldn't agree with the Mahayana viewpoint that the *Arahat* was only out for his/her own benefit.

So how was I able to integrate Mindfulness or Tranquillity meditation with Insight meditation? I thought it would be a problem for me but it wasn't. At first I just continued to practice Mindfulness meditation. As I became familiar with the form of Insight meditation I found myself gently moving back and forth. I would often start out calming my mind, gaining focus, listening without thinking, and then gradually I would switch to meditating on a specific object such as pain, suffering, old age, death, or impermanence. If my mind began to wander, I would switch to Tranquillity meditation and then I would flow back into Insight meditation. Eventually, I found myself doing this automatically as the need arose.

I would do the same in terms of whether or not I would keep my eyes opened slightly or closed completely. If I felt tired or as if I would fall asleep, I would open my eyes slightly and focus some three or four feet in front of me on the floor. If I was alert and focused, I would either keep my eyes open or some times I would close my eyes. It had reached a point where it no longer mattered. Therefor I did as I felt appropriate at the time.

Through my experience, I found that the basic teachings and practices are the same. There was/is no conflict, no problem. I go to the Wat each week to meditate, as I once went to the *Zendo* each week in Hawaii. In both cases I am with fellow human beings on the same path. I may be in another state, another building, a different Buddha Hall, but I still just continue to sit and "look within."

Chapter 39
Bhante Rahula

Several weeks prior to this particular Tuesday evening, there had been some excitement in the meditation group. Bhante Rahula was coming to our *Sangha* and as the time drew near, the anticipatory excitement also grew. Who Bhante Rahula was I hadn't a clue. All I knew was that he was an American monk, ordained in the Sri Lankan tradition and that he was in residence at the Bhavana Society monastery in West Virginia. Margeuritte assured me that it would be an awesome experience to attend meditation with Bhante Rahula. For one thing, she told me, he knew English and so the Dharma talk would be especially good. Plus, he was well versed in Buddhism, had written a couple of books and was considered an excellent teacher. She further advised me that he had been trained in yoga techniques and so he began meditation with yoga exercises first (which was not the usual in Buddhist circles).

I had hoped to be at the Wat early. However, I had been delayed and so arrived later than expected. It was a warm summer evening and the birds were busily chirping and flying back to their nests in their favorite trees, for their night of rest. As I walked toward the Wat entrance I noticed that no one was inside. As I walked around the left side of the house I saw that a large piece of plastic had been spread on the ground under a large shade tree. Men and women were moving in unison in various yoga positions being lead by a very thin, bald, American man draped in the long saffron robes of a Theravada Buddhist monk.

I quietly walked to the back of the group, took my shoes off and set them to the side. I placed my *zafu* near the edge of the plastic ground covering and took my place. As I looked up I noticed that Bhante Rahula was looking at me. I thought I had noticed a small smile but I couldn't really tell in the semi-darkness of the early evening. But one thing I was sure of; his eyes were calm and accepting. His eyes definitely smiled. I watched intently and copied the postures and motions that Bhante Rahula was demonstrating.

After the yoga session was completed, we took our places on our zafu and began formal meditation. I couldn't help but watch as Bhante Rahula gracefully sat down next to a large, gnarled tree trunk of a giant shade tree. He moved his legs into a crossed position and tucked his saffron robe around himself. Following his lead, all of us did the same and the stillness filled the night as we listened to the cricket sounds and wind blowing in the branches above and around us.

I had never meditated out doors before. It had always been indoors in a *zendo* or meditation hall. Initially I became easily distracted by the many sounds and smells I was experiencing around me. I would feel a breeze pass and I would find myself "thinking" about the wind. I would hear a distant birdcall and I would find myself wondering what bird it came from. The scent of flowers would enter my nostrils and I'd become lost in the fragrance.

My mind would flutter as the leaves did. Eventually, however, my mind started to still. I noticed the rhythmic flow of the approaching night. With my eyes closed I could sense when the darkness had finally descended, when the sun had finally set. The air felt differently on my skin. I could hear different night sounds besides those of cricket music. And, underlying all of this was the stillness. I found that my concentration became more focused, my meditation deepened.

Before I knew it the 45 or 50 minutes of sitting meditation had ending and everyone was stretching and standing for walking meditation. I slowly stood up and started to walk. My bare feet touched the cool, moist grass. I had done *kinhin* or walking meditation on tile, wood, and even carpeted floors, but never on the bare earth itself.

I had to be extremely mindful as I walked each step. The ground wasn't even and, if I didn't pay careful attention, I would stumble or fall. Once in awhile I would feel a root or stone under the sole of my foot and I would try to lightly step over it without interrupting the stillness filling the contours of my mind.

I became aware of a mosquito flying around my head and then landing on my shoulder. Normally, I would have become agitated and even attempted to strike the mosquito. But my mind was still and I observed the flying creature within my mind, watched it in my minds eye as it took a meal from my flesh while I remained still within. I continued to step forward and inhale, to exhale, step forward. I felt the air as it slipped through the inner passage of my nostrils and disappeared.

Eventually I noticed from the corner of my eye, the steady movement of the others as they made their way back toward the Wat. I did the same and joined the others in a sitting position on the carpeted floor of the shrine room. Incense had been lit and the pungent scent greeted us as we walked inside. The lack of any air movement was suddenly noticeable as we stepped indoors.

Bhante Rahula took his place on the raised platform and adjusted his robe. He then sat peacefully until everyone else had come in from their meditation and was seated. Once more everything was quiet and still. I wondered if he intended for us to meditate, again, as he sat motionless with his eyes closed for quite some time. Just as I was settling into the still pool of No-Thought, he started to speak to the group.

I followed his voice as he spoke about various components of meditation. He asked for questions, received them, expanded on them, and made sure he answered them to the questioner's satisfaction. I started to notice a pattern. It seemed to me as if he sensed when someone had something to ask and so he would turn his focus to that individual. No one raised a hand, as one would usually do in a classroom when one desired to be acknowledged by a teacher. No one spoke first to Bhante Rahula, he always knew when to direct his attention to someone and to ask if they had a question or concern for him.

After his discourse, tea was offered to him as well as the two Thai monks from the Wat who had joined us. The rest of the *Sangha* was offered tea as well, and told they could stay and talk if they wished. Margeuritte came up to me.

"Karen, I'm glad you were able to make it. What do you think of Bhante?" she asked.

"So far I think he's very good." I answered, "But I'm not into judging the monks. Let's say that I'm glad I came, too."

"Tell me," Margeuritte began, "would you be available during the day tomorrow?"

"I have no plans for tomorrow." I advised her.

"Good." she responded. "Would you want to join me in taking Bhante Rahula back to Bhavana? It's better if two people accompany him, especially if one is a woman. Plus, it would be a wonderful opportunity for you to get a chance to talk with him. For several hours he'd be trapped in the car with us. Just think of the conversation and learning we might experience."

"Sounds fine with me." I answered smiling. "What time do we meet and where?"

"We should be on the road no later than 9 o'clock in the morning. Meet me at the Wat at 8:30 and we will leave as soon as we can. Would you mind very much doing the driving? I just did a round trip last week."

"No problem." I agreed. "I don't mind driving at all as long as someone can give me directions. I've never been there before."

"No problem." Margeuritte responded. "I've driven there a lot. We just have to make sure we get there before lunch so that Bhante doesn't miss his main meal. Then we can hang out for a while before returning back. Should be home by 4-4:30pm if we don't encounter any problems."

After finishing my cup of tea and helping to clean up, Margeuritte brought me over to Bhante Rahula and introduced me. I bowed from the waist with my hands pressed together.

"Karen will be joining me in driving you back to the Wat." Margeuritte told him.

"That's very kind of you." Bhante replied looking at me.

For several minutes Bhante asked me questions about where I lived, if I had been coming to the Wat for a very long time, and how often I did meditation. At that point I felt it was time for me to leave and so I bowed once again and turned to go. Before parting I sought out the other monks and bowed in farewell to them as well. Margeuritte followed me to the door, thanked me for coming, and told me she'd see me in the morning. The moon looked very full as I opened my car door.

Chapter 40
Bhavana Society

A s I pulled into the entrance to the Wat I saw Margeuritte's car already parked in front. Since she lived much further away from the Wat than I did, I figured she must have left at an incredibly early time, as it was only 8:25a.m. I parked my car and made my way to the front door. Margeuritte was busily moving bags and boxes from the kitchen toward the door.

"What's up?" I asked her once I was inside the door.

"Oh, Hi Karen." She turned to look at me as she put one of the boxes down next to the wall. "These are donations of paper goods and food items that the Wat wants us to take back to Bhavana with Bhante Rahula. I told them we would take as much as we can. I know you have food products in your trunk, already, to take to Bhavana so I don't think we will be able to take it all."

Looking over the supplies I responded, "Well, maybe it will all fit since we have half the back seat available, too."

We set to work packing up the car and then we told Bhante that we were ready to leave. As we walked up to my car Margeuritte suggested that she sit in the back seat so that Bhante Rahula would have more legroom sitting up front. It was a nice offer, but I knew it was for my benefit, not Bhante's. She wanted me to have every opportunity to speak with him.

We headed north on Route 28, and then turned onto Leesburg Pike west. From the directions Margeuritte had, it looked like a pretty straight shot to West Virginia. The weather was beautiful. It was a nice and sunny day. Perfect for a drive.

I didn't turn on the radio or put any tapes into the tape player. I hadn't been told about this, but I knew that Theravada monks were not supposed to listen to music. Margeuritte, having made this trip before, was perfectly at ease and immediately started asking Bhante questions. From time to time we would grow silent and I would hear the whir of the tires as we moved swiftly along the pavement.

I turned briefly and looked at Bhante Rahula as he sat beside me. I decided to venture a question or two.

"May I ask you a question, Bhante?" I asked.

"Of coarse." he replied.

"I was wondering. What made you decide to become a Buddhist monk and how did you go about it?" I looked ahead at the road and waited for a response.

"Actually, it was a choice that sort of evolved over time." Bhante began, "I had a fairly wild youth. No one would have ever thought I would become a Buddhist or a monk."

He briefly described his life as a sort of hippie globetrotter. He believed in free love and lots of drugs. He was restless and searching, but really didn't know for what.

"I wrote a book about that part of my life." he volunteered. "It's called One Night's Shelter. You can pick up a copy at Bhavana if you are really interested."

"Thanks," I responded, "I just might do that."

Then the conversation focused on his asking me questions on how I became a Buddhist and what my experiences were. It evolved into questions concerning Buddhism and Buddhist practices and how Mahayana differed from Theravada. With only one stop along the way to use the bathroom, we made very good time and arrived almost an hour before the main meal was to begin for the *Sangha*.

I parked as close to the main building as I could as we had so much to unload for them. As we started to take the boxes and bags out of the car, other monks and lay people came to help us. Everyone seemed please to see Bhante Rahula back.

After the supplies were taken care of Margeuritte offered to show me around. We walked back outside and she gave me a mini tour of the monastery. It was cool up there in the mountains of West Virginia and it was with pleasure that I walked along the narrow paths zigzagging away from the main building.

The main building housed the kitchen, storage areas, current meditation hall which was also used for taking meals, with a women's dormitory on the left side and the men's dormitory quarters on the right side of the meditation hall. All areas were connected by enclosed walkways. The meditation hall had countless books displayed on shelves to the left of the main entrance. I had instantly gravitated toward the books, but Margeuritte suggested we walk around the grounds first.

Following her suggestion we walked on one of the dirt paths up past a small mountain stream. A couple of other monks, also wearing saffron robes, were busily working on a structure that appeared to be another meditation hall. As we walked closer we were invited inside.

"This is the new meditation hall." Margeuritte explained to me. "It's going to be a beautiful structure."

We walked inside and, even though it still had more to be completed, it was a very handsome structure. A stained glass window of a green Bodhi leaf had already been installed on the far wall where I assumed the altar was to be. Above the main entrance was a circular stained glass window of a red lotus. The building was constructed entirely of wood and the ceiling arched skyward, the beams coming together to a point at the top of the roofline.

To the left of the main entrance was a smaller room with a terra-cotta tile floor and totally enclosed with plate glass windows. Someone had already placed some potted plants inside. It was obvious that it was being used as a nursery. Later, I was told that this sunroom was initially designed to enhance the solar heating of the hall as well as to be a warm location to store the Bodhi tree during the cold winter months. The building had been built on a north/south axis in order to maximize the suns' warming light. As a by-product, so to speak, the sunroom became another environment in which to go to meditate. The Sri Lankan order is of the forest meditation tradition and so having a warm place to go with lots of plants during the frigid winter months was certainly helpful.

The sun, even though filtered through the full branches of the many trees surrounding this building, was still very bright as it cascaded down to the earth toned, tile floor. The air was warm and moist. It reminded me of the tropics and I could visualize it full of exotic foliage. Yes, this was the place I would probably gravitate to if I were to do meditation here.

As I looked at the plant life currently brought in, I noticed in a corner a potted plant that looked familiar somehow. As I walked closer, I realized it was a very small Bodhi tree. I had seen a Bodhi tree on the University of Hawaii's Manoa campus. It was a gigantic tree with beautifully curved, emerald green leaves. It cast a deep shade on the ground below it and I remember sitting under it, sometimes, while between classes. I had loved that tree. This miniature intrigued me.

"Ah, I see you have found our Bodhi plant." Bhante Rahula stated as he stepped down into the alcove.

"Yes," I replied a little startled, as I hadn't noticed his arrival. "It's so small. I recall the Bodhi tree on the University of Hawaii (UH) campus where I attended undergraduate school, it was very large."

"We are very pleased to have this cutting." Bhante Rahula went on. "It was brought over from Sri Lanka from a tree that was grown from a cutting of the original Bodhi tree that Gautama Buddha was sitting under, in Bodh Gaya, when he realized Enlightenment. We are optimistic that this cutting will grow over time into a large tree as well."

I was duly impressed. I hadn't seen a Bodhi tree, large or small, since leaving the islands. I hadn't anticipated seeing one now, especially such a tiny cutting, and in West Virginia. Looking at it a few moments longer, I envisioned it as the tall, majestic tree I had sat under so many times.

At this point Margeuritte led me out of the building and we walked some of the dirt paths crisscrossing the monastery grounds. We passed small, one room, wooden structures on stilts. She explained to me that they were *kuti* or individual dwellings for the monks and nuns. It consisted of only one room with a door and a couple of windows to let in some light. There was no plumbing or electricity. Most of the *kuti* had kerosene heaters for use during the cold months. Some *kuti* had wood burning stoves. Both had to be used very carefully so as not to cause fire or asphyxiation of the occupant.

Because of the lack of plumbing, most of the women preferred to occupy the dormitory adjacent to the kitchen facility. The monks preferred to inhabit the kuti for the additional seclusion it offered. For them, toilet facilities didn't seem to be as important. In either case, the men's *kuti's* were located higher up the mountainside and women were not supposed to venture up there unless accompanied by a monk or other male member of the community.

The women's *kuti* were located near the main buildings. It was apparent that this was for a two-fold purpose. It offered more security, and it was more convenient to the bathrooms located in the main building.

Our tour was interrupted when a passing monk advised us that it was now time for the mid-day meal and it was suggested that we might want to go back to the main building. Since we had been listening to the growling of our stomachs for some time now, we decided that it was, indeed, a good idea. Promising to continue our explorations after lunch, we quickly made our way back down the narrow dirt path to the meditation hall where the meal was to be served.

Margeuritte and I bowed at the entrance to the hall and quietly walked over to a short bench to the left where we were being directed. Black cushions had been placed along the long, narrow, wooden bench and it was apparent that we were to sit on a cushion, using the bench as a table. I sat down, crossed my legs, and sat up straight. Other monks and nuns walked in and took their assigned places along the walls nearest the altar. The lay people who worked and/or lived at the monastery also took their places along the far wall.

After everyone had taken a place to sit and it was silent, the head monk began chanting. As he chanted the other monks and nuns joined in. We sat with the palms of our hands pressed together in front of us and listened. Some of the lay-people knew the chant and joined the monks and nuns in their recitation. At the conclusion of the chanting, the monks slowly stood up, picked up their bowls, and silently walked in line to the kitchen.

I noticed that there was a definite order to the process. First the monks went to procure their food. They went in order of seniority with the oldest/most senior monk going first. Behind the monks followed the nuns, also in order of the most senior member proceeding first. After they had been served, guests were allowed to go to the kitchen, and then the other lay people followed suit.

As we moved in a steady, quiet flow into the kitchen we picked up a plate and eating utensils as well as a napkin all of which had been placed on the table along the edge closest to the entrance. We then moved clockwise around the table helping ourselves to whatever food items appealed to us. It was, however, tacitly understood that whatever we selected we were expected to eat.

On the way out of the kitchen we could pour ourselves some tea or take a cold beverage. The line moved steadily into the kitchen, around the table, and back out into the hall where everyone, once again, sat down at their place. By the time I had sat down, the monks

Picture 40.1: Kuti at Bhavana Society

and nuns had already started eating from their bowls. I bowed to my plate and commenced eating myself.

I was pleasantly surprised at how good the food items were although I was ignorant as to what most of them were. Some were spicy and, although I tried to avoid serving myself anything I thought may be spicy, I found I had placed some on my plate. I mixed in some of the bland rice and slowly, methodically consumed my lunch.

Once again chanting began. This time it was to express thanks and gratitude for the donations and offering of food that all had enjoyed. The monks and nuns had finished eating and were bringing their bowls and utensils back to the kitchen for cleaning. We were advised to stop eating during the chanting, but that we could continue eating and even go into the kitchen for more food, after the monks filed out of the hall.

As we finished our meal we, also, filed into the kitchen to clean our plates and utensils. Various lay people had volunteered and were already in the kitchen washing, sanitizing, rinsing, and drying the bowls, plates, silverware, and serving platters used for the meal. All was silent as they went about this chore and continued until the last item was returned to its proper place in a drawer, cupboard, or on a shelf.

After the meal, Margeuritte and I returned to the hall to look over the many books and tapes I had seen earlier when we had first arrived. There were countless books on all aspects of Theravada Buddhism. Many books were for free distribution. Others were for sale. Tapes of *Dharma* talks given over the years were also available for a donation. I don't know how long I spent looking at everything, but I walked out with ten books and two cassette tapes.

I had taken an envelope and discretely placed my donation inside and then sealed the envelope. When I was alone, I brought it over to the donation box and slipped it into the slot. I had wanted to donate something even if I hadn't collected so many books to take back with me, but I didn't want anyone to see me making the donation.

According to Maimonides ladder of giving (Maimonides or Moses ben Maimon, also known in Jewish circles as the Rambam, was a highly esteemed Jewish scholar of the eleventh century who wrote Guide of the Perplexed), the highest form was when neither the donor nor the recipient knew of each other. It had made perfect sense to me and I couldn't understand those good people who gave, but wanted to make sure every one knew they had made a donation and for how much.

Synagogue and Temple walls were often covered in plaques engraved with the names of the generous donors. There were also small plaques placed on the back of the seats in the sanctuary, itself. And even the prayer books weren't left unscathed. Inside many book covers, could be found nameplates inscribed with the donor's name including whom the donation was made in honor of.

After slipping in my own donation envelope, I made a quick retreat outdoors to meet up with Margeuritte who had decided to sit outside while I continued to look over the books and pamphlets. She was sitting on a small rock facing the trees and watching as the birds and other wildlife passed by. I quietly sat down next to her. After a while, she turned to me and asked if I would like to meet some of the others who lived at Bhavana. When I replied in the affirmative, we both stood up and I followed Margeuritte's lead.

I was to have the honor of meeting many of the monks and nuns, as well as the resident lay people who lived and worked at Bhavana Society. Unfortunately, the founder and head monk, Bhante Henepola Gunaratana, was not in residence at that time as he was traveling. The kindness and graciousness I felt from everyone I met impressed me a lot. They appeared genuinely interested in us, were open to any questions we may have had, and patiently answered any inquiries we asked of them.

As we walked back to our car, with books, cassettes, and other reading materials in our arms, I felt a deep calm and sense of wellbeing. This monastery, in the mountains on the eastern edge of West Virginia, and hidden from view, was truly a jewel for the Buddhist community. As I drove back down the mountain road toward home, I promised myself that one-day I would return. One day, I would stay for a retreat and really get to know this place, and myself, better.

Chapter 41
Meditation Hall Dedication

When I had left the Bhavana Society grounds, I had no idea that I would be returning just a couple of months later to attend the dedication of the newly constructed Meditation Hall. I was already enrolled to attend a weekend meditation retreat just a little over a month later and was actually pleased to be able to visit again prior to the retreat.

Margeuritte and I decided to attend together, as we were to go to the weekend retreat together as well. Over the last year or so we had become friends, enjoying one another's company and the fact that we were both Buddhists. We understood one another in a way the others in our life couldn't.

Fortunately, it was warm and sunny as we drove up the stone driveway onto the Bhavana's grounds. We were impressed with the large number of cars already parked and the many groups of people who had already gathered for the celebration. We saw *bhikkhus* (monks) and *bhikkhunis* (nuns) from the various monasteries in the Washington, D.C. area as well as from as far away as Korea and Sri Lanka. Lay people from areas around the world were also present.

I saw the monks from Yarnna Rangsee, the Wat I went to every Tuesday evening for my formal meditation practice. I bowed to each of them with the palms of my hands pressed together. I was pleased to see their familiar faces. I saw other lay people whom I recognized and others that Margeuritte knew and introduced to me.

Margeuritte was asked to go around to all the *bhikkhus* and *bhikkhunis* and to find out their names. She was a little overcome with the responsibility, but agreed to do so. In this way she was able to meet everyone. As she busily tried to intercept each and every monk and nun in the area, I roamed the monastery grounds, spoke to various people along the way, and looked forward to the dedication ceremony.

There would be refreshments after the dedication, and groups of lay people were busily setting up the tables outside. Others were arranging the food and drink to be offered, while others congregated in the kitchen cleaning and arranging other items to be served. I would not be able to taste any of the traditional and exotic foods I saw being placed on the serving tables. It was Passover and I was not to eat anything that may not be kosher for Passover, which meant anything that had been in proximity or made with leavening (such as leavened bread).

Meanwhile, it was announced that everyone should proceed to the Meditation Hall for the dedication. As I entered the large room I was enthralled by its simplicity and beauty. Totally constructed of light, knotted yellow and white pine, the ceiling beams came to a point as the wooden planks arched up from the walls to the top of the roof. The matching wood pillars also gracefully curved up to the roof.

Directly in front as you made your way into the hall, was a beautiful stained glass window above the large, golden statue of Gautama Buddha sitting in meditation. The luminescent green Bodhi leaf curved upward in unison with the pillars and ceiling. Across the hall and above the entrance was another stained glass window of a red lotus flower. The hall was covered wall-to-wall in light brown carpeting, and the many windows that lined the three walls let in a soft light.

To the left was the atrium or sunroom, separated from the main hall by two glass doors and a water wall constructed of twenty (20), 7 foot high water tubes used for the manufacture of solar energy. It was light and warm and the plants added an additional feel of outdoors and serenity. I would walk out there often in order to feel the warmth and look at the small, transplanted Bodhi trees in their oversized pots.

The dedication went smoothly. The *Bhikkhus* and *Bhikkhunis* sat at the front of the Hall while the lay people sat throughout the hall primarily on meditation cushions although quite a few sat on chairs toward the rear of the hall. Various *Bhikkhus* and lay people spoke, thanking everyone who supported the undertaking and effort to build the hall and recounting how it came about that there would be a monastery in West Virginia. How it all had been designed and built was also reiterated. I was surprised to learn that Bhante Rahula had designed the new meditation hall that was being officially opened this

Picture 41.1: Outside the Meditation Hall at Bhavana

day.

     Briefly, the Bhavana Society was formed on May 13, 1982. On May 4, 1984, a thirteen-acre parcel of land was purchased in a secluded, forested area in West Virginia and was given the name "Dhamma Village." As time went by, more land was purchased and some land was even donated to the society. Today it encompasses forty-two acres near High View, West Virginia, approximately two hours west of Washington, D.C.

     We were allowed a brief time for meditation and then everyone was invited to partake of the food and drink that was set up outdoors for our enjoyment. As everyone slowly walked out of the meditation hall, I located Margeuritte. We decided to wait a while in the sunroom until the other guests had had a chance to eat. It was

Picture 41.2: Venerable Henepola Gunaratana and Bhante Rahula

peacefully quiet and we both remained silent taking in the scenery outside the windows and the peacefulness we were feeling within.

I looked wistfully around me. I had that warm feeling of being at home. I closed my eyes, felt the warmth of the sunlight folding itself around me, and slowly inhaled the earth smell of growing plants. I stood
silently this way for awhile, then I stretched out my hand and carefully caressed one of the deep green leaves of the Bodhi tree in a pot next to my feet. For a moment I felt I knew what the Buddha must have experienced while sitting under the majestic Bodhi tree in the park of Varannasi.

Bodh Gaya, where the Buddha first attained enlightenment, is located approximately 80 kilometers south of the modern Indian City of Patna (near modern Bihar). It is one of the four sites a Buddhist should visit. Perhaps one day I would be able to make a pilgrimage to that exact spot.

My reverie was interrupted when others came into the sunroom. They had also come to admire the beauty, and feel the serenity, of this place. I looked at Margeuritte. She smiled and we both walked out of the room together to make our way outside where most of the people had gathered to select and taste the many foods prepared for the occasion. The air was filled with the many sounds of voices in conversation, but I still heard a bird sing and the tinkle of a small mountain stream making its way toward the east and the Potomac River.

Chapter 42
Karma (*Kamma*) and the Holocaust

Kamma (Pali), Karma (Sanskrit):
"Actions, the law of consequences which inevitably follow
upon actions [either good or bad]."

Vipaka (Sanskrit):
"Action and its result. Vipaka can be called the fruit of our
actions, whilst karma is the seeds that we ourselves sow."

(quotes taken from the glossary in <u>Selling Water by the River</u>, by Jiyu
Kennett)

For any Jew, the Holocaust is a major tragedy not easily
dealt with. For me, the concept of *kamma* becomes
problematic when looking at such a horrific event. And
so, I grapple with the problem of the concept of karma and the
Holocaust. Millions of innocent men, women, children and infants
were captured, enslaved, tormented, tortured, and murdered. Was it
their karma? Was it merely a manifestation of their prior actions and
its fruition? Did all of these millions merely reap what they had sown
during their current or past existences?

Karma (*Kamma*) is mental volition and *vipaka* is its result, a
process also known as cause and effect. If every consequence can be
explained as having come about due to a prior action, then does this
mean that any unfortunate harm we experience is due to some action
we initiated in the past? Not necessarily. The doctrine of
Karma/*Kamma* is very complex. Not everything can be explained in

terms of past action. There are some experiences such as common illnesses/sicknesses, and minor injuries that are solely the result of having a material body.

Is there ever a time when a sentient being is subject to some cruel act, or is killed, due to some other beings bad karma and through no fault of their own? Could it be that the Nazis and their collaborators, as a manifestation of total evil, inflicted their harm on others solely because of their own bad karma? Such inhumane, inconceivable evil, must/will surely result in horrendous consequences for those who harmed others with such evil intent.

Hitler developed his evil plan, found an outlet for its manifestation, found others who felt and believed the same way as he did and were willing to follow him. Add to this the acceptance of his diabolic scheme by the surrounding population, and he was able to carry out his evil intent on an unbelievable scale. The unmitigated evil of those who would inflict such pain, suffering, cruelty, and death, did so solely on their own volition.

However, these actions were originally set in motion due to past conditioning (*kamma*). Their choices were made within a field of influence involving their own past tendencies (i.e., anti-Semitism, a strong belief in their own Aryan supremacy, and the perceived threat to this supremacy posed by another group such as the Jewish people). And yet, their actions were also initiated and imposed on their victims as a manifestation of another universal law involving the order of the mind, the psychic law involving consciousness and conscience (or the lack thereof). Man, ultimately having freewill, in this case, chose the dark path.

But, again, what about the millions (and not only Jews) who perished at their hands? Is there no room in Buddhist doctrine for the concept of total innocence? Could not a horrible event take place for which you were blameless, having planted no seeds of karma? Could a person be consumed by another person's "bad" karma while he, him self, was innocent?

Kamma is difficult to pin down. As finite beings we can hardly comprehend that which is infinite in all directions: past, present, and future. To say that the victim's karma played no part in historic events would be to ignore the reality of karma. Could it be that these millions who were born into Jewish families, who lived in those countries (that would eventually be taken over by Nazi rule), were there because of past karma (that determined that they were to be born into such a family, at that location, and at that particular time period)?

This doesn't necessarily presume that the victims knew what was to transpire during their lifetime, but that their past karma did, indeed, influence the conditions of their rebirth. As such, the victim unwittingly placed him/herself in harms way as a manifestation of his/her past conditioning, attachments, and desires. In this way the victims cannot be thought of as entirely innocent (although the term innocent is not quite the right word for it), and yet no blame must be placed on the victim either. The situation of his/her birth was just a manifestation of the reality of ignorance, and attachment to that which is familiar and comfortable.

There is, therefore, no blame to place on the victim, no karmic finger to point. Do we blame the victims because they were unable to foresee the unmitigated evil that was about to surround them? Do we blame the victims for the murderous intent and actions inflicted on them? We could, I suppose, say that because of ignorance the victim might have stayed in harms way when, perhaps, there was an opportunity to avoid it. But is that ignorance a reason to place blame on the victim?

Karma is neither good nor bad. It is merely the manifestation of a prior mental volition or action. It is a continuous stream. However, not all situations can be accounted for by using karma as an explanation. Many causes of events can be traced back to such things as a lack of mindfulness. For example, you trip over a step and fall. It was a lack of awareness (or mindfulness) that caused the mishap, not "bad" karma. Karma can also be neutral. In this case, being born into a Jewish family who is living in an East European country during the time frame of Hitler's rise to power was due to karma. Hitler's rise to power and he's being able to gain so many followers, was also due to past karma. Unfortunately, these two groups coming together during that particular moment in time resulted in a most unspeakable horror.

How does one explain this? One doesn't. As Dr. Rewata Dhamma has stated on page 13 of his book, The First Discourse of the Buddha,

> "The Buddha's doctrine of causal relations does not postulate
> merely a single cause for any given event. Rather,
> phenomena or events are the product of a multiplicity of
> causes or conditions. There is no single cause nor any first

cause which conditions a particular effect. The question of the cause of a first event does not arise because a first event can never be discovered."

Man's cruelty and inhumanity has, unfortunately, manifested itself many times during the course of history: the Roman's treatment of the Christians as they fed them to the lions for sport. The Chinese villagers being raped, tortured, and murdered at the hands of their Japanese conquerors. The cruelty displayed by the Chinese military against the Tibetans after they had aggressively occupied Tibet. The Croatians and the Serbs. The list goes on and on, including the government's who enacted atrocities upon their very own citizens.

Unfortunately, atrocities are not difficult to find. The only hope appears to be in mankind developing compassion and loving-kindness toward all beings. As Dr. Dhamma further wrote on page 16 of his book,

"He [Buddha] taught that greed, anger, and delusion are latent mental dispositions in the human mind. Because of greed, anger, and delusion, one cannot discriminate right from wrong and consequently one undertakes unwholesome actions. If the mind is pure, influenced by loving-kindness (*metta*), compassion (*karuna*), and wisdom (*panna*), one's actions also become pure and wholesome."

Yes, there is horror, but there is also hope.

"Not to do any evil, to cultivate good, to purify one's mind. This is the teaching of the buddhas."

(Dhammapada Verse 185)

Chapter 43
Meditation Retreat at Bhavana

I t was now June. The weather had gotten considerably hotter and more humid. Margeuritte and I were to drive up to Bhavana to attend a weekend retreat together. Both our husbands had generously offered to watch our sons and to hold down the fort until our return. I met Margeuritte at the Wat where I transferred my belongings to her car as she decided to drive. We had both been looking forward to this opportunity to stay at Bhavana and to have several days to devote solely to meditation.

Prior to the Meditation Retreat, we were given a booklet of guidelines to read over concerning what to expect and how to conduct one self while residing at the monastery. We were told that we should observe the Eight Precepts while there, and that a vegetarian diet was to be followed. No food was to be eaten after twelve noon and we were to observe silence at all times. It was expected that there would be no physical contact between attendees and that modesty was to be consistently maintained.

It advised us what personal items we should bring with us, what to leave behind. We were told not to bring any radios, musical instruments, writing materials, newspapers, magazines or secular books. Alcoholic beverages and illegal drugs were forbidden. We were asked to bring our own linens such as sheets, pillows, blankets, towels, etc.

It instructed us as to what proper etiquette was required when in the presence of a monk or nun. Eating procedures were listed in detail as well as how we were expected to keep our living quarters and bath facilities clean. We were also told that we would be expected to attend all of the group meditation sessions each day and the *Dhamma* talk held in the evenings. Those guests not attending a retreat were required to attend a minimum of two hours in a group meditation session each day.

Margeuritte and I arrived around mid-afternoon on that Friday. We wanted to get there in plenty of time to get settled into our quarters and to be able to walk around the grounds a bit before the retreat formally began and the rule of silence would be in effect. The air was refreshingly cool up here in the mountains. It was so still and quiet that we could hear the running water in the brook that transverses the monastery's grounds. We had brought up with us some tea, coffee, and some approved food items. I had made sure we brought up lots of chocolate, including hot chocolate. Food I could do without, chocolate, no way. Not eating after 12 noon didn't concern me so long as I could have a cup of tea and a piece or two of chocolate. Margeuritte had brought some healthy snacks with her. We indulged before the retreat began, afraid we may become hungry during meditation that evening and our stomachs would growl noisily.

As the evening drew closer more and more people arrived for the retreat. We were surprised at how many people showed up. Our expectation had been that not many would find their way up here, but we had been wrong. Men and women from other areas of Virginia, as well as from other parts of the United States, were arriving and setting themselves up for the weekend. Every room and bed was taken. We had thought we would have a room to ourselves, but when asked if another woman could take the third bed we knew it was to be a full house.

The gong sounded announcing the start of the retreat, that Noble Silence was now to be observed, and that our first group meditation was to begin shortly in the new Meditation Hall. Everyone quickly and silently made their way out of their rooms and down the hallways to the Buddha Hall. Wine red *zabutons* and *zafus* had already been set up across the floor so all we had to do was select our place to sit. I had brought my own *zafu*, so I carefully placed the *zafu* that was already there to one side.

I quietly sat down on my *zafu* and arranged myself in the half lotus position, right foot resting across my left thigh. I placed my palms upward with my right hand resting inside the palm of my left. Rotating in a clockwise, circular motion, I found a comfortable position and stopped. I noticed that Margeuritte had taken the cushion directly in front of me. I heard the stirring of others finding their places and getting into position. Then it was silent.

The sun was setting and the fading light slipped threw the

stained glass window above the Buddha altar. The soft light gave the meditation hall a very spiritual as well as mystical quality. The stillness was complete. At home I would hear cars drive by or children playing. No sounds of civilization penetrated our sanctuary, here within the folds of the mountains of West Virginia.

I became aware of the stillness growing deep inside me. I was relaxed, alert, and comfortable. Easily I sat in meditation. Nothing was forced. When it was time for walking meditation I remained where I was, sitting. I couldn't bring myself to move. Being enveloped in a peace and solitude I rarely experienced, I was reluctant to change my position. Afraid I would break whatever spell I was under. Since I wasn't feeling any discomfort in my legs or back, I continued to sit.

At other times I would rise to do walking meditation. Usually, it was because I had a sense that I should continue my meditation outdoors, under the trees and open sky. As I walked slowly along the stone pathways that intersected the monastery grounds, I would become absorbed in the landscape forgetting that I was even walking, some times even forgetting that I was there.

At times I would spontaneously stop and just stand in place listening and watching nature around me. I watched the water ripple down a small stream. It made small waves and ripples pass along the surface of the water, sometimes carrying small forest objects with it such as a bird's feather or a fallen leaf. My mind's eye would feel the coolness of the water, the smooth edges of the pebbles and stones the water flowed over, and the softness of the moist soil on its embankments. I felt as if I was being carried down stream where I would eventually merge with the waters of the great Atlantic Ocean.

Looking up, I would feel as if I was soaring high up in the clouds. Birds were my companions and they taught me how to fly. I felt the wind tossing my hair and moving down across my body. It helped to lift me into the air. I added my voice to the songs being sung by the birds', crickets, and frogs. Yet, I was silent.

Maintaining Noble Silence was easy. I had no desire to converse. I was actually relieved that we weren't supposed to talk. It took away the burden of having to force myself to do so. I was in another place, and yet I was still where I was. I took it all in with my eyes, my skin, my breath. I feared I might be becoming attached to meditation, itself.

The routine was similar to that which I had experienced at

Shasta Abbey, but with many more opportunities for meditation. The daily schedule was basically as follows:

5:00 AM	Wake-up gong
5:30-6:30	Group meditation (sitting)
6:30-7:00	Group meditation (walking)
7:00-7:40	Breakfast
7:40-11:00	Group meditation (sit/walk)
11:00-12:00N	Lunch
12:00-2:00 PM	Work, rest, meditation
2:00-5:00	Group meditation (sit/walk)
5:00-6:00	Yoga or meditation
6:00-7:00	Work, rest, meditation
7:00-8:00	Group meditation (sitting)
8:00-close	Dhamma talk, discussion

There was a sign-up list outside the kitchen area on a table. One list was for volunteering for after lunch clean up, the other for an opportunity to speak with a monk or nun. Margeuritte and I signed up to wash the dirty dishes, utensils, pots, and pans after lunch on Saturday. When I found the list for signing into a time slot to speak with a monk or nun, all the slots were filled. I decided it wasn't a big deal as I had access to a monk most of the time at the Wat. Better that the others, who might live far away from a Wat or monastery, have the opportunity.

In the evening, after the *Dhamma* talk, we would be free to move about, have some tea or hot chocolate, shower, get ready for bed. It was at this time that I would have my tea and some chocolate. Some times I would take my tea outside under the warm night sky filled with more stars than I had ever thought possible. Without the competing light from street lamps, car headlights, shop windows, and the like, the stars manifested themselves in intense brightness. I listened to the night sounds of the forest while looking up at the sky. I even saw a comet as it whisked across the darkness and then disappeared.

The briefness of the comet's light brought to my mind the transience of life, the impermanence of all things. Occasionally, I would fall into meditation while sitting on a step, a rock, or on a ledge. So calm, so peaceful, and yet countless events were taking place, not only in this forest, but also around the world right at this very moment. I shut my eyes and embraced the universe.

Sleeping in strange surroundings, on a regular mattress (I'm used to a waterbed), was difficult enough. Add to this the necessity of getting up countless times to use the bathroom while trying not to disturb anyone, and you can well imagine the challenge. I tried to make it a time of quiet, although sleepy, reflection. Several times, after returning from one of my many trips, I would lie on the bed on my back with my hands folded across my stomach, and would meditate until I fell asleep once again.

The following day I had the same experience during meditation. I continued to sit while the rest of the group stood up for walking meditation. Some went outside to meditate, a few went to the sunroom, while others remained in the meditation hall and walked between the empty spaces along the walls. I sat on my *zafu*, completely empty, feeling the light streaming in, hearing the soft footsteps of those walking near me, calm, and aware.

Time had no reality. Time didn't matter. A minute could stretch into an hour and an hour could appear to be no more then a few seconds. Time-less-ness. Fall would come and the leaves would lose their vitality, turn into a vast spectrum of primary colors, fall to the ground below, turn brown, dry, and crumble into dust. New leaves would take their place the following spring. Trees would fall and die, others would grow more branches up toward the sunlight. I would die and even the indentations of my footsteps on the earth's thin mantle disappeared in a rainfall. My children would grow and have children of their own who would have more children. So the cycle would continue over time, the illusion of time.

I felt the warmth of a hand press lightly on my left shoulder. It was Margeuritte. I focused my eyes outward, slowly moved back and forth, uncrossed my legs, and knelt next to my meditation cushion. I gently rolled my *zafu* and plumped it up then returned it to the *zabuton*. The meditation hall was empty except for us. I stood up and followed Margeuritte outside.

"Wow, you were really into it" she whispered. "I just couldn't sit that long, my legs."

I nodded, we continued along the pathway toward the kitchen building in silence.

Margeuritte went inside to attend to something. I decided to remain outside, to walk around, and to come back down to earth. I smiled to myself as I thought that. I aimlessly walked toward the driveway, going wherever my feet decided to lead me. As I came closer to the drive, Bhante Rahula stepped into my field of vision. He smiled at me as I looked up and recognized him. He slowly walked towards me. I walked towards him. I was to meet with a monk after all.

"I saw you still sitting during walking meditation." he commented. "You were still sitting when we left the hall. Is everything all right?"

"Yes," I replied, finding it a little difficult to talk after having been silent for so long, "Everything is fine. I was so into my meditation that I just didn't want to get up. I hope that was okay."

"Of coarse." Bhante Rahula responded.

"It was a very good meditation session for me." I decided to continue, to try and explain although I knew I really didn't have to. "I felt, it felt, well, so, well, complete. I can't describe it."

"I know you can't." he replied as he looked past me into the trees.

I made *gassho* (bowed) to him, he nodded his head in a bow to me, we smiled and we each went our own way. I continued up the drive toward the trees he had glanced up at a moment earlier.

Chapter 44
Wonder of Equanimity

To come to that place where everything is in balance, the scale neither tipping right nor left, is equanimity. A distressing event occurs, someone is insulting and rude, you are aware of this, do what has to be done, and move on. You don't become unglued, you don't become angry or out of control. You are very much in control. Calm, focused, able to discern the problem or problems, to come to a solution, and to execute it dispassionately. This is equanimity.

You are being fawned over, praised, and people are thrilled just to be in the same room with you. Gracious, in harmony, without excess ego and pride, you get on with whatever you have to do without becoming overwhelmed with self- importance. You help others through acts of loving-kindness and compassion whether they appear deserving of it or not, whether they anger you or please you. This is equanimity, too.

Equanimity comes from an inner balance and calm. It bathes you in peace of mind. No need to worry over that which you have no control, and no need to worry over what you can enact change to, if necessary, because you have the clarity to see what needs to be done and faith in your ability to rise to the occasion. Your feathers rarely get ruffled. You are still, calm, and transparent. Like a clear lake on a sunny day, you are able to reflect the landscape, to carry a boat on your surface, to support life.

In Pali, equanimity is called *upekkha*. It is a state of mindfulness and non-attachment. Being neither happy nor sad, dwelling within inner peace and joy. Equanimity is the ultimate embodiment of The Middle Way, avoiding extremes and encompassing all elements of the Noble Eight-Fold Path. It is realized through the cultivation of mind. And how does one begin this cultivation of mind? By practicing Meditation. First the development of a calm, tranquil, focused mind, and then the penetrating, intimate experience of inner awareness and wisdom brought about through *vipassana* or insight meditation.

In Hebrew, the Kabbalist's refer to equanimity as *hishtavvut.* It is when the soul is indifferent to either praise or blame. It is one of the three ranks of *Devekut* (individual enlightenment or bliss). It is realized through the practice of meditation. It can also be developed through the activity of prayer so long as it is done with *kavvanah* (mystical intention) that would elevate the act of prayer to that of meditation. It is a necessary element in reaching *Devekut* and, thereby, initiating and continuing the process of *Tikkun Olam* or world repair.

As I stand under a starlit sky, or watch the sunlight filter through the softness of pastel clouds during sunset, or experience the power of a crashing ocean wave, I can't help but to be overwhelmed by the greatness of it all. I am a people watcher, too. I can just sit and watch the world go by for hours without moving. I'm constantly amazed at the diversity, and the compassion and love I often see manifested even between and for strangers.

Every religious tradition has its names, traditions, values, labels and laws. But does it really matter? What one calls oneself is really quite secondary to how one lives ones life, how you manifest your life. The actions taken in order to better the world and to help other living beings speaks much louder then any words that could be used or preached.

In the final analysis, and there is rarely ever a final analysis, you realize that to live in balance, in a state of equanimity, requires an inner integrity. To have a sense of integrity you must know yourself inside and out. You must experience Reality as it is, not reality as you would have it be. You must be willing to let go of your ego, yourself. You must be other minded. You must reside within the active mind of meditation.

Chapter 45
A Buddhist-Jew

So, where do I reside? How do I live my life as a Buddhist-Jew? Can I integrate the two systems or must I forever swing from one side to the next like the pendulum on an old grandfather's clock? It is true, that for most of my life I have swung back and forth like that pendulum. First, immersing myself in Buddhist customs and ritual. Meditating with a fervor bordering on fanaticism. Then, seemingly turning my back on Buddhist principles and meditation practices and delving into the history of my people as written in the Torah and in history books. Celebrating each Jewish holiday as it came up around the calendar. Cooking all the traditional foods.

I have found myself in demand as a Jewish religious schoolteacher, and respected as a supplementary religious school principal. My opinion had been sought when there were questions dealing with Judaism. I've developed curriculum for all age levels covering every major topic in Judaism that one could possibly think of. I've been asked to teach, and taught, adults the basics of Jewish mysticism.

I have been solicited to sit on Buddhist educational boards and committees and invited to lecture at Buddhist retreats. I've been asked to write articles on some aspect or other of Buddhist concern, and I've participated in the religious components of practice. I've taught meditation techniques to students and have sat, myself, for well over a quarter of a century.

At the same time I've read countless books on Judaism, Kabbalah, Buddhism, meditation, and meditation methods. I've traveled to Buddhist holy places as well as to the sacred Jewish locations in the land of Israel. I've walked the path of the Buddha and I've walked the path of Abraham. I've grappled with the problem of suffering in the world and within myself, and I've grappled with the frustration of trying to "know" G-d.

I've sat for hours in meditation trying to shut up the chatter in my mind so as to be able to hear that small, still voice of G-d. I know G-d is always speaking, if I could only learn how to sit silently and to just listen. I have pursued the experience of no-thing-ness, the void. I've felt G-d within the empty mind, within the void, in this no-thing-ness, within the never-ending, eternal potential of this peaceful state of no-thing-ness. From emptiness all that can be imagined, rarely imagined, or never imagined has the potential of existence, of being manifested.

I have blended Buddhism and Judaism into a workable hybrid of sorts. I believe in the one G-d. I recite, and feel the truth of my conviction whenever I declare, "Shema, Israel, Adonai Elohainu, Adonai Ehud. (Hear, Oh Israel, the Lord is our G-d, the Lord is One)." I long to know G-d as the ancient Patriachs and prophets knew G-d. I want to experience the reality that is One and is G-d. I have read the Tanach (Bible) several times and have spoken to numerous Rabbis. I have tried to understand the teachings and I've become familiar with the *Mitzvot* (613 "divine precepts", laws and/or deeds of loving-kindness, good works expected of a Jew), and continually strive to live by that standard.

I have learned how to sit in meditation as the Buddha did. I have learned how to still that inner-chatter, how to listen, to manifest compassion and loving-kindness to all sentient beings. I have read various translations of the *Dharma* (Sanskrit)/*Dhamma*(Pali) or teachings of the Buddha. I'm aware of the 108 precepts (in Mahayana Zen) and 227 precepts (in Theravada) of the Buddha's and I try to live according to the Five Basic Precepts for lay Buddhists. I follow the Eight Precepts when attending a weekend or two -week long Buddhist meditation re-treat where I have an opportunity to practice even more intensely. I've sought a connection point between these two seemingly different religious systems.

I will probably be trying to merge the two my entire life. I am fortunate, however, that I discovered and learned about Jewish mysticism and Kabbalah. This awareness did much to build a sturdy bridge between Buddhism and Judaism on which I am able to walk upon to experience both sides of the riverbank, while always being aware that it crosses the same river. I have discovered that there is more similarity between the two, than there are differences.

Believing that all paths eventually lead to the same destination, what does it matter which path you follow? To develop morally, to be kind and compassionate to all other beings whether human or not, to do good deeds/actions and to avoid doing any harm. Both are advocated in the teachings of Buddhism and Judaism (and most other 'isms as well).

I follow the footsteps of my Jewish ancestors and never forget that I'm a link in that very long historic chain of Hebrews/Israelites/Jews who lived their lives on this same earth thousands of years before me and believed in the one G-d. I practice the Way of the Buddha as a means of becoming a better person, cultivating good, avoiding evil and to learn how to be silent, still, and alone with my G-d.

Judaism and Christianity could be described as religions of prayer. Man seeks freedom from suffering and sorrow in the world through the power of the Absolute Being, G-d. Abraham discovered the One G-d. He went against his father's belief system as well as the belief system of his countrymen. So strong was his faith in the one G-d that he took his wife, and nephew, and left his homeland for an unknown fate in an unknown land solely at G-d's request.

Buddhism could be called the religion of Enlightenment. Man strives to realize the Absolute within himself. He strives to experience the unity of the Absolute and the individual. Sakyamuni Buddha (Buddha meaning "The Awakened One") discovered the *Dharma/Dhamma* or the teaching leading to the cultivation of Mind, The Four Noble Truths concerning suffering and the path leading one out of this life of suffering called the Noble Eight-Fold Way. Yet, it isn't enough to know Buddhism, one has to become a Buddha (i.e., enlightened).

Could I find a meeting point between these two systems? I believe I did. G-d, the Infinite Being, is Ultimate No-thing-ness. In Kabbalah He/She/It is known as *Ein-Sof* or *Ayin* (One or No-thing-ness) or YHVH ("Yod, Hay, Vav, Hay," the unpronounceable, real name of G-d). Unpronounceable because to know G-d's name is to know G-d, and how is infinite no-thing-ness to be known by something finite?

Union with the Absolute (which is no-thing-ness) is referred to as *Yechidah.* In Buddhism the ultimate realization is also spoken of in terms of no-thing-ness. Not nothingness in the negative sense of being empty, "void," or of all things being lacking, but the no-thing-ness of total potential, open to all experience, totally clear and pure. This Ultimate No-thing-ness is referred to as *Parinibbana* in Pali (*Parinirvana* in Sanskrit).

In Jewish mysticism, Kabbalah, the enlightened saint or sage is called a *Tzaddik*. The term for enlightened is *maskil*. The *Tzaddik* follows the teachings of the <u>Torah</u>, <u>Tanach</u>, <u>Talmud</u>, and upholds the 613 divine precepts. The *Tzaddik* "knows" G-d. His/her eyes are fully opened.

In Buddhism the "Supremely Awakened One" is called *Samma Sambuddha*, or The Buddha "The Enlightened One," the World Teacher. The *Samma Sambuddha* is the "Supremely **Self** Enlightened Buddha," or Siddharta Gotama, himself. *Savaka* Buddha's or *Arahants* who are fully enlightened (but are not "the" Buddha) follow the *Dhamma* (Pali)/ *Dharma* (Sanskrit), the teachings of the Buddha, and live by the 108 (Mahayana)/227 (Theravada) precepts, and are fully awake.

I have been told, repeatedly, that being a Buddhist meant I was getting involved with idol worship. In Judaism this is considered extremely grave and is an act of apostasy. In Jewish law this is enough to separate a Jew from his fellows, to be cut off and shunned by the entire Jewish community. Another concern, whether or not the Buddha even felt there was a G-d to begin with. To not believe in G-d was not to be a Jew, but an unbeliever, an apostate.

Buddha was a man like all men. He was not, nor was he looked upon as, a god. Siddhartha was a prince who struggled with the concept of suffering, eventually left the pampered and sheltered life of a prince, lived as an ascetic in the forest, and some six years later through his own resolve and hard work discovered the Way and taught this *Dhamma* to others.

The Buddha neither confirmed nor denied the existence of a Supreme Being. When the question of whether or not gods did exist was asked of him, he would merely state that it was of no consequence, of no benefit to a being striving to end the cause of suffering and to become "fully awake." This must also be understood within the context of the time in history in which the Buddha lived. The primary religion of his time was Hinduism. Hindu's believe in many gods, the head god being Brahma. Their deity (and definition of their god) is not the same as that of the Jewish people or people who are monotheistic. There was no belief in only one god, a god who was absolute and full of the no-thing-ness of total potential and all things.

Lesser deities or angels may be a more accurate term to use in their case

The Buddha did not speculate on what occurred prior to birth or after death. His sole concern was with what Beings did during their current life span, after birth and just prior to death. How a Being's actions would affect his/her current and future existence. What actions would affect the end of a Beings endless cycle of *samsara* (the round of birth and death and the suffering experienced within each round)?

This being the case, I could follow the teachings of the Buddha without worrying about having to accept the Buddha as a god as he was not a god. I could also follow the path of the Buddha without a conflict of interest concerning the existence of, and my strong belief in, the G-d of Abraham, Isaac, and Joseph. Buddha was concerned with the time frame after birth and just prior to death. In many ways, so is Judaism.

I incorporate both of these elements into my practice. I use Buddhist meditation techniques to get in touch with and become one with G-d. G-d is the unifying force, creativity, universal potential, and no-thing-ness. I strive to become one with G-d as a Buddhist strives to become one in no-thing-ness. G-d is No-thing-ness in terms of a definition meaning complete potential, not complete emptiness in terms of something lacking. Realization of *Ein-Sof* becomes realization of *Nibbana* (Nirvana). Both are No-thing-ness.

There appears to be many paths with the potential to lead to the same destination. If there is only one Truth, and Truth is Truth no matter what label is placed on it, and from whatever tradition it is cast in, does it really matter which path you follow so long as you arrive at the correct destination? If it is Reality we seek to experience and know, and there is only one "real" Reality, free from illusion and delusion, totally pure and clear of all distortion and blemish, is the path more important than the destination?

I believe that the path one leads is a reflection of the Reality you seek. Or, minimally, a reflection of the path you are on even if you are traveling on that path mindlessly, unaware of the consequences of your choices. If you are walking a path of morality, manifesting compassion and loving-kindness, doing good and avoiding evil these characteristics reflect the destination you are traveling toward. The same holds true if you tread a path of immorality, selfishness, cruelty, and manifesting an unsympathetic and aloof attitude. Each path is a reflection of the destination being sought (or destination mindlessly being traveled toward). Of course, which path to follow should be done consciously, as a choice which is up to each individual to make for themselves which will ultimately present its inevitable consequences either immediately, or some time in the future, in this life or the next. That is the ideal of being mindful, truly conscious and aware, being fully awake.

Unfortunately, many people live unconsciously. They travel the highways and byways of life rarely questioning why they are walking down any road at all. They make choices based on immediate gratification, or what is easiest to do, or solely in reaction to a prior action or event. Or they make no choice and wait for circumstances to make the final decision for them.

What path is selected not only depends on the destination you seek, but is also dependent on a person's personality, temperament, and socialization within his/her community. Most of us are taught about the path our parents, and their parents before them, followed. Most of us continue to follow the path our ancestors followed without much questioning. It's the path best known to us, the most accepted by our family, and the most comfortable for us to follow. But is it the only legitimate pathway to the Truth, to a direct knowledge of Reality, toward cultivating a compassionate heart, and being able to reach out in loving-kindness to other living things in order to make life better for all beings on this planet, including our selves?

For me it is more important how a person lives and actively manifests his/her life then the name of the path he/she follows. As my great-grandmother, Jessie Horowitz Kane used to say, talk is cheap. I don't care about the words you use, the religious order you believe in, traditions you uphold and observe, or the lifestyle you chose to live. I do care about how you treat other beings, whether you are a kind, compassionate, warm person who strives to help others, or whether you act selfishly for your own gain, with no regard for other living creatures.

Your actions reflect the reality of your destination (whether consciously or unconsciously), not the religion you profess to follow. The path you follow is, therefor, a true indicator of your perception of reality and the destination you are traveling toward (hopefully an informed and conscious goal you aspire to). If you attend synagogue or church each week, and pray every day, but during your daily actions you are self-centered, manipulative, judgmental, and ego-bound, how has attending a house of worship helped you become a better person? Or, are your actions just habits performed unconsciously?

Just being in a religious environment doesn't make you a religious, spiritual or better person. It's what you do with the learning and understanding that determines that. Sitting in a church or synagogue doesn't make you a better person. Your choices made moment by moment create the person you are and will become. Just attending or affiliating with a church or synagogue doesn't magically make you moral, kind, giving, and compassionate. You have to work on yourself to gain these characteristics. All the religions of the world can but point the way, but you, alone, must walk the path step-by-step, cultivating self. To do this you must be **fully awake** and you must **consciously** make decisions and choices realizing the ramifications of every choice you make and every action you take.

So how do I put Buddhist and Jewish principles into practice on a daily basis? It isn't as difficult as I had originally thought. In fact, it is progressing smoothly. I say progressing because it is an ongoing process. Continually working on one self, looking within, focusing outward, growing, experiencing, and learning. Life is constantly unfolding and so we constantly experience life. Life is dynamic and so must our practice be dynamic.

Would I sit in a half lotus position on the *bimah*, in meditation, during a Shabbat service in a synagogue? Probably not. Although I have caught myself meditating during services, dwelling within the silence between the words being chanted in prayer. I've felt the presence of G-d within me and around me as I stood silently listening. I see G-d in every being's eyes, in everything I see around me, in creation, itself.

Would I suddenly stand inside a Buddhist Temple and start praying in Hebrew, the holy tongue of G-d, while swaying back and forth in deep concentration? I think not. It just wouldn't be appropriate and would probably greatly disturb any others who may be trying to meditate. Yet, I know there are no walls between the Buddhist Temple and the Synagogue. I have come to realize that meditation is meditation no matter what tradition it's clothed in. The goal, if it can be referred to as such, is the same in either case. It's to connect with the wholeness, the oneness, the "no-thing-ness" of Reality.

As for my path, it remains the same in either case. I live by the precepts, both the *mitzvot* of Judaism and the precepts of the

Buddha, the best I can while always striving to do better. I sit in meditation either in a Buddhist meditation hall or at home. Quietly being still, being silent, letting go, and listening for that still, small voice of G-d, that sound of no sound. Experiencing the wholeness of no-thing-ness, the totality of complete and perfect potential, of all that was, is, and that will be, which I call G-d.

So if I'm in a Buddhist temple or a Jewish temple, it is of no consequence. The experience I am having, the world that I see is the same in either place. A building is a building, a room is a room, traditions are enacted, and wisdom is always cultivated and honored. Silence and awareness are the gateways to enlightenment. Whatever you decide to call something, or whatever path or tradition you chose to follow, Enlightenment will always be Enlightenment. The experience will be the same no matter what wall you are going through or what stream you are crossing.

Appendix 1

Similar Terminology

English	Pali	Hebrew
compassion	karuna	rahamin a tef'eret
giving/generosity	dana	zedakkah
equanimity	upekkha	hishtivvut
loving-kindness	metta	chesed
enlightened being	Buddha	Tzaddik
path of purification	visuddhimagga	mitzvot
ultimate enlightenment	parinibbana (after death)	ruach ha kodesh
enlightenment	nibbana (while living)	devekut
celestial beings/angels	devas	chayot or cherubs
demonic beings (like a devil)	mara	shedim
insight meditation	vipassana	hitbonenut
tranquility meditation	samatha bhavana	hitbodedut
teachings	Dhamma	Tanach
founder/discoverer	Siddharta/Gotama	Abram
-after discovery	Gotama Buddha	Abraham

Bibliography

Dhamma,Ven. Dr. Rewata, The First Discourse of the Buddha.
Boston: Wisdom Publications, 1997.

Humphreys,Christmas, Concentration and Meditation. New York:
Penguin Books, 1935.

Humphreys,Christmas, Zen Buddhism. New York: The MacMillan
Co., 1959.

Johnson,Paul, A History of the Jews. New York: Harper & Row,
Publishers, 1987.

Kalupahana,David J. and Indrani, The Way of Siddharta: A Life of
the Buddha. Boulder, Colorado: Shambhala Publications,1982.

Kamenetz,Rodger, The Jew in the Lotus. New York: HarperCollins
Publishers, 1994.

Kaplan,Aryeh, Jewish Meditation: A Practical Guide. New York:
Schocken Books, 1985.

Kaplan,Aryeh, Meditation and Kabbalah. York Beach, Maine:
Samuel Weisner, Inc., 1982.

Kennett,Jiyu, Selling Water by the River: A Manual of Zen Training.
New York: Pantheon Books, 1972.

Michener, James A. The Source. Greenwich, Connecticut: Fawcett
Publications, Inc., 1965.

Rahula,Walpola, What the Buddha Taught. New York: Grove Press,
Inc., 1959.

Scholem,Gershom, Kabbalah. New York: Meridian Books, 1974.

Scholem, Gershom, On the Kabbalah and Its Symbolism, translated
by Ralph Manheim. New York: Schocken Books, 1960.

The Zohar, Volumes 1-5. Translated by Harry Sperling and Maurice
    Simon. London: The Soncino Press, 1984.

Warren, Henry Clarke. Buddhism in Translations. Boston: Harvard
    University Press, 1896.

BOOK LIST

Buddhist Topics

Conze, Edward. Buddhist Meditation. New York: Harper
Torchbooks, 1956.

Dhamma, Ven. Dr. Rewata. The First Discourse of the Buddha.
Boston: Wisdom Publications, 1997.

de Bary, Wm. Theodore. The Buddhist Tradition. New York: The
Modern Library, 1969.

Gunaratana, Ven. Henepola. Mindfulness in Plain English. Boston:
Wisdom Publications, 1991

Humphreys, Christmas. Concentration and Meditation. New York:
Penquin Books, 1935.

Humphreys, Christmas. Concentration and Meditation: A Manual of
Mind Development. New York: Penquin Books, 1968.

Humphreys, Christmas. Zen Buddhism. New York: The MacMillan
Co., 1968.

Kalupahana, David J. & Indrani. The Way of Siddharta: A Life of the
Buddha. Boulder, Colorado: Shambhala Publications, 1982.

Kennett, Jiyu. Selling Water by the River: A Manual of Zen Training
New York: Pantheon Books, a division of Random House,
Inc., 1972.

Rahula, Walpola. What the Buddha Taught. New York: Grove Press,
Inc., 1959.

Rajneesh, Bhagwan Shree. Meditation: The Art of Ecstasy, ed. by Ma
Satya Bharti. New York: Harper Colophon Books, 1976.

Sekida, Katsuki. Zen Training: Methods and Philosophy. New York: John Weatherhill, Inc., 1975.

Suzuki, D. T. An Introduction to Zen Buddhism. New York: Grove Press, Inc., 1964.

Suzuki, D. T. Essays in Zen Buddhism, First Series. New York, Grove Press, Inc., 1949.

Suzuki, D. T. Studies in Zen. New York: Dell Publishing Co., Inc., 1955.

Suzuki, D. T. The Field of Zen. New York: Harper Row, Publishers, 1969.

Suzuki, D. T. What is Zen? New York: Harper Row, Publishers, 1971.

Trungpa, Chogyam. Meditation in Action. Boulder, Colorado: Shambala Publications, 1969.

Watts, Alan. Meditation. Millbrae, California: Celestial Arts, 1974.

Yamaoka, Haruo. Meditation Gut Enlightenment: The Way of Hara. San Francisco: Heian International Publishing Co., 1976.

Jewish Mysticism/Kabbalah Topics

Ben Shimon Halevi, Z'ev. A Kabbalistic Universe. York Beach, Maine: Samuel Weiser, Inc., 1977.

Ben Shimon Halevi, Z'ev. The Work of the Kabbalist. York Beach, Maine: Samuel Weiser, Inc., 1986.

Cooper, David A., Rabbi. God is a Verb: Kabbalah and the Practice of Mystical Judaism. New York: Riverhead Books, 1997.

Heifetz, Harold, compiled by. Zen and Hasidism. Wheaton, Illinois: The Theosophical Publishing House, 1978.

Hoffman, Edward. The Heavenly Ladder: Kabbalistic Techniques for
    Inner Growth. East Meadow, New York: Four Worlds Press,
    1985.

Hoffman, Edward. The Way of Splendor: Jewish Mysticism and
    Modern Psychology. Northvale, New Jersey: Jason Aronson,
    Inc., 1981, 1989.

Kaplan, Aryeh. If You Were God. New York: NCSY/Orthodox
    Union, 1983.

Kaplan, Aryeh. Jewish Meditation: A Practical Guide. New York:
    Schocken Books, 1985.

Kaplan, Aryeh. Meditation and Kabbalah. York Beach, Maine:
    Samuel Weiser, Inc., 1982.

Kaplan, Aryeh. The Infinite Light: A Book About God. New York:
    NCSY/Orthodox Union, 1981.

Kushner, Harold. To Life!: A Celebration of Jewish Being and
    Thinking. Boston: Little, Brown and Company, 1993.

Raz, Simcha. A Tzaddik in Our Time: The Life of Rabbi Aryeh
    Levin, translated from the Hebrew by Charles Wengrov.
    Jerusalem: Feldheim Publishers, 1976.

Scholem, Gershom. Kabbalah. New York: Meridian Books, 1974.

Scholem, Gershom. Major Trends in Jewish Mysticism. New York:
    Schocken Books, 1941.

Scholem, Gershom. On the Kabbalah and Its Symbolism, translated
    by Ralph Manheim. New York: Schocken Books, 1960.

Scholem, Gershom. On the Mystical Shape of the Godhead: Basic
    Concepts in the Kabbalah. Translated by Joachim
    Neugroschel. Edited by Jonathan Chipman. New York:
    Schocken Books, 1991.

The Zohar, Volumes 1-5, translated by Harry Sperling & Maurice
     Simon. London: The Soncino Press, 1984.

Weiner, Herbert. 9 1/2 Mystics: The Kabbala Today. New York:
     Collier Books, 1969.

General

Boorstein, Sylvia. That's Funny, You Don't Look Buddhist: On Being
     a Faithful Jew and a Passionate Buddhist. New York:
     HarperCollins Publishers, 1997.

Kamenetz, Rodger. The Jew in the Lotus. San Francisco: Harper
     San Francisco, 1994.

Addresses and Web Sites
(of meditation halls/monasteries, yeshivot, etc.)

1. Rabbi Ariel Bar Tzadok
    Yeshivat Bnei Neviim
    P.O. Box 59-700
    Chicago, IL 60659
    Telephone: 312-274-3777
    (Ultra-orthodox, Sephardic outreach program teaching
    spiritual/meditative aspects of Judaism. Also publishes a
    magazine called "Panu Derekh" or "Prepare the Way")

2. Rabbi Harold Swiss
    Little Synagogue
    155 East 22nd Street
    New York, NY
    (teacher of Kabbalah)

3. Cambridge Insight Meditation Center
    331 Broadway
    Cambridge, MA 02139
    Telephone: 617-491-5070 (Colette Bourassa)
    FAX: 617-441-9038
    www: **http://world.std.com/~cimc/**

4. Barre Center for Buddhist Studies
    149 Lockwood Road
    Barre, MA 01005
    Telephone: 508-355-2347 (Mu Soeng)
    FAX: 508-355-2798
    www: **http://www.dharma.org/bcbs.htm**

5. Insight Meditation Society
    1230 Pleasant Street
    Barre, MA 01005
    Telephone: 508-355-4378
    FAX: 508-355-6398
    www: **http://www.dharma.org/ims.htm**

6. Bhavana Society   (monastery and meditation center)
    RT. 1 Box 218-3
    High View, WV 26808
    Telephone: 304-856-3241
    FAX: 304-856-2111
    e-mail: bhavana@access.mountain.net
    web site: **http://www.bhavanasociety.org**

7. General World Wide Web entry for listing of many Buddhist
    Centers in the USA:
    http://world.std.com/~metta/centers/usa-ctr/ctrma.html

8. General Kabbalah category matches on Yahoo search engine
    http://search.yahoo.com/bin/search?p=kabbala&hc=0&hs=0

9. Links with Theravadan Buddhist temples around the world and is
    also a source for teachings on Theravada Buddhism.
    http://www.thaiways.com/buddhism/index.htm

10. Buddhist Virtual Library:
    www.ciolek.com/WWWVL-buddhism.html

11. Selected bibliography on Kabbalah:
    www.acs.ucalgary.ca/~elsegal/RelS_365/Kabbalah_Guide.html

12. Index to Kabbalah, Mysticism, and Messianism reading:
    www.shamash.org/lists/scj-faq/HTML/rl/mys-index.html
    Mysticism reading list:
    http:shamash.org/listarchives/scj-faq/reading-lists/mysticism

13. Cherub Press, publisher of Jewish mystical literature:
    msabrams@pluto.mscc.huji.ac.il (mailing list)

14. Jewish Spirituality Links: **http://kavannah.org/links.html**
    Resources for Kabbalah & Jewish Meditation by Michael
    Sidlofsky: **http://kavannah.org/meditation.html**

15. Extensive listing of Kabbalah web sites:
    http://search.yahoo.com/bin/search?p=kabbalah&hc=0&hs=0

INDEX

Moses ben Maimon. See
Maimonides
Moses de Leon. See Rabbi
Moses de Leon
Moyel, 127, 128, 130
mystical intention. See
kavvanah.

N

Nefesh, 164
Neshamah, 164
Nibbana (Nirvana). See
enlightenment
Nirodha, 19
Nirvana, 32. See Nibbana.
Noble Eightfold Path, 5, 17,
18, 19, 20, 21, 226
Noble Eightfold Way, 197, 230
Noble Silence, 221, 222

O

Obaku, 29
Old Testament, 14

P

Pali, 22, 29, 54, 61, 92, 102,
192, 216, 226, 229, 230, 231
Pardes, 161
Parinibbana, 61, 230
Parinirvana. See Parinibbana.
prayer, 13, 14, 16, 54, 57, 58,
71, 108, 116, 157, 163, 164,
166, 210, 227, 230, 234
prayer shawl, 87, 102
Precepts, 30, 34, 38, 39, 42, 43,
47, 48, 91, 102, 189, 197,

220, 229, 231, 234; Ten
Precepts, 37
Professor Scholem. See
Gershom Scholem

R

Rabbi Akiva, 162
Rabbi Chaim Vital, 78
Rabbi Isaac Luria. See the Ari
Rabbi Luria. See the Ari
Rabbi Moses de Leon, 60
Rabbi Moshe Benshemon, 77
Rabbi Moshe Cordevero. See
the Ramak
Rahula, 18
Rambam. See Maimonides
reincarnation, 79
Reverend Ichinose, 5, 6, 34, 35
Reverend Keido Chisan Koho
Zenji, 35, 42
Reverend Master Jiyu-Kennett.
See Jiyu Kennett Roshi
Rinzai, 29, 42
Ruach. See enlightenment.
Ruach HaKodesh, 56, 61
Ruah, 164

S

Safed, 75, 77, 78, 81, 91
Sakyamuni Buddha. See
Gautama Buddha
Samadhi, 29, 32
Sambodhi, 61
Samma Sambuddha. See
Guatama Buddha.
samsara, 232
Samudaya, 19
Sanga, 42, 44